MW00815121

The Body and Embodiment

The Body and Embodiment

A *Philosophical Guide*

Frank Chouraqui

ROWMAN & LITTLEFIELD
Lanham • Boulder • New York • London

Published by Rowman & Littlefield
An imprint of The Rowman & Littlefield Publishing Group, Inc.
4501 Forbes Boulevard, Suite 200, Lanham, Maryland 20706
www.rowman.com

6 Tinworth Street, London SE11 5AL, United Kingdom

Copyright © 2021 by Frank Chouraqui

All rights reserved. No part of this book may be reproduced in any form or by any
electronic or mechanical means, including information storage and retrieval systems,
without written permission from the publisher, except by a reviewer who may quote
passages in a review.

British Library Cataloguing in Publication Information Available

ISBN: HB 978-1-78660-974-8
       PB 978-1-78660-975-5

Library of Congress Cataloging-in-Publication Data

Names: Chouraqui, Frank, author.
Title: The body and embodiment : a philosophical guide / Frank Chouraqui.
Description: Lanham : Rowman & Littlefield, [2021] | Includes bibliographical
    references and index.
Identifiers: LCCN 2020056995 (print) | LCCN 2020056996 (ebook) | ISBN
    9781786609748 (hardback) | ISBN 9781786609755 (paperback) | ISBN
    9781786609762 (epub)
Subjects: LCSH: Human body (Philosophy)
Classification: LCC B105.B64 C49 2021 (print) | LCC B105.B64 (ebook) | DDC
    128/.6—dc23
LC record available at https://lccn.loc.gov/2020056995
LC ebook record available at https://lccn.loc.gov/2020056996

♾️™ The paper used in this publication meets the minimum requirements of
American National Standard for Information Sciences—Permanence of Paper
for Printed Library Materials, ANSI/NISO Z39.48-1992.

To Natalie Heller

Contents

Chapter 11   Race, Visibility and Power   181

Chapter 12   Female Disempowerment   193

               Conclusion   213

               Glossary   217

               Bibliography   225

               Index   237

~

Acknowledgements

This book is the result of several iterations of my course on the Body and Embodiment at the University of Leiden in the fall semester of 2015, the spring semester of 2018, and the spring semester of 2019. It bears the marks of each student who took part in these classes. Without their encouragements, I would never have ambitioned to put this material in writing. They allowed my thinking to come together, and this book is interlaced with flashes of their personalities, of their generosity, their patience and their philosophical audacity. This book has a special connection to Marianthi Michaelidou, the thought of whom remained with me as I worked on it, as the thought of an ideal reader. I have benefitted hugely from the always reliable, indefatigable and thoughtful help of Laurens Koops who dealt with much of the thankless work of transcription, and from the unblinking writer's eye of Sascha Luinenburg. This book was made possible by the generosity of the Institute of Philosophy at the University of Leiden, in particular its management team, James McAllister and Carolyn de Greef. Many warm thanks also go to my friends and colleagues at Leiden for making such a wonderful home, in particular Doug Berger, Michael Eze and Ryan van Nood for their helpful bibliographical advice. I am thankful to my editors at Rowman & Littlefield: Isobel Cowper-Coles and Frankie Mace for their trust in this project, and to seven careful and constructive reviewers. Happiness always feels the urge of writing its name on every wall. This book, like everything that comes from my happiness, is dedicated to Natalie Heller. Her tireless investigation in the embodied condition persuaded me that embodiment contains all insights. Finally, the growing souls and physical presence of Marianne and Julia are painted all over this book, and as far as I am concerned, all over everything else too.

CHAPTER ONE

~

Introduction

You have a body. So do I. This is why we're here, you reading and I writing. Take this away from us, and my thoughts would never reach you. Take this away from us, and we will never meet, through words on the page, through shaking hands or staring into each other's eyes. Having a body is our way of being here. But of course, we're not both here, or if we are, we are *here* in different senses: I am here writing, and you are here reading. Probably I am here writing *before* you are here reading, and probably, the place is different. I am here writing at my desk, in my study, but most likely, you're here, as I wish for you and for this book, on a sunny terrace, with a coffee cup at hand. And yet, it is not absurd to say that right now, we are encountering each other. Except, we are encountering each other indirectly, via objects in the world, ink on the page, vibrations in the air between the pages and your eyes, on your side, and on my side, via my fingers typing, via the keyboard, the computer, and in-between, via the entire production process of a book, chemical reactions, cogwheels, the mechanics that only bodily things can know. So our bodies make us present to each other, and with it comes the fact that they make us present to all sorts of physical processes, the very ones we rely on to read, communicate, but also orient ourselves, the ones your hand is using when reaching for that cup.

Our body is the great assumption of our lives: the fact that I am in a body, or that I have a body which is mine, is implied in everything I do, everything I expect and plan to do, and in everything I see and understand. Our body is so obvious that anything we appeal to in order to understand it would be less

1

obvious, less certain that this: I have a body, I am a body. The body explains rather than is explained. The fact that I have a body is primary.

So, you have a body, and so do I. This is not an issue. Interestingly though, the obviousness of the fact that we have bodies is in complete conflict with the difficulty of explaining what this means. We have a body, yes but what is a *body*? What is it to *be* embodied? What does it mean to *have* a body? The challenge of the philosophy of the body has always been to reconcile this certainty—I have a body—with this puzzlement—what does this mean? Does the certainty of being embodied contain any insight into what having a body is? This is the predicament that philosophers find themselves facing.

But they're facing it on all our behalf: because if it is an obvious fact about us that we have bodies, it is also an obvious fact that our lives are lived according to this fact. And so living in a body always means having to live in a body, taking the trouble to live in a body, dragging a body around. The ethical responsibility of the human is to learn to live as she is given to herself; as this body that she didn't choose and yet is. A body we haven't chosen, whose presence is so fundamental to us that we cannot conceive of our existence without it, and yet, something that is not truly ours since it forces us, prevents us, gives us away, and demands things of us, sometimes, tyrannizes us. Although the fact of embodiment is primary, we have yet to learn to live according to this fact. And this begins with thinking. This is the task that philosophers have been taking up for us.

In the process, they have liberated us and allowed us to better understand this obvious but mysterious fact of embodiment. In the process, they have also done the reverse, pressing us into corners, into uncomfortable ideas about what our embodied lives *should* look like, how we should live in them, whether and how much we should value them, how we should move in them, what we should impose on them, how we should care for them, or deny them, what we should and shouldn't do with them, and so on. It is this adventure, the philosophical adventure that taught us the joy and the discomfort to live in our bodies, which this book is about.

* * *

This book is meant to play a part in helping us understand how we came to live in our bodies the way we do. How we live in our bodies partly depends on how we and others think of embodiment. The way you think about your body depends on your understanding of what having a body is, and this understanding depends on the view of embodiment passed down to you through your culture and imposed upon you by the others, other people as well as institutions and cultural structures. We live in our bodies according to the philosophy of the body we are born in. Even further, we live in our bodies according to the worldview that has been passed down to us. One of the points of this book is to show that this worldview itself depends on the way we conceive of our bodies too: because the world that is the object of this worldview is the world of our body, and the way we think of ourselves as living in it is dependent on the way we think of our embodiment, it determines the way we see the world itself. Asking about the history of the notion of embodiment therefore also involves asking about how we ended up living in our bodies in this way. In short, the philosophy of the body is special because it is not distinguishable from our experience of life and of culture; when it comes to embodiment, the distinction between history of ideas, cultural history, existential analysis and philosophy in the technical sense is blurred, and thankfully so.

This is true at the collective level: there is a modern, Western way of living in our bodies, which is loosely identifiable, but identifiable nonetheless, with its rhetoric of domination, with its organisation around aesthetic, gendered, racial and age lines, one which is probably most marked by conflict and oppression. Conflict between myself and my body, but also conflict between identifying with our bodies and rejecting our affiliation with it, resulting for example in attempts to glorify our bodies, to repossess or to beat them into submission, through practices where the one becomes hard to distinguish from the other; think of plastic surgery, fitness practices, fashion, tattoos, scarification, makeup, and so on. This is also something that can be regarded individually, and I hope that perhaps your relationship with your own body could become a touch clearer to you thanks to this book, as I hope mine does to me. Some of the tropes we explore, tropes that were either created or taken up and systematised by the sleepwalking philosophical heroes this book is devoted to, have left their trace inside us, some of their conflicts of ideas have resulted in existential conflicts within us, some of us carry our bodies in defiance of the Platonic-Christian order, some of us in defiance of the materialism that sought to eradicate that order, and most of us are living in our bodies in composite ways, trying to find breathing room at the heart of these tensions between the conflicting and incompatible crushing noises of commands, theories, demands and injunctions all based on some fantastical interpretation of this simple fact: you have a body. The result is this creature limping through life, dragging their bodies along, letting them drag them along, remaining out of step with themselves, this creature with their constant exposure to fracture: you and me.

* * *

This book traces the history of the philosophy of the body in the West, it provides a narrative line to contextualise the most determinant moments in this tradition. What allows me to unify a diverse, rich, and often divergent tradition in such a way is, I think, the previous point related to cultural history. In spite of such differences, and distinctions, we still meaningfully (if admittedly, not correctly) talk of the "Western tradition," "Western culture," and the like, to refer to a diverse, rich, changeable and Protean cultural context which although it is loosely defined, remained identifiable. Our thinking about the body, in the same way, has been passed down to us through a selective process that has organised it in coherent ways, and made certain key changes count not as ad hoc philosophical innovation, but as paradigmatic ones. As a consequence, any talk of a narrative must be, if it is to be responsible, general enough to accommodate a number of divergent views, and precise enough that it allows us to order what would otherwise look like chaotic diversity.

* * *

This book gives us a basis to think of the body in new ways, outside the Western tradition. This book focuses on the Western tradition with a view to establishing its strengths and weaknesses, its arbitrary turning points as well as the ways this tradition has had a normalising impact on our lives. As such, its intention is not to reinforce or glorify this tradition, but rather, to offer some clues and insight on how, given the tradition we inherited, new ways to think of embodiment, and therefore new ways to live in our bodies are possible. The paradigm we inherited, one that hesitates between sanctifying and criminalising the body, one that hesitates between dominating, repressing and embracing embodiment, and one that fostered a sense of alienation from our bodies as well as a host of practices to care for them, is succumbing before our very eyes under the weight of its own contradictions. Two current developments could serve as examples of the pressure that has been applied to these contradictions. The first is the increased interaction between embodiment and technologies, including questions regarding plastic surgery, restorative surgery, cloning, transplants, and the like. The second is the increased claims of those minority communities defined in relation to their embodiment, body practices, racial features, gender or sexuality. The moral and political decisions that are at stake in these developments will be decided on the basis of our implicit, culturally inherited understanding of the body, of embodiment, of what bodies can and should do and be. In looking back therefore, this book is meant to help us look ahead. In this function, it can only serve as a starting point. Although it attempts to initiate a transition towards the question of somatic oppression in the last two chapters that focus on racial and gendered embodiment, it falls woefully short of a developed account of the rich and growing literature on such current subjects.

These are the two areas most visibly missing in the book, and for the investigation of which it can only offer a starting point. The philosophies of identity represent a rich and active field for reasons philosophical, moral, social and political, and it is premised on the view that our identity and our embodiment are mutually related, and that this means that discourses about bodies influence identity and that debates about identity influence embodiment. This leads into subtle, but very real oppression, including sexual oppression, racism, sexism, homophobia and discrimination on the basis of ability or age. As we shall see in chapters 11 and 12, this oppression is both reliant on the Western tradition that this book chronicles, and a response to it.

Second, this book should serve as a starting point to investigate body practices, including dance and performance art, sports studies, the philosophy of human enhancement, medicine, sexual practices, asceticism, fashion and cosmetic practices. Again, all of these and more are the focus of lively debate in philosophy, cultural studies, psychology, anthropology and many other fields in some cases. As these studies show well, there is more than our bodies at stake in such practices, and yet, the fact that they are embodied means that they always carry with them the metaphysical self-apprehension that philosophers have taught us, via our cultural environment. This book focuses on the general experience of embodiment as a preparation for an investigation of specific bodies or specific embodied experiences.

Synopsis

For the reasons outlined previously, this book cannot do its purported philosophical job without also doing some work in the history of culture. It can only justify its narrative structure by appealing to a loosely unified cultural context that illustrates the fact that the history of Western thought about the body is more than one doctrine after another, but rather has some sort of internal logic that can be traced, retrospectively at least. This, of course, is at the cost of a more pedestrian survey of doctrines and authors. This book doesn't take for granted that authors need to be surveyed just because they are great authors. Those authors that appear in the book have justified their presence in it not because they are much-talked-about (although many of them are), or because they are great authors in the canon (they all are), or even because they are correct about the body. On the contrary, they have been chosen because without the ideas they present or illustrate, how you are feeling in your body right now would not be intelligible. Conversely, many authors you might expect to see in any survey of Western philosophy on the body or on other themes only make a small cameo in it. This may be because their thought hasn't influenced culture in the same way, or because they have influenced it in ways similar to that of another author who does appear in the book (regardless of whether, to a scholarly historian of philosophy, the differences between their views cannot be ignored). This means that Plotinus, for example, has become squeezed between Plato and Augustine; that Sartre and Fanon and Beauvoir have been implicitly reduced to satellites of Descartes (although in the case of Beauvoir especially, there is some left over, which I hope is addressed with reference to Iris Marion Young); why Agamben only makes a small appearance in reference to Kantorowicz and Freud; and why a very influential tradition of cognitive science is also implicitly accounted for by Descartes.

The same goes for the choice of texts. Although each chapter focuses on providing a faithful account of one or two authors' views on the body and embodiment, it does so by emphasising some texts over some others, and some ideas over some others. It does so according to two criteria, the first is accuracy and representativity, and the second is usability. The two criteria often clash: some of the most useful insights gathered by reading an author may not be the insights found in the author themselves. The first three chapters, which emphasise the insights gained by the failure of some authors to do away with the body, are an example of this. Some other times, the important insight is implicit, or peripheral to a given author, like when Freud acknowledges only implicitly and to an extent anticipates the insights of the phenomenology of the body. This doesn't take anything away from the importance of these thoughts.

So, this book forced me to carry out a selection between authors, texts and insights, and to bring out a narrative line whose purpose is to square the circle of *presenting* the history of thought as it is on the one hand, and making *sense of it* on the other, that is to say, using each part of it as a context in which the other parts fit. This is, of course, a cause for suspicion: with such tools in hand; by granting myself such discretion, I may have allowed many biases to sneak in: philosophical biases, historical ones, ethnocentric ones, gendered ones as well as pedagogical ones. This is the quandary of any guide: they guide you by making choices for you. All that can be done is to point out what these choices are, and hold oneself accountable to the one criterion that's left: does my experience of being embodied become clarified, even ever so slightly, by reading this book?

* * *

The grand arc of the book is simple: it chronicles the way an entire tradition moved from making the separation of body and soul a fundamental dogma to making their unity—embodiment—fundamental. The book is organised in three sequences. The first sequence (chapters 2–4) explores the initial thrust of Western philosophy in terms of an attempt at reducing the fact of embodiment to another, more fundamental fact, be it the soul, god, or the duality of body and soul. The second (chapters 5–8) explores the consequence of the failure of this attempt, and how the resistance of embodiment forces a refoundation of metaphysics in general: not only the meaning of being human must now change, so too does the meaning of the world and the meaning of truth. The third sequence (chapters 9–12) explores the consequences of embodiment for political thought. It argues that just like the fact of embodiment changes our view of the world, it should also change our view of politics. In particular, it changes what we call 'power' by questioning the notion of sovereignty.

Part I

The common idea according to which the Platonic-Christian tradition represents a sustained effort to avoid the fact of embodiment is correct. However, we find in the same authors the roots of a thread of thought that recognises the paradoxes that dualism entail and the difficulties involved with both an integrated and a dualistic account, leading into a much more serious engagement with embodiment. Part I examines the thoughts of three of the great architects of the Western worldview. It begins with Plato's attempts at reducing the body to a mere restriction of the soul, and his realisation that such a reductive project is doomed to failure. It continues with Augustine's Christian reworking of Plato and his realisation that embodiment is best seen as a possibility of self-determination which Augustine calls "sin" and which is itself irreducible. Finally, we examine Descartes' attempts at presenting embodiment as secondary by emphasising that mind and matter are naturally distinct, and we chronicle how this attempt also fails. Taken as a whole, this first sequence shows *ad absurdum* that any attempt at doing away with the fact of embodiment leads to an impossible worldview. This results in the insight that (a) embodiment is a primary fact, and (b) this fact carries consequences for not only an account of the body, or of the human, but of the world itself.

Part II

The minor thread in Platonism-Christianity proposed (mostly in order to reject them) a series of discussions surrounding what the unity of soul and body might entail. It comes to full flourishing in phenomenology and embodied cognition theories, both of which take this unity as the primary given. Just like anthropological dualism founded a dualistic metaphysics, an integrated anthropology informs a non-dualist metaphysics. Therefore, part II examines the implications of taking seriously the fact of embodiment. It begins in chapter 5 with Husserl's attempt at granting a central place to the fact of embodiment via the theme of reciprocity: to be a body means to be in the world, and embodiment grants us access to the world of experience as well as it grants the world access to us: embodiment establishes a reciprocal relationship between the subject and the world. This is furthered in chapters 6 and 7 by Merleau-Ponty's systematisation of these insights, which shows that the natural consequence of such reciprocity is that we must think of embodiment as an ontological factor: being embodied is the mode of being of Being. As a result, Merleau-Ponty shows, we must think of our body no longer as a thing, or a spatio-temporal object, but rather as a *force* of affecting and being affected. The body is the pervasive style of our life; as such, it is taken for granted in the present and always only understood retrospectively, as the structuring dimension of whatever just happened. The lesson of phenomenology is that the world and the objects in it should no longer be conceived as things that interact with each other, but they should be defined in terms of their interaction. Gibson's famed theory of affordances is a direct result of his concern for embodiment (chapter 8), which leads him to reduce the world and the objects in it to their surface, and in turn to reduce surfaces to meanings: the surface of an object is what is exposed of it to my gaze and I will interact with it in terms of what it means to me. Largely on the basis of some of the questions left open by Gibson, the enactivist tradition proposes that a stronger way to think of body and mind—and of meaning and physicality—together, is by appealing to the notion of activity. In this enactivist view of the mind (chapter 8), perception and action are mutually constitutive. The chapter concludes by pointing out that the unity of meaning and physicality advocated by phenomenologists and enactivists alike leads to a view of objects and of humans as open, indeterminate and partly virtual, and therefore constitutes an appeal to the notion of historicity: bodies are essentially transformable through experience and representation and herefore, they are historical. As we see in the next part, this draws attention to the political dimension of embodiment.

Part III

The effort of modern political theory in the West is to establish a strong notion of sovereignty through a removal of the ambiguity of embodiment.

Sovereignty is pure power, power without resistance, feedback or response, power without reciprocity. The fact of embodiment which makes all powers embodied and all embodiment reciprocal exposes this illusion by showing that it needs to more or less forcibly separate the active and the passive principles which phenomenology and embodied cognition have shown to be intertwined. Part III therefore investigates both the strategies that have been developed to maintain the fantasy of sovereignty, and the foundations of critical projects that expose its very fantastical character, analyse its origins and its impact, and confront it to an analysis of oppression and alienation that relies not on domination premised on sovereignty but on normalisation premised on a softer, more embodied, notion of power. Just like chapters 2 through 4 examined the attempts at constructing a fantastical metaphysics that explained away the fact of embodiment, chapter 9 begins with an analysis of the fictional ways in which the phenomenological insight of the reversibility of embodiment, was anxiously covered up and fictionally resolved. In the process, it exposes this anxiety as a fundamental motivation in the construction of the Western focus on sovereignty. Chapter 9 begins this investigation with an analysis of the rhetoric of the body politic in classical political thought and in particular in political theology. Chapter 10 examines the theories of alienation put forward by Marx and Foucault and how they implicitly point to the fact that the metaphysical tradition has taught us to live in our bodies in a way that deprives us of our agency; showing that oppression was not the result of sovereignty, but of soft power. Chapter 11 examines the case of the racialisation of bodies (and therefore of the embodied experience of racialised people) as a historically constructed mode of embodiment which expresses and reinforces political oppression not via domination but via internalisation. Chapter 12 examines the same trope as it plays out in the case of gender and the oppression of women's embodied experience.

As a whole, this journey yields three kinds of insights: historical, cultural and philosophical. Historically, it substantiates the claim that Western philosophy is organised around an ambivalence towards the fact of embodiment. Culturally, it shows that this theoretical ambivalence in turn has become embodied, leading to a certain discomfort of the Western subject, caught in the crosshairs of the supposed rivalry between body and mind, subjectivity and objectivity, passivity and activity. Philosophically speaking it shows that:

- Embodiment is best understood as localisation and commensurability.
- The body changes everything: the self and the world are co-embodied.

- The body is best understood as a *force* rather than a *thing*, and therefore that the body is a theme that has the potential to dissolve the traditional oppositions of subject and the object, the self and the other, the active and the passive.
- As a result, the body problematises the idea of power as sovereignty.

Using This Book

This book is designed to be useful to students and anyone with an interest in asking the question of embodiment from a theoretical point of view. It is also designed to be used as a course companion. Indeed, this is how I've used this material over the years. As such, it covers a typical thirteen sessions semester, and each chapter is organised around a series of readings. The readings have been chosen for representativity, readability and length. They are quoted in the most reliable and most widely accessible editions (please see the bibliography for more details). I have tried to make the primary readings manageable, and they usually number ten to twenty pages (with some rare exceptions). These are mentioned in the first text box of each chapter. Unless otherwise noted, the quotations used in the body of each chapter refer to the primary readings announced in the first textbox of the chapter. Other boxes provide some additional readings, which students or convenors can use for further context or as sources for their essays, and that the reader in general can find interesting. Indeed, they contain many truly exciting texts. In the spirit of succinctness, each chapter is meant to be readable in one hour, although in spite of my best efforts, many of them certainly bear re-reading. Additionally, the contents of the chapters are meant to constitute an organic unity with the texts themselves, and they presuppose some familiarity with the readings. For the sake of succinctness, I focus on commenting, not outlining or rehearsing the contents of the readings. This allows me to bring out the implications and presuppositions of the text, and thereby, to bring out the connections between texts that sometimes may not appear at first sight to be related. To make the match between primary texts and chapters easier, I have placed the important passages in text boxes alongside the relevant commentary. These are designed to give context to the core claims of each chapter by showing how these claims are laid out by each author, and hopefully, the primary text and the commentary are mutually illuminating. Finally, the reader will notice that I have striven to break up each chapter into bite-size paragraphs, often numbered, to help the reader follow the argument step-by-step. Finally, the book also offers some help for those who wish to dig further, with a list of further primary readings in the final text box of each chapter and secondary readings at the end of the book. The closing apparatus contains an index, a short glossary and a list of further readings especially geared towards helping you make the next move: to zero in on your specific areas of interest, hopefully beyond the Western classical canon.

* * *

I began by suggesting that this book aims to propose a few lines to help us think and live according to the fact of embodiment. We would be wrong to think that our well-being alone is at play in this refoundation of the world. More is at stake. Earlier, I described sovereignty as pure power and suggested that as such, the fact of embodiment exposes the fantastical nature of any notion of sovereignty. This is not so much to do with the nature of power; it is to do with the nature of purity. As Descartes saw clearly, any emphasis on embodiment threatens any notion of purity, it threatens any possibility to match our ideas with reality: for our ideas are categorically distinct from each other and categorically self-identical, pure. From this perspective, experience is an inacceptable mixture. After Descartes, whose nuanced experiments with thoughts were transformed into *doxa* by a culture desperate for simple answers, the disease of modernity, and perhaps the original sin of Western Judeo-Christian thought in general has lain in a fetish for purity. Pure races, the essence of the nation, the essence of your gender, pure morality, territorial integrity and all the fiction-based institutions put into place not for the sake of protecting such fantastical purity but in order to desperately breathe life into it, and keep up the illusion of its existence, have coalesced into violence, abuse and self-abuse on the grand and the microscopic scale, resulting in an amputation of the Western soul's ability to respond to experience. A nasty, brutish and short-sighted ideal, "purity" is nowadays rearing its ugly head again. Embodiment has always been the pebble in the shoe of purism: it affirms the admixture of the pure soul and the pure body, of the self and the other, of thinking and feeling. Taking the fact of embodiment as a starting point is the necessary first step towards curing ourselves from the disease of purity and towards learning to live impure and honest lives. And we must begin at the beginning.

PART I

FOUNDATIONS
AND PARADIGM

CHAPTER TWO

~

The Irreducibility
of the Body 1: Plato

Readings
Plato, *Cratylus*, 399a–400d.
Plato, *Phaedo*, 69e–72d and 95a–104c.
Plato, *Phaedrus*, 246a–250d.

Beginning with Plato: A Disclaimer

We begin with Plato. Although it remains the right place to start, it requires a few explanations. Beginning with Plato has been a tradition in Western philosophy, ever since Plato himself. But of course, it contains its share of philosophical and cultural assumptions, several of which are relevant to the way philosophy has treated the body. The first problem when beginning with Plato is that this presumes that the beginning of philosophy is the beginning of Western philosophy in Greece. This *de facto* places any non-Western philosophy in a derivative position, one which, it goes without saying, is incorrect, both philosophically and historically, and nefarious culturally and politically. The second problem is that it ignores earlier philosophers even in the Western tradition. Even assuming that philosophy indeed began in Greece at sunrise around 6:30 a.m., Plato came along for breakfast a bit after 8 a.m. This means that beginning with him is ignoring all that took place in between, especially all the cooking that made breakfast with him possible at all. Finally, there is a problem that combines both problems, namely, that the ethnocentrism of beginning in the West is combined with the historical error of beginning so late in the day, when we consider non-Western philosophies which are, themselves, more ancient than Greek philosophy. It's good to remember that the Buddha is about one century older than Plato, so was Confucius, and that the Hebrews, the Persians, the Assyrians and the Egyptians all had elaborate systems of natural philosophy well before Plato came along. Indeed, he may have been influenced by them.

Yet, we still begin with him. One reason is pedagogical: part of what this book does is take the history of philosophy as it has become enshrined into a canon, try to make it accessible, and hopefully, make you want to read more, including read more about how this canon came to be constituted. And because Plato has always been used as the start, Plato has influenced the way philosophy has been done in the West in structural ways. Beginning with Plato therefore allows us to clarify some views that will later become common habits of thought. Ironically, it is this millenary yet arbitrary habit of beginning with Plato that has made beginning with Plato indispensable. Second, and correlatedly, Plato was a major formative intellectual influence on Christianity which in turn, is the single most important intellectual influence in the way we in the West have come to think about our bodies and live in them. As you remember, understanding how this thinking and this mode of being came about is crucial for us, and it takes us back to Plato. This is all the more ironic as we will see that Plato himself has a view of the body which is much more complex and ambiguous than its treatment by way of Christianity filtered through everyday culture would suggest.

Introduction

This chapter discusses three Platonic themes that are seminal for subsequent developments:

1. The first is the introduction of the dualism of mind (or soul) and body. Plato believes that body and soul are made of different stuff. This means that they have different essential properties, in particular, that the body is subjected to mortality and the soul isn't, that they have different relations to becoming and transformation (the soul only changes through recollection, while the body changes entirely through time, by way of aging, disease, amputation, growth, etc.), and finally, and importantly, that they are in a hierarchical relation with each other (they are engaged in a rivalry for dominance) as well as a

normative relation (the soul is superior to the body and therefore it should dominate it).

2. The second is the theme of the Fall. If our body and our soul are distinct and have different origins: how did they come together? Plato says that this is because the soul "fell" into a body at the moment of birth. As we shall see, this Fall, which will be crucial for the Christian worldview (replete with mentions of the Fall of man and Fallen angels) involves in fact two "falls": first, our soul falls from the spiritual realm to the physical realm, it becomes involved with physical things. Second, it falls into individuation, from the general (Plato says the soul-world) to the particular: the soul doesn't only become involved with body in general, it becomes involved with *a certain body*, this or that body, your body, or my body. In the process, it becomes one soul, the soul of this body, your soul, my soul.

3. The third insight we can gather from examining Plato's struggles with the notion of embodiment is Plato's failure to maintain the first two positions, and how as a consequence, Plato's doctrine of the body is ambiguous, expressed less through arguments than through examples, myths and stories, and in the end, how the body cannot be fully explained if we maintain its inferiority to and dependence on the soul. In the same way as Augustine and Descartes later, Plato turned out to be unable to overcome the fact that the body needs a separate account and that this account changes everything: we can no longer account for the soul, for the truth, for the world or for human nature without referring to the body.

As you can already see, the first two of these claims (the dualist claim and the account of the Fall) offer a clear and familiar view of the relations between body and soul, one that fits the now widespread complaint that Western thought throws a stigma on the body. The last one makes things more complicated and goes against much of what Platonism has come to mean for us.

Plato's Ambivalence

As discussed in the introduction to this book, a commonplace idea is that we live in our bodies in a Judeo-Christian way, but one can only say this if we begin Christianity with Plato. Indeed, this has become a common view. A lot of philosophers, starting in ancient times, thought that Plato had Christian revelations before the fact. That's how closely Platonism and Christianity are weaved together—from a cultural perspective at least. In fact, we should say that the link between Platonism and Christianity concerns only *one* strand of Platonism, the one that emphasises the first point: the soul and the body are naturally distinct, the body threatens the purity of the soul, and the soul should dominate the body.

However, there is another strand of Platonism, which doesn't settle for such a division, but emphasises the problems involved with the relation of body and soul. That strand hasn't been taken up by Christianity. Yet, it needs to be done justice to as well. For Plato begins with a paradox, as a way to build intellectual energy, by arousing our curiosity. Before proposing the hierarchical account that will be taken up by Christianity, Plato's initial concern is about the body and the soul as *different yet related* entities. There are two things, body and soul, that need to be put together (because we encounter them together in our everyday life), but whose union at the same time cannot be understood. So, Plato's first contribution is to raise a problem. Here already, we move from the sort of dogmatic reading of Plato that says Plato is about *repressing* the body, to a more generous reading, that says, Plato is *confronted with a problem*, for which he does not have a simple solution.

In order to take a broad view of Plato's contribution therefore, we must understand the three views outlined previously and investigate how (and to what extent) they belong together. To see this, we will focus on three texts (with some help from others): The early *Cratylus*, the middle *Phaedo* and the later *Phaedrus*. We will also use context from the *Symposium*, the *Meno* and the *Republic*.[1]

Many people are most familiar with the *Republic*, so let's begin there. In the famous myth of the Cave and related passages, the *Republic* informed us that there are ways to move from the visible to the invisible, from illusion to truth. In the myth of the cave, the philosopher is seen *going up* towards the light. There seems to be a difficult, but linear and unbroken path between the world of illusion and the world of truth. Indeed, Plato claims that the cave dwellers are not plagued with ignorance, but with *partial* knowledge. They contemplate shadows of imitations of the real things. This is low-level knowledge to be sure, but the difference between this low-level knowledge and the knowledge acquired through the philosopher's ascent towards the light is a difference of *degrees*. In other words, there is a linearity between the shadows, the imitations, and the real things, between illusion and truth. This is important because it already means that Plato will have to work to show how the body which is the seat of illusion, is not disconnected from the soul, which is the seat of *theoria*, truthful contemplation. Alongside *Meno* and even *Phaedo*, therefore, the *Republic* establishes a linearity which *allows* us to go up, which contains the promise of the achievement of progress. This linearity gives us the opportunity to transcend our state into the next one. Similarly, in the *Symposium*, lust (the love for bodies) leads to love (for a person), love leads to understanding of the other, which leads to understanding of the world, which in turn leads to wisdom. Here, the body is understood both as object and as subject. As an object, the body is understood as an object of interest in the sense that loving someone's body leads you to love the soul of the person, and later, it leads you to love souls in general. As a subject, the body loves other bodies and then teaches our soul to love spiritual things. Here, it is the body which is doing the loving, not just the soul of the body. There too, although in the context of love rather than perception, the linearity between error and knowledge suggests a continuity between body and soul. One can therefore see that even in the most well-known Platonic allegories, the entire stress is placed on continuity. Plato puts the continuity of body and soul at the centre of his metaphysics.

And yet, we know from other texts that he also put the *discontinuity* between body and soul at the centre of its metaphysics. These are the texts that argue that the soul existed before the body and will exist after it, that the body and the soul are in a struggle to the death, etc. From this tension, one might conclude that Plato simply did not finish his work or that he was a bad philosopher. But this, of course, is not the case. His ambivalence is the sign of a problem whose seriousness cannot be avoided. We should understand this contradiction as an energetic concentration, the energetic concentration that has created the explosion of Western philosophy. It is this very problem, the impossibility to think of the body and the soul together or apart, that has been the fuel for Western philosophy from the start.

Cratylus: The Superiority of the Soul and the Necessity of the Body

This basic problem already appears in the earlier dialogue *Cratylus*. There, Plato recognises that body and soul should be taken as distinct and that the soul should be given axiological priority over the body. Yet, the body is a hindrance to the fulfilment of the soul at the same time as it is indispensable to it. He asks: how can we square the view that the body is inferior to the soul with the view that the body is an indispensable instrument for the well-being of the soul?

Analogies

To come closer to a clarification of this paradox, Plato, characteristically, uses a series of three analogies. One could argue that the body is to the soul

"Thus some people say that the body is the tomb of the soul, on the grounds that it is entombed in its present life, while others say that it is correctly called 'a sign' because the soul signifies whatever it wants to signify by means of the body. I think it is most likely the followers of Orpheus who gave the body its name, with the idea that the soul is being punished for something, and that the body is an enclosure or prison in which the soul is securely kept—as the name itself suggests—until the penalty is paid." —Plato, *Cratylus*, 400b–c

what the word is to the meaning, what the deceased is to their grave and what the prisoner is to their "cage." All three analogies betray Plato's discomfort with the fact of embodiment.

The Word Analogy

Plato begins by suggesting that the body could be conceived as a *natural meaning* (or a "natural fit" 399d). That is to say, that the relations of body and soul could be understood in terms of the relationships of word and meaning. The word, he says, is the body of the meaning, and the meaning is the soul of the word.[2] What might this mean? First, let's examine how the word can be construed as the body of the meaning. I think we can get an idea of that fairly easily. Just like bodies, words seem to be subjected to the laws of physics. They can be seen, heard, written, they can be erased, they can be misheard. They are dependent on the vibrations in the air when we're talking. They are dependent on light when we are reading them. They are dependent on your pen when you are writing. In short, they are spatio-temporal. But of course, the word is not the meaning, because if you had a little ant walking on a manuscript by Plato, the little ant would not learn what Plato thought or said, and will not understand the meanings of the words. It will *see* the words but not read them, let alone understand them. Socrates declares: "the other animals do not investigate or reason about anything they see . . . , but a human being no sooner sees something, than he observes it closely and reasons about it" (399c). In short, man sees *and* understands, but animals only see. Already, we see some sort of hierarchy: the words are less important than the meanings for it is our interaction with meaning that makes us more than mere animals. Additionally, it seems the dependence of meaning on words is rather loose. For example, most meanings can be conveyed in fairly satisfactory ways even when using different words. Similarly, their physical characteristics are usually seen as secondary: writing a sentence or saying it amounts to similar meanings (although they have nothing in common physically). Likewise, the meaning of a sentence is unaffected by saying it with a high-pitched or deep voice. The same goes for variations in fonts, even spelling in some cases, etc. Words, like bodies, are subjected to change and variation, in ways that meanings, like souls, aren't. Plato concludes that the meaning is more important than the word, and that it is the standard for the choice and use of the word, for it is stable throughout all variations. This seems to establish the priority of the soul. Yet, the analogy also emphasises that just like the word is indispensable to the meaning, so is the body indispensable for the soul.

For the body is necessary to the soul in three ways.

First, the body expresses the soul just like the word expresses the meaning: it is there to make the soul visible (facial expressions, but also physical acts such as speaking, writing etc. involve the body).

Second, the proper use of our body is determined by our soul (just like the meaning is the standard for the word-choice): for example, we shouldn't allow our body to hurt another or to engage in debauchery because this is damaging to the moral nature and purpose of our soul; and there are ways to use our bodies that foster the moral progress of our soul (this includes ascetic exercises but also appreciating the arts, even reading and studying).

Third, the body is there to allow us to access the soul of others, through reading or listening. Understanding therefore, seems to involve an influx of life (meaning) into a text (words). Your text, your book, is dead until you open it and read it yet, it only has a chance of coming alive thanks to the presence of the words on the page.

The Grave Analogy

This is why Plato encounters the analogy of life and death (399d–399e). It looks like, for Plato, we should think of the body as something that is dead until the soul comes into it. He will later call this "ensoulment," an influx of life. At this stage, Plato uses the analogy of the grave. The word is the gravestone of the meaning, the body is the gravestone of the soul. What is a grave? Why do people have gravestones? People have gravestones, it seems, to remember. The grave is always the sign of a presence. It's the sign of the presence of something that cannot manifest itself on its own. The dead cannot present themselves, something else needs to do it *for them*. And so, in this sense the grave evidences the presence of the dead. In other words, it bridges the divide between life and death: It makes the dead continue to live, at the level of meaning, as something we think about, something we remember. And that's why we *read* graves. Almost all graves have signs that are codified to be read (most of the time it's the alphabet, but not always). And those signs are there to allow the reader to restore the dead to life for a moment. In a sense therefore, the body as grave makes the soul separate from other souls. On the other hand, it immediately compensates by offering itself as an interface through which souls can communicate.

The Cage Analogy

The next analogy is that of the body as a cage: the soul, Plato suggests, is locked up in the body and serving time. This means that the body controls or restricts the soul. So, if the soul is in the body just like the person is in the prison cell, this suggests that the body represents an interference and a disruption to the expression of the soul. The body, just like the word and the grave, is now censured as an obstacle to the life of the soul.

Yet, this third analogy is richer than the first two, for it introduces a legal undertone to Plato's discussion. Not only do we have a distinction between body and soul, we also have an account of their relation as a relation of oppression (confinement) and of punishment (imprisonment), suggesting a hierarchical and penal connection between body and soul (this is developed in the *Phaedo* and throughout Christianity: we live in our body as penalty for the Fall). This seems to place added emphasis on the negative valence of embodiment, but in fact, it also reproduces the movement of the two previous analogies, for punishment, Plato says in *Cratylus* and in many other places, offers the chance of redemption. In the *Gorgias*, for example, Socrates famously demands punishment for his mistakes, a punishment he calls education, and regards as redemptive.

So it seems that Plato plays on the notion of punishment: having a body means being punished, but does this make having a body undesirable (punishments are undesirable) or desirable (punishments are redemptive)? Thanks to this ambivalent notion of punishment, Plato seems to come to a first approach of the ambivalence of embodiment. It is not clear if our embodiment is simply the sign of a crime we committed before being embodied (therefore, it is the soul that committed the crime, not the body, which is sinful); or if the evil of our life comes from our being caged up in our bodies. This is a tension he will return to in much more explicit terms in the *Phaedrus*.

Finally, Plato brings out a third dimension of imprisonment. Incarceration can also mean *keeping safe*. Plato says: "The body is an enclosure in which the soul is securely kept" (400d).The prison of the soul *protects* the soul in three ways.

First, it prevents it from doing further harm (as one would perhaps incarcerate a drunk for the night).

Second, it protects it from external aggression (as one would incarcerate a key witness before a trial, or as we shall see with Freud, a King who is under threat). If you're going to have to be in this world, to be taken away from the spiritual world, then you're going to need protection.

Third, it allows it the time to learn. And that's what the body does too. Later (in the *Gorgias*, *Meno* and the *Republic*), this theme of rehabilitation through punishment is worked out in terms of a kind of education where bodily perception is instrumental in regaining knowledge. The body re-educates the soul by allowing it to learn about virtue again. This shall be achieved by moving from sensual perception to higher understanding. In short, the body will provide the soul with access to the true world, and only the body can do this, because for those who, as a result of their fall, have forgotten about the higher intelligible objects called the forms, the only way to be reminded is to observe objects of the physical world, which are imitations of the higher forms and remind us of them. In short, for the fallen, embodied soul, the only access to the intelligible is via the sensible, and our only access to the sensible is by being sensible ourselves.

* * *

This series of analogies can therefore serve to help us set the scene of Plato's problem of embodiment, just like it set the scene for Plato himself. In the *Cratylus*, we have a confused picture that shows the lines according to which Plato will have to clarify his thinking:

First, the analogies suggest that the soul is better than the body but cannot do away with it.

Second, it looks like the body has a rehabilitative relationship to the soul. The punishment for the soul is necessary for its restoration and the body is entrusted with carrying out this job. As a cage, the body restricts the soul to one corner of the world, to a specific point of view, whereas without a body, this soul could contemplate the entire world all at once. Yet, without a body, our soul would be unable to interact with other souls, to manifest itself, or even to *learn*.

This is the third point: it looks like the body is essential to visibility and vision and that visibility and vision are essential to the well-being of the soul. The body is a way of allowing the soul to express itself in the world, or access the world.

For Plato is operating a shift. If the body really is like a grave, if the body really is like a word, the body is essentially indispensable. It fulfils a necessary function of *making visible*. And, of course, this is the beginning of a very long history of the body being connected to perception. What does that mean?

Two things. First, the body perceives, however, this is not what Plato talks about at this moment. What Plato is talking about here, is the second point, that the body *is* perceived, perceptible. What do I see of you? I see your body. Being there for each other requires manifestation.

And there, we see Plato, as the great philosopher that he is, struggling with himself: It's not as easy as he thought. Getting rid of the body is also removing visibility, it's also removing access. And Plato is a philosopher of access. The great philosophical question for him is "How can I access the world of ideas?" The body is both isolation—it imprisons us, takes us away from each other—and access, it makes us visible to each other. So, here, we see Plato gradually giving weight to the possibility that the body would possess a positive value, that it may be impossible to define it as *lack* only.

The Positivity of the World of Illusion

Plato's analysis of appearances led him to the recognition that the limited cannot be reduced to some pure lack. This is an insight systematised in the late dialogue *The Sophist*, where Plato argues the following: If a sophist is a fake philosopher, then a sophist is someone who *appears* to be a philosopher without being one. A sophist's power therefore, lies in appearance. And this power is not nothing, because it killed Socrates (the Tyrants who sentenced Socrates to death are meant to have been influenced by the Sophists). As a result, appearances have power. Now, to have power over things that exist, you need to exist (as per the "Eleatic principle" exposed in *The Sophist* [248c]), so, Plato concludes, appearances exist. And of course, to exist *as appearances*, to appear, is a distinct mode of being that is irreducible to other modes of being. In other words, there is a positivity to appearances: appearances are not accidental.

The problem for Plato is that this conflicts with his famous theory of forms. On that view, the spatio-temporal is purely accidental. As a result, any appearances are accidental too, and they therefore cannot be essential and constitutive in the ways outlined earlier. The theory of forms posits that all things that exist have an ideal form: this would suggest that there are forms of appearances as such. Not only does this sound hard to conceive, but this has knock-on effects for the rest of Plato's philosophy: for example, for his moral theory which presupposes that the good involves living according to the forms and that evil is illusion. This is the deepest tension there is in Plato. It's expressed in many different ways in many different places. Plato keeps hesitating between valuing the visible because the visible *is* the way that we can learn and learning is the objective of life, and disvaluing the visible because the visible is illusion, and therefore the opposite of learning.

Why is there this ambivalence? Surely not because Plato cannot decide. The ambivalence prevails because visibility itself is ambiguous. Visibility is always both *illusion* (I called it interference previously) and *access*.

As a result, the question becomes pressing: is the body the result or the cause of our removal from the truth, and therefore, of illusion? The *Cratylus* text shows us that Plato is aware, almost from the start, that this is a key question. From a point of view of intellectual history, it is interesting to note that the dominant story about Platonism would suggest that this is an open-and-shut case: the body lures us towards sin, case closed. But Plato doesn't close the case at all. On the contrary, he writes two competing dialogues, each of which takes one of the two options (although both texts have hints of the other position). The *Phaedo* makes the general argument that we fall *because* of our bodies. The body is the sin and the cause of the crime. *Phaedrus* makes the opposite point: our souls are damaged, they are insufficient to start with, and that's why we fall into our bodies. Our bodies are therefore the consequence of our sin.

Phaedo: The Body Is the Source of Imperfection

In this section, we examine Plato's most focused attempt at doing away with the ambivalence of embodiment by rejecting the idea that the fall into the

All these things will necessarily make the true philosophers believe and say to each other something like this: "There is likely to be something such as a path to guide us out of our confusion, because as long as we have a body and our soul is fused with such an evil we shall never adequately attain what we desire, which we affirm to be the truth. The body keeps us busy in a thousand ways because of its need for nurture. Moreover, if certain diseases befall it, they impede our search for the truth. It fills us with wants, desires, fears, all sorts of illusions and much nonsense, so that, as it is said, in truth and in fact no thought of any kind ever comes to us from the body. Only the body and its desires cause war, civil discord and battles, for all wars are due to the desire to acquire wealth, and it is the body and the care of it, to which we are enslaved, which compel us to acquire wealth, and all this makes us too busy to practice philosophy. Worst of all, if we do get some respite from it and turn to some investigation, everywhere in our investigations the body is present and makes for confusion and fear, so that it prevents us from seeing the truth."—Plato, *Phaedo*, 58b–d body is caused by sin: rather, it is embodiment that causes sin, the body is not necessary to the soul, but only a hindrance to it. Interestingly, *Phaedo*, which makes the more canonical argument according to which the body is the downfall of the soul, is the earlier of the two dialogues; which may suggest that *Phaedrus* represents a more accomplished position of Plato's (although, again, dating is uncertain in the case of Plato's works).

Early in the dialogue, Socrates associates the body with Evil. He declares that illusion is caused by the body and that the body can have no part in redeeming it. Here, in the *Phaedo*, Plato decisively cuts the Gordian knot he had tied up himself in *Cratylus*: the body cannot offer us redemption or learning. He even goes as far as to suggest that even souls that have shed their bodies and died, if they retain any sin, do so because of their past bodies (81d–e).

Further, Socrates argues that the soul is pure and as such, harmonious, that is to say, simple. This means, as he points out, that all souls are the same and participate in one great element called Soul (he sometimes talks about the soul-world). It also means, most importantly, that evil, which is disharmony, cannot come from the soul (which is one), and that whatever introduces evil in our lives is by nature different from the soul. For Plato, this is a way of killing two birds with one stone. Proving at once that the soul is distinct from the body and that the body, not the soul, is the source of evil (95ff.) Of course, the cost of this view is a certain emphasis on the distinction of body and soul, and with it, a weakening of Plato's ability to account for their interaction, and further, to provide any account of education as a movement from embodied ignorance to disembodied contemplation: any such movement would have to return to the linearity of the *Republic* (discussed previously) and of the *Meno*, and it would rely on the body's ability to grasp physical objects. These are problems that remain unsolved in the *Phaedo* and which motivate much of Plato's later work.

Phaedrus: The Body Is the Sign of Imperfection

In this section, we examine in what ways Plato moves beyond the *Phaedo*'s position to distance himself from the view that the body can be done away with. In keeping with the alternative presented earlier, it does so by suggesting that the problems that the body resolves have been caused *before* embodiment. This emphasises the necessity of the body and returns us to the *Cratylus* problem. Faced with the connection *and* distinction of body and soul, the *Phaedo* emphasised the separation. The later dialogue *Phaedrus* obeys exactly the opposite logic. It seeks to account not for the *separation*, but for the *connection* of body and soul. The famous myth of the Fall of the soul presented in stunning language in the *Phaedrus* is Plato's indirect way to deal with a problem that he is coming to recognise as crucial for the functioning of his philosophy in general. The myth tells the story of an originary fall of the soul into the body. The fall, he says, is the result of the soul's inability to live in a divine way: it is the direct result of the fact that the soul is, after all, not unified (as is the case in the *Phaedo*), but composite, and not harmonious, but rather the locus of internal tensions. Plato describes this tension as a conflict between two horses with different inclinations. This means that in *Phaedrus*, Plato exonerates the body from the charges brought by the *Phaedo*, namely, the charge of being the *source* of evil. Rather, it is now suggested that evil exists in the souls that fall in the first place.

The text in question is especially difficult to deal with because it's a myth. It's also incredibly beautiful, one of the great texts of the Greek civilisation. In it, there is a sensitive edge which betrays the existential motivations of Plato. Plato's philosophy never ignores the suffering of life. And he knows injustice, he knows the sense of the tragic, and he embraces the natural human tendency which is to get beyond suffering. The text offers an allegorical description of what it is to be a human being. And what it is to be a human being, he argues, is to suffer, to refuse the suffering, and to have a chance or a fantasy for redemption. It is very hard to visualise what Plato is talking about. Our souls, he says, are riding on chariots taking part in a big procession, the big cosmic procession that contains all the souls in the world. Each soul has a charioteer and two winged horses. This procession is led by the gods. It's probably best to think of it a bit like a solar system. It's the dance of the planets. And there are higher planets and lower planets. There are those that are comets, and we, imperfect humans, are like the comets, we don't obey the rules of the universe, which would be to orbit endlessly. But we, like comets, have another style of motion: we fall. The Gods, by contrast, are absolutely in control. But what does it mean to be in control? It means that their nature and nature in general are the same thing: in the language of the *Phaedo*, they are in harmony with themselves and with the rest of reality. And therefore, they follow the order of nature, and hold their place in the procession, in an orderly manner, like stars in the sky. And then there is poor little us. Here is our curse: we are close enough to divinity to believe that we can be like the Gods. This is because our soul has a divine horse. That divine horse wants to go up, towards the Gods, it pulls us towards divinity. But then, we also have a bad horse. And the bad horse just drags his feet. It doesn't want to go anywhere, and it is lazy. Note that in this view, the wicked horse, which is a purely spiritual entity, plays the role attributed to the body in the *Phaedo*. He wants to fall down. He's heavy. He doesn't know how to fly. Finally, there is a charioteer who is supposed to get the bad horse in line.[3]

The *Phaedrus* examines the way in which the disharmony at the heart of the soul is what makes the soul fall *on earth*. By claiming that we fall into an earthly body, Plato treats two falls in one fell swoop.

> Let us then liken the soul to the natural union of a team of winged horses and their charioteer. The gods have horses and charioteers that are themselves all good and come from good stock besides, while everyone else has a mixture. To begin with, our driver is in charge of a pair of horses; second, one of his horses is beautiful and good and from stock of the same sort, while the other is the opposite and has the opposite sort of bloodline. This means that chariot-driving in our case is inevitably a painfully difficult business. And now I should try to tell you why living things are said to include both mortal and immortal beings. All soul looks after all that lacks a soul, and patrols all of heaven, taking different shapes at different times. So long as its wings are in perfect condition it flies high, and the entire universe is its dominion; but a soul that sheds its wings wanders until it lights on something solid, where it settles and takes on an earthly body, which then, owing to the power of this soul, seems to move itself. The whole combination of soul and body is called a living thing, or animal, and has the designation "mortal" as well. Such a combination cannot be immortal, not on any reasonable account.—Plato, *Phaedrus*, 246b–d
>
> Besides, the law of Destiny is this: If any soul becomes a companion to a god and catches sight of any true thing, it will be unharmed until the next circuit; and if it is able to do this every time, it will always be safe. If, on the other hand, it does not see anything true because it could not keep up, and by some accident takes on a burden of forgetfulness and wrongdoing, then it is weighed down, sheds its wings and falls to earth. At that point, according to the law, the soul is not born into a wild animal in its first incarnation; but a soul that has seen the most will be planted in the seed of a man.—Plato, *Phaedrus*, 248c–d

First, to fall on earth means to fall into a body because it means to exist in the spatiotemporal (or sublunar) world. Here, the earth is defined as the realm of the laws of physics. But to be subjected to the law of physics, we must be a physical thing ourselves. This involves that the soul becomes embodied, it becomes part of a field of interaction regulated by the laws of physics.

Interestingly, as this happens, a second thing happens: the soul cannot be part of the physical world without acquiring a certain spatio-temporal location. Not only does it acquire physical substance, it also acquires *this* body and not *that* body, that is to say, a *certain* body, and not body in general. Interestingly, this is something that Plato takes for granted: to fall into the spatio-temporal immediately means the acquisition of a body, of localisation and of individuation. This shows well that for Plato (and for the tradition after him) the physical world is not just the world of the *tangible*, but it is also the world of the *individuated*. To be physical, one must cease to be intangible, but one must cease to be universal too: to have a body means to be somewhere and not everywhere, at a certain time and not at another. So, the fall into embodiment is also a fall into individuation. This is why we must speak of two falls.

The Positive Status of Embodiment

This suggests that Plato regards the Fall of the soul as the acquisition of *a point of view*, a vantage point from which to look at the world. Here, Plato displays his awareness of a theme that will become central for phenomenologists of embodiment twenty-five centuries later: only a body allows us to have a world of perception, because it is only by having a body that we have an angle of vision onto the world. Remember, before acquiring a body, our soul was floating over the world, shapeless, and therefore everything in the world appeared to be in front of everything else, above or below everything else, left or right of everything else, none of it coalescing into any meaningfully organised vision. Left, right, front, back, up and down all are necessary for creating any image of the world around us and yet they are all relative to our point of view. Without a body, no perception is possible. This is not only true pragmatically (actual things that perceive also have bodies) it is also true necessarily: you cannot perceive without being or having a body. In short, our body makes us into perceptual beings. At the same time, this acquisition of a world of perception goes along with our reduction to one single point of view: it allows us to see and at the same time it restricts our ability to see. The fall reduces us to *one* point of view. But it also bestows upon us the *acquisition* of a point of view. For having all the points of views or none, in either case, vision is impossible. The right number of points of views for the world to appear is exactly one. Without a point of view, we would have no restriction, but we would have no access. It looks therefore that when it comes to perception, partiality is indispensable.

Plato's next problem therefore will be: is this acquisition of a body a good or a bad thing? What is the net result if we measure the ability to see against the restrictions in our vision that come with our acquiring a body? More fundamentally for Plato, can the advantage of vision be maintained without losing the advantage of universal omnipresence? The analysis of perception implicit in the myth of the Fall therefore comes close to threatening Plato's doctrine of the congruence of all goods because perception seems to suggest that there is a conflict between different aspects of goodness: we cannot have all the benefit of having *no* point of view without losing the benefit of having *a* point of view. Should we therefore bite the bullet and simply reject the idea that perception, our ability to see the spatio-temporal world, is a good in any way? Certainly, this is strongly suggested in the *Phaedo*. It is worth returning to it, as it will allow us to get a better grasp of what the positivity of embodiment—the fact that we cannot reduce the fact of embodiment to any other, more fundamental fact—means. In the *Phaedo*, Plato takes a quantitative view to the question of value, and this allows him to define the spatio-temporal as restriction: what the body gives us access to is the same world that the soul had access to, simply it is now *restricted* to one single point of view. For Plato, the sensible world is an *imitation* of the intelligible world and its contents are imitations of the contents of the intelligible world (the forms, including souls). The right way to frame the question therefore is to ask whether there is added value in imitation. The *Phaedo* and *Republic* try to answer no. In keeping with the view of restriction as nothingness, they argue that the original (the ideal) contains everything that the imitation contains *and then some*, namely, at least, its being the original. In this view, it is not so much that the world of perception turns up for us (this is also the case in the spiritual world), rather, it is that the world turns up *in a perceptual way*. Therefore, seeing it appear in a perceptual way is not an added bonus. On the contrary, Plato says, this new way is a lesser way. Knowing the world through perception is a less perfect way to know the world than the way of intellectual, disembodied contemplation. Imagine going to buy ice cream. There are two ice cream parlours in town. One of them, called Phaedrus's Scoops offers pistachio, chocolate, coffee and vanilla flavours. The second, Phaedo's delight, offers all of the above *in addition to* strawberry and mango. It seems that Phaedrus's Scoops is only different from Phaedo's delight by virtue of the fact that its range is more restricted. Yet, nobody would count this as an argument for going to Phaedrus's Scoops. After all, it's distinguishing feature is not an added good, but a lack. Going to Phaedo's delight certainly involves forfeiting the experience of going to Phaedrus's ice cream, but this only means missing out on the *absence* of strawberry and mango. In short, Phaedrus has more absent flavours than Phaedo's and missing out on it means missing out on absence. Hardly a disadvantage. In this view, the restriction involved in perception amounts, literally, to nothing: a lack. This will be crucial to Augustine's notion of Evil in the next chapter. Note that here the argument relies on the idea that the difference between the two modes of life is reducible to one single scale, in which the greater contains all the goodness of the smaller and in which consequently, the thesis of the unity of all goods remains unharmed. In the same vein, the famous idea of the *Symposium* (another middle dialogue), is that the beauty of soul *contains* the beauty of individual souls. And the beauty of individual souls contains and supersedes the beauty of bodies. In other words: physical beauty is reducible to spiritual beauty. It doesn't have anything specific to it.

So, why does Plato go back on this view in the *Phaedrus*? This is a question that has worried many of his followers, not least Plotinus, who concluded that Plato became aware that beauty and especially the beauty of colours, could not be a good derived from other intelligible goods (i.e., goods that could be enjoyed by disembodied souls). For Plato, the reasons are multiple, but let's return to the ice cream argument. Note that this is an argument that only works if (a) the difference between the two ice cream parlours is quantitative and not qualitative (only a matter of how many flavours are available, not quality, décor, etc.), and (b) if Phaedo's Delight indeed carries exactly the same ice cream flavours as Phaedrus' Scoops *in addition to* strawberry and mango. Plato gradually comes to the realisation that neither of these two premises hold. The perceptual world is qualitatively different from the intelligible world (Plotinus's reference to colour is a nod to this: in the intelligible world, we never experience the qualitative experience of colour), and it contains some properties that the intelligible world doesn't.

As this has been often noted by Plato readers, this problem regarding the reducibility of the perceptual realm to the intelligible realm is signalled by Plato's self-defeating use of perceptual language to discuss intelligible processes. For example, he calls the highest exercise of the soul *theoria*, that is to say some sort of perfect "vision" or "contemplation." Similarly, he talks of intelligible objects in terms of their "beauty" and of philosophy in terms of its "insights," he also likens intellectual pleasure to sensual pleasures. Now, all of this could be dismissed as stylistic and rhetorical strategies if it weren't for the fact that Plato has no other way to talk about the intelligible than to use references to the perceptual. In other words, Plato is implicitly acknowledging that the intelligible *means* nothing to us if it is not represented in sensuous terms: meaning comes from embodied experience. In the *Phaedrus* itself, we have this interesting discussion, where Plato, always the honest and self-critical philosopher, stages his own contradictions for our benefit. Wisdom, he declares, is the most desirable, but in order for us to know that, we need to see that it is as desirable as sensuously beautiful things. "The loveliness of wisdom would have been transporting if there had been a visible image of her and the other ideas." In other words, the fact that we are more interested in pretty people than in wisdom is because wisdom is invisible. But in fact, if wisdom was a person it would be the most beautiful person. The problem is that most of us do not see the beauty of the invisible, "and instead of being awed at the sight of wisdom" we pursue "earthly pleasure." The problem, for Plato, is that the beauty of wisdom is not recognised by embodied beings. There is a lack that prevents embodied beings from recognising the beauty of wisdom. This lack could be attributed to embodied beings themselves: because we are embodied, we are fascinated with perceptual objects and forget about invisible beauty. But does this solve Plato's problem? It remains that, in an environment made of embodied beings, wisdom is *less* powerful than images. The power of images therefore seems to be a good that cannot be accounted for by the intelligible notion of goodness.

One might object that this is a good that is of a lower quality, because it is only necessary to those who are blinded by prejudice and perceptual illusion. This is true, and indeed, Plato affirms this many times: beautiful objects are a way to teach us to love beauty in general. But even in this reading, images retain some power: as discussed briefly, the power that images have and that the intelligible lacks is a pedagogical power. Images *teach* us to learn. In this sense, images are not perfection itself, since they only exist when imperfection (i.e., ignorance) exists. The problem with this view is that it implies a sort of quietism: the view that there is no need for those living in the world of experience to attain enlightenment because the world of experience is contemptible. Perfection is not affected by what takes place in the world of experience. This is a consequence that Plato is not willing to draw however, and so for two reasons. First, because one of the goods that participate in perfection is being. What this means is that everything that *is* should be contained in the notion of perfection. Now, either the world of perception exists and therefore it belongs to perfection and needs to be made perfect, or it doesn't exist. In comes the second reason why this is not a desirable outcome for Plato: we cannot say that the world of experience doesn't exist, as this would be the same as saying that learning is not possible (we know everything since ignorance only belongs in the non-existent world of perception) or desirable (getting rid of ignorance would constitute, rigorously speaking, no progress at all). This shows that the only possible defence of the *Phaedo* argument, would involve a strict reading of Plato's idea that we should *not* have bodies, and lead us to sacrifice the whole of Plato's theory of education which is almost all of his philosophy. This discussion is pursued in the *Sophist*.

For our current purposes we can see that what this means about the body is that taking embodiment as a positive fact means taking the ability to learn to be primary. It's the lowest ability to learn there is, because we only learn about bodily things which are the lowest kind of things there are. But it is an indispensable starting point. And so, we need to maintain this sort of ambivalence where the body is both the beginning, the source of learning, and an impairment on learning, because it binds us to the spatio-temporal. It makes it impossible for us not to learn, *and* it becomes a limitation, it prevents us, at a certain point, from learning more. Why is it impossible for us *not* to learn when we have a body? Because having a body exposes us to the easiest kind of wisdom there is. Because our senses are curious before we are. Just because we have a body, we have senses, because we have senses, we're open to the world. And so, there will always be a day where we will be surprised by something. Maybe a flash of light, or maybe a certain movement, or a piece of music grabs our attention and we're already humanising ourselves. So, this leaves us with two upshots.

First, everything in the spatiotemporal is a symbol of something in the world of ideas. What that means is that the spatiotemporal world is a laboratory for learning about the real world that is behind it. Second, more importantly for us in terms of the body, our body teaches us. It does the learning *for us* and we can't help that. Merleau-Ponty, later, as we will see, talks about the "prospective activity of consciousness," and what he means by that is that our ability to learn is never asleep. It's always reaching out for the world, it prospects, it pushes out to feel for things, to look for things. So of course, you can shut your eyes, but you cannot shut your eyes forever. You are exposed to the world, to the spatio-temporal world, because you have a body. But that's going back to the idea that the body is both restriction and access. It gives you access to the world, it also prevents you from transcending this access to the world. It prevents you from moving on to knowledge about things that are not in the world. But, this ability to learn about things that are not in the world has been trained by our interaction with the world. In the context of the discussion of the unity of virtues, Plato asks himself: Is there a certain way of being where we have everything? Where we have vision, the way that man in the real world has vision, *and* we have no illusion the way that souls in the world of ideas have no illusions. And Plato gradually comes to the realisation that you cannot have both. It is impossible to explain the beauty in the spatio-temporal world in terms of non-spatio-temporal beauty. It is impossible to reduce everything that's good about the spatio-temporal world to non-spatio-temporal things. In other words, there is an intrinsic value in the spatio-temporal. The beauty of a body for example, is always the beauty of an individual thing and something of that beauty is lost when this individuality is dissolved into the thin air of the sky of ideas. These are problems that Plato realises—slowly—cannot be solved.

What's important for us, because this book takes not only a history of philosophy outlook, but also a history of culture outlook, is that there is this tension. We have, basically the best mind available, Plato, discovering the best problem available, that we cannot explain the body away. Beyond questions of right and wrong, that's Plato's grand contribution: there is no state that combines all the goodness in the world, because some goodness contradicts some other goodness, namely the goodness of the spatiotemporal contradicts the goodness of the intelligible. Why? Because we have bodies.

Conclusion

Of course, the fact that Plato does not give a good reason for why we should overcome the body doesn't mean that culture hasn't received the message that we should do so. We may be tempted to complain that Plato did not prove that we should overcome the body. In the pursuit of this goal, he makes a philosophical discovery which is not only that his goal cannot be attained but even that it may be a *contradictory* goal, an attempt to do away with the spatio-temporal motivated by our experience of spatio-temporal existence.

This leaves us with three insights that will be seminal for the later tradition.

- The body is irreducible to the nonbodily, embodied life is *sui generis*.
- The body is defined as spatio-temporality that gives access to the spatio-temporal world.
- The fall of the soul is always two falls.
  - ○ The fall from one state of being to another, from the spiritual to the physical.
  - ○ The fall from the general to specific, or to the individual.

Taken together, these conclusions amount to this: the fact of embodiment pervades everything about us, and therefore, also about the world we live in so far as it is *our* world.

Additional Readings
Plato, *Symposium*, 201d–212c.
Plato, *Republic*, Book V.
Plato, *Gorgias*, 467a–468e.
Plato, *Sophist*, 258a–268c.
Aristotle, *Physics*, I, 9 and II, 1–3.
Aristotle, *On the Soul*.
R. S. Bluck, "The *Phaedrus* and Reincarnation."
D. D. McGibbon, "The Fall of the Soul in Plato's *Phaedrus*."
C. Zoller, *Plato and the Body: Reconsidering Socratic Asceticism*.

Key Ideas

The body is a principle of spatio-temporal localisation.

Embodiment is involved with imperfection: either as its cause (*Phaedo*), or or as its sign (*Phaedrus*).

The body separates us from the world and from each other and it gives us access to the world and to each other.

The body prevents the soul from flourishing (knowledge) but it offers the opportunity for learning.

The existence of the body means that the world is imperfect.

In spite of Plato's best efforts, the fact of embodiment is irreducible: embodiment is not an accident, it is a primary, fundamental and independent structure of the world as a whole.

Notes

1. It is very hard to chronologise Plato's dialogues. But there is more or less an agreement that the middle Plato includes the *Republic* and the *Phaedo*, and that the *Symposium* is somehow attached to the *Republic*. *Cratylus* seems to come before the *Republic*, and *Phaedrus* seems to come after the *Republic*. This gives us the following loose sequence: *Cratylus, Republic, Symposium, Phaedo, Phaedrus*.

2. This is a theme that returns to prominence in St Paul's *Letter to the Corinthians*, for example.

3. This is the replay of the myth of Phaeton, who is the son of Elios. Elios's job was to carry the sun across the horizon in one day and every morning he gets up to his chariot to carry the sun across the horizon. And one day he is sick, and his son Phaeton begs him to let him try to drive the sun, and he tries, and fails. He has no control over the chariot, and goes too close to the ground, burning a whole expanse,

that's how we've got the Sahara desert and then he goes back up and the earth freezes over and we got glaciers. Phaeton lacks the strength of soul that his father has to control the power that he is carrying. Plato takes the story over and places it in a philosophical context.

CHAPTER THREE

~

The Irreducibility
of the Body 2: Augustine

Readings
The Bible, book of Genesis, Chapter 2.
Plotinus, *Second Enneads*, II, III, 14–16, *Fourth Ennead*, III, 8.
Augustine, *Confessions*, Book 1, Chapters 5 and 6.
Augustine, Letter 143 to Marcellinus.
Augustine, *The City of God*, Book XIV, Chapters 4–17.
Augustine, *Genesis, Against the Manichees*, II, Ch. 15.

In the previous chapter, we examined how Plato's entire philosophy had to be transformed before his reluctant discovery of the fact that embodiment couldn't be explained away. Although his early and middle thought presumes that the unlimited intelligible realm contains and exhausts the limited embodied realm, his later thought recognises that this would make him unable to account for perception, and therefore, for the entire spatio-temporal world. This carries the cost of losing any account of learning. After all, the soul is embodied as a result of a double fall from the general to the local and from the intelligible to the sensible, and embodiment is therefore a precondition to learning. A prominent neo-Platonist who took up the *Phaedo*'s project of reducing imperfection to nothingness was Plotinus, but he too came to the later Plato's conclusion, and resorted to calling the sensible world the "youngest child" of the intelligible, and the "manifestation of god." In Plotinus's view, the sensible world had to be recognised as making a specific contribution to

37

the cosmos that was irreducible to the intelligible, namely, "beauty" (*Ennead* V, 8–12). Plotinus is an intermediary figure between Plato and the great philosopher of early Christianity, Augustine of Hippo. He is not the only one, and between Plotinus and Augustine stand a number of fascinating, if lesser known figures, including Origen, who we will discuss in a moment.

Plotinus inherited Plato's problem, which is to account for the positivity of embodiment without repudiating the ethical, metaphysical and epistemological priority of the intelligible. Accordingly, Plotinus sees himself tasked with the project of recuperating the positivity of appearances and explaining how it participates in the unity of virtue. He brings out two claims that remain implicit in Plato's works. First, without appearances there would be no colours or beauty, both of which are obviously good. Second, this runs the risk of violating the doctrine of the unity of virtues by making perfection itself a contradictory concept, with some perfections incompossible or incompatible with others. Unity, for example, is a requirement of perfection. But appearances—at least when they are beautiful or colourful—are a necessary part of perfection also—that is, perfection without colour is less perfect. But perception and unity are mutually incompatible because in order to perceive you need a separation between the perceiver and the perceived. So, you will always have a perfection *lacking*, or a conflict between perfections. A lack or a conflict, are *imperfections*. This, in turn, raises two questions that become increasingly pressing after Plato, and especially in the Christian era: first, why does the world necessarily contain imperfection? And second, why does such a world not reflect badly on God?

This chapter explores how the Platonic legacy has shaped and influenced early Christian thought by focusing on the thought of Augustine. This question is important not only for philosophical reasons. Christianity is arguably the central cultural influence on Western culture; understanding its account of the body is essential to the historical ambitions of this book, but also to the existential question: asking how we have come to live in our bodies is also asking how the way we live in our bodies has been informed by Christianity. This chapter focuses on Augustine because he is a central figure for the establishment of Christianity as a worldview and a philosophical position, because Augustine himself made the question of the body central to his own work, and because Augustine is the major link between Platonism and Christianity.

The Problem of Theodicy

Augustine is famous for his doctrine of the original sin, and he has long been decried by those who argue that Christianity has placed a stigma on the body in general and on sexuality in particular, by associating the original sin to a sexual act. Of course, things are more complicated and if sex has anything to do with it, it is only because through it, humans give birth to new humans, and as we remember, to be born is to fall into a body. The problem with sex is that it reproduces embodiment, not, as is often contended, that it encourages the appetites. Augustine's philosophy is not directly animated by some sort of resentment towards embodiment. For him, embodiment becomes of concern only in the context of his attempt to account for evil. The problem, as I mentioned before, was present in Plato and became more pressing in Plotinus, and Origen, and reached a pitch of urgency with Augustine.

As a bishop in fourth-century North Africa, Augustine was surrounded by infidels, people with a very deep and elaborate pagan theology. And he knows that the problem of theodicy places Christianity at a disadvantage against paganism. This is because paganism offers much more flexibility precisely as regards the unity of virtues. In paganism, conflict is the norm. In Homer, for example, the gods fight. They constitute multiple and competing centres of value, of power, of justification, of legitimacy. And the world is made of conflicts because the gods fight.[1] Monotheism, on the other hand, also presents conceptual advantages: In general, unity is more elegant, theoretically speaking. But monotheism also paints itself into corners when it comes to the question of evil.

Beyond this historical context there is also for Augustine a philosophical question, which is about the value of the One. Not just about the unity of values, but about the unity of the world itself (the next chapter shall return to this concern, which re-emerges in almost the same way in Descartes' dualism). If there is evil, it looks like there is difference, if there is difference, the One is in fact not One. It's fragmented. Is the world one thing? Is knowledge always about the same thing? Is the knowledge of one part of the world and knowledge of another part of the world about the same world? Do the same rules apply all the time? Are there universal laws of nature? And therefore, is philosophy meant to be systematic?

For all these reasons, inherited from Plato but reactivated in the meantime, Augustine must explain how a world ruled and created by god can contain evil. Evil, Augustine assumes, following Plato, is connected to the Fall and like Plato, Augustine wonders if evil is the cause or the consequence of the fall into our body, and which aspect of the fall (the individualising or the materialising aspect) is involved with evil.

Augustine's project, therefore, is to produce a theodicy, to describe a world in which evil cannot be used as an objection to the existence or perfection of God. Generally speaking, theodicy is a response to the argument

> Here is the message of Lachesis, the maiden daughter of Necessity: 'Ephemeral souls, this is the beginning of another cycle that will end in death. Your daemon or guardian spirit will not be assigned to you by lot; you will choose him. The one who has the first lot will be the first to choose a life to which he will then be bound by necessity. Virtue knows no master; each will possess it to a greater or lesser degree, depending on whether he values or disdains it. The responsibility lies with the one who makes the choice; the god has none.' . . . Now it seems that it is here, Glaucon, that a human being faces the greatest danger of all. And because of this, each of us must neglect all other subjects and be most concerned to seek out and learn those that will enable him to distinguish the good life from the bad and always to make the best choice possible in every situation.—Plato, *Republic* X, 617d–621c.

from evil which asks, "if God is almighty and all good, how come there is evil?" If God is almighty, but there is evil, then he allowed for there to be evil, but that contradicts the principle of divine goodness. If God is all good but there is evil, that's because he was unable to prevent the existence of evil and this violates God's omnipotence. Power and goodness are both parts of perfection, and so we see how the argument from evil puts pressure on the doctrine of the unity of virtues.

In addition to the conceptual headache that comes with this question, Augustine needs to navigate his way between two positions that have been (then or since) declared heretical by the Church. The first is Manicheism, which questions the almightiness of god by positing that evil is a positive, existing entity. As we shall see, Augustine comes dangerously close to this view when he acknowledges that embodiment is a necessary evil. The other is Origenism, which follows the *Phaedrus* in claiming that souls aren't perfect, and have sinned before acquiring a body, and which takes over the metaphor of the prison from *Cratylus*. Augustine declares, "I do not believe, nor grant, nor consent to [Origen's] view that souls sin in another, higher life, and are cast thence into bodily prisons" (Letter 143). Between these two heretical positions, Augustine needs to find his narrow path. Interestingly, this position will resemble the one outlined by Plato himself at the end of the *Republic* in the myth of Er: evil is man's, not god's responsibility. But how can god not be responsible for man?

Here is how Augustine approaches the problem: God is a principle of goodness. Anything that *is*, is because of god, and therefore, to be is to be good. However, the body is connected to imperfection. So, the next question is, does the body exist? And that continues the tradition of the *Phaedo* that says: "God is not responsible for evil, because evil is nothing," and God is not responsible for nothing (remember the ice cream parlour scenario). Nobody is responsible for nothing. As we saw, the main difficulty for Platonism, which is not necessarily a religious form of thought, is not so much "How do we defend God against the charge of allowing evil" but rather that the difference between *being* and *nothingness* is not as strict as the Middle Plato (and Parmenides) thought, and this is why he takes the dramatic step of moving away from this doctrine in the *Sophist*. It is true, in a sense, that evil has less reality than goodness. But it doesn't mean that evil has no reality, or that it cannot defeat goodness.

At this stage, we can see that in much the same way as Plato had to reluctantly acknowledge the irreducibility of the body because of the irreducibility of perception, Augustine will be brought to acknowledge (a) that nothingness is irreducible, (b) that nothingness is, strictly speaking, evil, and (c) that the presence of nothingness in the world is embodiment. As a result, the body is irreducible by virtue of the irreducibility of evil. All of these accounts are complicated because they talk about embodiment negatively. As such, we can read in Augustine's complications about the fall an implicit understanding of how difficult it is to do away with the body: just as Plato cannot do away with the body because he cannot do away with the perceptual world, we shall see that Augustine cannot do away with the body because he cannot do away with sin.

The Fall

This means that we need to return to the notion of the Fall as this is the foundational event which accounts for the origin of imperfection (evil) and of restriction (nothingness) and raises the question of responsibility: is the body the source or the result of sin, and if it is the result, who or what is responsible for sin? Augustine begins with a neutral definition of the body, which is drawn from the two aspects of the fall of the soul, namely, that embodiment *materialises* and *individualises* the soul. And, as Plato declares, these two falls happen in one event, the event of birth. Augustine then asks: how can the fall be explained without making the body a principle of evil incompatible with God's goodness and power? Augustine argues: to be in a body is to no longer be everywhere all the time. It's to be naturally distinguished from God, the entity that is everywhere all the time. In other words, this fall is literally a fall *from* God. It's the breaking up of what Plato calls the soul-universe into bits of soul, each of which is given to a certain body. Just like Plato and Plotinus had to explain how the One could appear in the guise of the many (i.e., in the world of perception), Augustine must ask how God's universality can allow for localisation. Can localisation be a mode of universality, or is it separate from it? In either case, one must explain separation: how can localisation as distinct from universality exist within universality, or how can localisation exist outside of universality?

Now the serpent was more subtil than any beast of the field which the lord God had made. And he said unto the woman, Yea, hath God said, Ye shall not eat of every tree of the garden? And the woman said unto the serpent, we may eat of the fruit of the trees of the garden: But of the fruit of the tree which is in the midst of the garden, God hath said, Ye shall not eat of it, neither shall ye touch it, lest ye die. And the serpent said unto the woman, Ye shall not surely die: For God doth know that in the day ye eat thereof, then your eyes shall be opened, and ye shall be as gods, knowing good and evil. And when the woman saw that the tree was good for food, and that it was pleasant to the eyes, and a tree to be desired to make one wise, she took of the fruit thereof, and did eat, and gave also unto her husband with her; and he did eat. And the eyes of them both were opened, and they knew that they were naked; and they sewed fig leaves together, and made themselves aprons. And they heard the voice of the lord God walking in the garden in the cool of the day: and Adam and his wife hid themselves from the presence of the lord God amongst the trees of the garden. And the lord God called unto Adam, and said unto him, Where art thou? And he said, I heard thy voice in the garden, and I was afraid, because I was naked; and I hid myself. And he said, Who told thee that thou wast naked? Hast thou eaten of the tree, whereof I commanded thee that thou shouldest not eat? And the man said, The woman whom thou gavest to be with me, she gave me of the tree, and I did eat. And the lord God said unto the woman, What is this that thou hast done? And the woman said, The serpent beguiled me, and I did eat. And the lord God said unto the serpent, Because thou hast done this, thou art cursed. . . . And the lord God said, Behold, the man is become as one of us, to know good and evil: and now, lest he put forth his hand, and take also of the tree of life, and eat, and live for ever.—Genesis 2: 2–24.

In *On Free Choice* (3:59), Augustine returns to the debate between the *Phaedo* and the *Phaedrus*. He asks himself how we must understand the world before the fall: has it been created in a defective manner by God? He reviews four possible accounts of the fall: each of which corresponds to an ontological account of the world before the fall:

1. The first is the "Natural" (Traducian) account: That imperfection comes by way of generation (but this involves that sin can be passed down genetically from Adam—leading to questions about the first sin, and often, to falling back onto option four).
2. The second is the "Divine" account (Creationism): Evil is newly created when each person is born.
3. The third is the "sending" account: souls which pre-exist elsewhere are sent by God into the bodies of those who are born.
4. The fourth is the account from Freedom: Evil comes come down to us by way of our own will.

What is interesting, as the famous Letter 143 makes clear, is that Augustine's attitude to these competing theories is neutral, because he argues that there is no need to discuss the detail, when the problem is dealt with in all these views indifferently: for those views disagree about the *cause* of the Fall, when the true problem is its *possibility*.

This means that the Fall becomes regarded as a sign of a broken creation: even before there was any fall, there existed the possibility of a fall, and therefore there was a latent split in the world: some things were actual, and some were potential but not yet actual (i.e., the Fall). This is also Plato's idea, as you remember, because Plato himself recognised that for there to be a Fall, there has to be a mixture of actuality and potentiality in the world: the Fall shows that the Fall was possible, that existence is not fully perfect, because it can introduce imperfection via the Fall. This could be because this imperfection is primary as is the *Phaedrus*'s view (we have an imperfect soul made of conflicting instincts—represented by horses), or it could be because of some sin our soul had committed, or because of "chance" (*syntixia*). In any case, the fact that imperfection is possible should not be discounted, for this possibility *is* imperfection itself: a world where imperfection is possible is less perfect than a world where imperfection is impossible.

The question ends up revolving around the question of limitation: either our soul-limitation leads to our physical limitation as a punishment, or our body-limitation is the consequence of our soul-limitation. This might suggest, in the latter case, that the body is nothing but the *place* of the soul.

Indeed, that there is really only one substance. But, Augustine argues, this is impossible, as this would mean that God's only creation was the material of the soul-world later given to Adam as a "stock of soul." In other words that individuation is not of God's doing, which is exactly the conclusion that was to be avoided.

Free Will and Augustine's Modal Ontology

Letter 143 is a clarification of Augustine's discussion of Traducianism in *On Free Will*. The standard way that prior theodicies had justified evil was by saying: "evil is for the sake of a greater good, and this greater good is free will." As you remember, in the Platonic paradigm, difference involves imperfection: no two worlds could be equally perfect yet different, for this would mean one of three things: (a) that one of them has one more perfection than the other, (b) that each of them has a perfection that the other doesn't have, or (c) that the differences are about neutral contents, making it impossible to prefer one world to another. In short, any preference will compare two unequal worlds, and so, in order for choice to be possible at all, imperfections must exist. You cannot have freedom without the opportunity to make choices and therefore mistakes, the argument goes, but having freedom is a greater good for there to be in the world, than the evil that it causes. This, of course, immediately leads to two problems: first, this grants what is the core of the problem, namely that some perfections are incompossible, in this case, freedom and the perfection of the world. Second, in a theological context, this amounts to assuming that there are laws of non-contradiction that apply even to God. But God is almighty. He could have made it so that perfection is multiple, and that would have allowed us to have both free will and perfection all the time. As a result, the standard theodicy fails: there is a contradiction between a perfect world without the perfection called freedom and a perfect world with free will. The first is imperfect because it lacks free will; the second is imperfect in order to make room for choice. And so perfections contradict each other, and the unity of goodness is threatened.

In any case, this suggests that evil should be regarded as one of the intrinsic possibilities of free will, and therefore any new theodicy will need to come to a better understanding of what free will means. This is why Letter 143 is an important transitional moment between the texts on free will and the later *The City of God*. In it, we see Augustine struggling his way towards his mature position in which evil is defined as individualism, or, in Augustine's language: "living according to man." (secundum hominem). We'll return to this.

In the process of assessing the constraints imposed on any theodicy, Augustine comes to think about evil along ontological lines. Evil should be regarded as a *way to be*, perhaps even a way of being of the world, and the existence of evil changes how we should think of being in general. In particular, the existence of evil implies that we should make more room for nothingness into the world: we need an ontology in which nothingness is not nothing. Just like the later Plato had to recognise a positive existence to nothingness, Augustine recognises that nothingness exists in the world, as separation and restriction. This is important for us because it moves Augustine to systematise the view that the body is related to evil, as well as to bring out that the question of embodiment is ontological. On this basis, he will come to argue that the existence of individual embodiment is the locus of evil, and that if the fact of embodiment holds, then the whole world is changed.

The letter is focused on insisting that Augustine makes no commitment to any one particular account of the entrance of sin, but rather registers that all such accounts presuppose the possibility of sin in the world, whereas this possibility itself constitutes the evil that must be understood. This leads Augustine to ask how potentiality as such is itself related to evil, and how and if it stands up to God's will. Possibility, he argues, places the world as it is and the world as it could be in competition, reproducing the problem of free will whereby any separation between possible worlds threatens the unity of goodness and by extension, the divinity of God.

Augustine then focuses no longer on the question "who has sinned" which is about a specific instance of sin, but on the question "why is there sin" which is an ontological question about the structure of creation. The focus on this question therefore invites us to carry out an ontology, or at least a metaphysics of sin and no longer to pursue sin as a moral or psychological problem to do with people's souls. So, Augustine is after an abstract principle of sin, namely the possibility for the divine One to be separated into the Many. This, to Augustine, corresponds to an ontological split of the world between two realms, the realm of the actual and the realm of the possible. There is a way of thinking of the relations of the actual and the potential in spatio-temporal terms. In this view, the potential is the actual *elsewhere* or at *another time* (contemporary possible-world theory is an heir to this view). For example, it is possible to be a knight errant, but not now, only in the Middle Ages. Similarly, it is possible to live on Mars, but this simply means that *one day* in the future some people will live on Mars. Similarly, it is possible to see the Polar Lights but this means that it is the case that people are seeing Polar Lights right now, simply, they are elsewhere, say in Lapland, Keralia or Antarctica. In other words, the actual and the potential are separated by space and time alone. Since time and space are introduced by embodiment, this means that the split of the world into the actual and the possible coincides with the fact of embodiment. Following Plato's *Sophist*, Augustine argues that this initial, modal division between the actual and the possible is originary insofar as it is bound to impose its style of being to any further event. Once there is a division between the potential and the actual, all things will be marked by it (i.e., they will exist in time). As such, the modal division grounds the possibility of embodiment, since the basic possibility is the possibility of the fall.

It also carries evil with it because being embodied is a *restriction* of the sovereignty of the soul, the adjunction of nothingness to the soul, which surrounds it with emptiness, an alienation from the rest of creation that needs to be redeemed. The soul governs the body in a now restricted manner. This restriction, Augustine shows, is signalled by our experience of passivity: via our body, our soul becomes subject to the laws of the universe. Evil, in this view, is an element that structures the universe. This brings Augustine close to the heretical position of Manicheism, which sees evil as an irreducible cosmic force, and Augustine explores to what extent Manicheism can be avoided. This is one of the tasks of *The City of God*.

Sin Is Individualism

Augustine is often regarded as an existential thinker, that is to say, a thinker who is interested in how it feels to be separated from the world and from oneself. In true existentialist fashion, Augustine explains the experience of being alive in terms of conflicts, tensions, discomforts, anxieties. The tradition, since Augustine, thinks that all these conflicts are the result or the expressions of inner separation. You cannot have conflict without separation. We can now see how central this question of separation is to his philosophy. For Augustine comes to conceive sin as the separation of the part from the whole; of us individuals, from God. As a result, the internal tension which works the human subject and defines their experience of existence is the conflict between their divine essence and their individual character. God is universal. The human is both universal and individuated and that conflict *defines* human existence.

The question of how to make the divine part of us triumph over the individual part is the motivating theme of *The City of God*. There, Augustine will have to walk the fine line between denying the existence of evil (for our individual part is nothing but our divine part + restriction) and affirming it as an irreducible force (for this restriction cannot be brought to nought) the way the Manicheans do. His solution is to emphasise that sin exists, but not as a positive force (like the Manicheans) but only as nothingness.[2]

We can already see how this will lead to the strange implication that nothingness exists. We can immediately see that these intellectual acrobatics force Augustine to say at once that separation is nothing, and therefore not a positive force the way the Manicheans say, and yet real enough to account for the existence of sin. Ultimately, and for this reason, his account is untenable, but in the process, it will have been seminal for the rest of Western history.

> We must carefully consider how the serpent persuaded them to sin, since this question is especially pertinent to our salvation. Scripture reports these things precisely so that we might now avoid them. For, when she was asked, the woman told him what they had been commanded. [The serpent] said, "You will not die the death. For God knew that on the day that you eat from it your eyes will be opened and you will be like gods, knowing good and evil." We see from these words that they were persuaded to sin through pride, for this is the meaning of the statement "You will be like gods." So too he said, "For God knew that on the day that you eat from it, your eyes will be opened." What does this mean but they were persuaded to refuse to be under God and to want rather to be in their own power without God? Thus they refused to obey his Law as if, by his prohibition, he jealously begrudged them an autonomy that had no need of his interior light, but used only their own providence, like their own eyes, to distinguish good and evil. This is what they were persuaded to do: to love to excess their own power. And, since they wanted to be equal to God, they used wrongly, that is, against the Law of God, that middle rank by which they were subject to God and held their bodies in subjection. This middle rank was like the fruit of the tree placed in the middle of paradise. Thus they lost what they had received in wanting to seize what they had not received. For the nature of man did not receive the capability of being happy by its own power without God ruling it. Only God can be happy by his own power with no one ruling.—Augustine, *Genesis, Against the Manichees*, II, Ch. 15.

One of Augustine's intuitions in thinking about the presence of evil is that there is a truth common to the Judeo-Christian belief in the Fall as told in chapter 2 of the book of Genesis, and the Fall as told by Plato. And this,

Augustine contends, can be synthesised, in the first verse of Genesis 2 where the serpent says: "Did God really say that you shouldn't eat the fruit of the tree of good and evil?" For Augustine, this suggests that the Fall can be identified with our ability to question the order established by God. After all, the only sin committed by the serpent is to ask a question. The fall is described as a reflective moment. But this is a dramatic moment, because once the question has been asked, it is no longer god who can answer, but man who is to decide whether they endorse the word of god by answering "yes, this is god's command" or rather by saying: "I'm not sure," "I forgot," etc. What the fall introduces, therefore, is reflective thinking, critical thinking, and imagination, that is to say, along the lines sketched earlier, a relation to the *potential*. The serpent puts Eve before a choice between her ability to live according to God, and her ability to live according to her own individuality, all by asking a question. All it takes is it saying: "Yes, you've been living according to God all this time, but you know there are other ways," and then he leaves his question lingering. He walks off leaving Eve wondering: "I didn't know there were other ways!" And what becomes problematic is the difference and irreconcilability between several possible ways to be: the sin of the serpent is this, the introduction of choice, and the coincidental implication that the human can think of themselves as an autonomous subject, entitled to make choices, something Augustine calls "pride." This is a theme that has had a long legacy. Perhaps one clarifying example is to be found in Rousseau's *Second Discourse*. There, Rousseau asks, how did we come out of the state of nature? And he answers: because we had too much imagination. And that was our downfall, for Rousseau uses the word fall also. For Augustine like for Rousseau, imagination, that is to say, an encounter with the possible, was the downfall. For Augustine the fall consists in "pride" which is for the humans to "use only their own providence, like their own eyes, to distinguish good and evil" to rely on themselves in order to know the truth and to guide their actions. The fall consists in "thinking for oneself," as the English language says so well. The serpent is a critical thinker (On *Genesis*, II, chapter 15). And disobedience amounts to taking one's separation from God seriously: thinking for oneself instead of thinking according to God.

So this means that the Fall has something to do with (a) the appearing, through imagination, of a new way of living, one that Augustine calls autonomous or individualistic, and which he later calls "living according to man," and (b) with our ability to think of this new way as a competitor to our natural way, which is to "live according to God." These important phrases deserve elaboration:

Living according to Man and living according to God

When, therefore, man lives according to man, not according to God, he is like the devil. Because not even an angel might live according to an angel, but only according to God, if he was to abide in the truth, and speak God's truth and not his own lie. And of man, too, the same apostle says in another place, "If the truth of God hath more abounded through my lie"; "my lie," he said, and "God's truth." When, then, a man lives according to the truth, he lives not according to himself, but according to God; for He was God who said, "I am the truth." When, therefore, man lives according to himself—that is, according to man, not according to God—assuredly he lives according to a lie; not that man himself is a lie, for God is his author and creator, who is certainly not the author and creator of a lie, but because man was made upright, that he might not live according to himself, but according to Him that made him, in other words, that he might do His will and not his own; and not to live as he was made to live, that is a lie. For he certainly desires to be blessed even by not living so that he may be blessed. And what is a lie if this desire be not? Wherefore it is not without meaning said that all sin is a lie. For no sin is committed save by that desire or will by which we desire that it be well with us, and shrink from it being ill with us. That, therefore, is a lie which we do in order that it may be well with us, but which makes us more miserable than we were. And why is this, but because the source of man's happiness lies only in God, whom he abandons when he sins, and not in himself, by living according to whom he sins? In enunciating this proposition of ours, then, that because some live according to the flesh and others according to the spirit, there have arisen two diverse and conflicting cities, we might equally well have said, "because some live according to man, others according to God." For Paul says very plainly to the Corinthians, "For whereas there is among you envying and strife, are ye not carnal, and walk according to man?"—Augustine, *The City of God*, Chapter 4

- By "Living according to man," Augustine means living according to the individual man that one is, setting one's own rules and goals, living as if one were not part of a greater whole. In other words, living according to what is particular in us. A modern thinker would call this living according to our particular will, and our identity (gender, age, socio-political status, etc.).

- By "Living according to God," Augustine means living according to the whole, in particular, living according to universal rules (the Enlightenment thinkers make the same point by simply replacing god with "universal reason" not much of a stretch since god is defined as a principle of universality in Augustine too). In the *Confessions*, Augustine presents a succinct description of living according to God: "only wanting what god gives." This is a useful formulation because it evidences the Platonic inheritance of the notion of "living according" to man. In the *Gorgias*, Plato defined evil as the act of confusing the natural with the unnatural. As natural humans, our needs are fulfiled naturally. Our desires, on the contrary, are artificial and based not on need but on imagination (we would now say fantasy). As a result, living according to man involves pursuing our desires as if they were our needs, and strictly speaking, this is Plato's definition of evil. Augustine recasts this in terms of the story of *Genesis*: in the garden, God fulfils all our needs. We don't *need* to eat the fruit of knowledge of good and evil, but we *can*, and it is our faculty of imagination that makes us aware of the fact that that we can, and opens us up to temptation.

The distinction between the two modes of living introduced in *The City of God* is therefore instrumental in completing the work begun in *On Free Will* and evidenced in Letter 143, namely, the work of accounting for evil as possibility. Now, living "according [secundum] to man," can be formulated as *living as if man was a legitimate entity*, and this shows—intuitively—why it is connected to sin. If I truly believe that the fact that I am me, and therefore not you, and therefore not God, is justified, then my taking care of my own interests is justified. The fact that your interests don't counterbalance mine, the fact that God's interests or God's will, does not counterbalance mine, is legitimate. Evil is separation, sin is living according to the separation. And in fact, this connects quite well to the everyday notion of evil as egoism: believing that my being me has legitimate normative implications. It is therefore thanks to this distinction between the two modes of life that Augustine synthesises the notions of evil in the following way: evil is the possibility of separation of man from God.

This separation is, strictly speaking, a certain imagining: the imaginary identification with a spatio-temporal structure which we imaginarily identify as *our body*. Sin, now defined as living in imagination, carries with it a basic pre-definition of the body: to be embodied is to be able to imagine oneself as truly occupying a point of view different from the universal point of view of god. This also seals the connection between the body and sin: embodied life is always the practice of identifying with the limitations that our embodiment involves, it is living according to the illusion that the possibilities *of my body* are the possibilities *of me*. To insist on the connection of sin as living according to man and the body, Augustine himself goes to the trouble of explaining that the Paulinian expression "flesh" which designates the body, is best understood as the way of life involved in "living according to man": "In enunciating this proposition of ours, then, that because some live according to the flesh and others according to the spirit, there have arisen two diverse and conflicting cities, we might equally well have said, "because some live according to man, others according to God . . . so that to walk according to man and to be carnal are the same; for by *flesh*, that is, by a part of man, man is meant." So, flesh is a part of our individuality, but we use it to mean the whole of our individuality because of the work of identification carried out by the imagination. Interestingly this vindicates the body itself, which is not responsible for sin. Augustine writes: "There is no need, therefore, that in our sins and vices we accuse the nature of the flesh to the injury of the Creator, for in its own kind and degree the flesh is good." So, what is reprehensible is not the flesh per se, but the flesh when it's *not* in its own kind and degree. In other words, it's when we give undue importance to the flesh. When the flesh is not kept in its rightful place. Sin is not the flesh, but the judgement that my flesh is me, the act of imaginative identification, is. This can only make sense if we understand how radical Augustine is being: far from the modern notion which would regard the body as real because tangible, physical and concrete, Augustine argues that there is nothing to the body but a tendency to believe we are separate. This tendency is enough to account for all the phenomena we call physical, for feeling by way of our body is the same as feeling that we are here and the thing we feel is not us, and over there. We shall return to this view in the discussion of Husserl. For Augustine therefore, imagination is not only a relation to the potential, it is, in its form of identification, also a form of deception: it makes us believe that our body, which is the principle of our individuation, is real. He writes: "When, therefore, man lives according to himself, that is, according to man, not according to God, assuredly he lives according to a lie. . . . When, then, a man lives according to the truth, he lives not according to himself, but according to God."

This is strikingly illustrated in the famous story of Genesis, which reminds the reader that before committing the sin of beginning a life lived according to man, in response to the temptation of the serpent, Adam and Eve "were naked and they had no shame." The eating of the fruit brings them shame, however, and this can only be explained by pointing out that once they start living according to man, they begin to identify with their bodies, seeing their bodies as themselves, the nakedness of their body as *their* nakedness. Only this moment of identification can explain the resulting shame. Anyone who has seen a small child in a bath knows that their lack of self-consciousness is related to their inability to think of themselves reflectively, as "being" their body. The appearance of shame, in this light, should be seen as the first experience of *being seen*. This is, the Scriptures tell us, not the first time their bodies were seen, but it is rather, the first time that the experience of having their bodies seen was felt as the experience of being seen. Indeed, Adam and Eve's first response is to hide from God. This moment of identification to our body is sin.

Conclusion

Augustine associates sin to separation and defines the body as localisation. As a result, he discovered a necessary and systematic connection between sin and embodiment: they are two sides of the single phenomenon of individuality. Of course, this carries with it an entire set of presuppositions and insights about the body that are worth unpacking.

- First, the body is understood as a principle of localisation: it is my insertion into the spatio-temporal world.
- Second, this insertion is reciprocal: in order to have access to the spatio-temporal, I need to be spatio-temporal myself.
- Third, the body is the expression (neither result nor cause) of a fractured world. It is associated with sin as a sign of it, but not held responsible for it.
- Fourth, the body is connected to imagination. Because the body is local, it interacts with the world that is present around it by organising it into images, and with the potential world by imagining it. Imagination usually denotes an interaction with images (image-making) and a relation with the potential; Augustine argues that the body is involved in both.
- Fifth, this suggests that embodiment, the experience of having a body, or the matching of a body to a soul is guaranteed by an imaginative process of identification. To recognise a body as ours is an act of imagination.

More broadly, this also carries consequences for the rest of Western intellectual history. Augustine's legacy has set up a paradigm for thinking not just about embodiment, but about Creation in general.

It establishes the groundwork for a dualistic ontology because embodiment carries with it the idea of a fractured universe, one in which the intelligible and the sensible cannot exhaust each other.

Within this metaphysical dualism lurks an ontological account of the relations between being and nothingness: nothingness restricts being, resulting in localisation. This means that there is some sort of positive existence to nothingness and that any account of the world that ignores it will be guilty of quietism.

As a result, we must think of embodiment as a restriction of our natural powers because the body restricts our freedom, by being subjected to the laws of nature. But we must also think of it as what enables us to achieve results in the sensible world. And if we are to leave quietism behind, acting in the sensible world remains a divine requirement. This leads Augustine to an analysis of the subject as a point of equilibrium between activity and passivity and between freedom and restriction. To have a body gives us power and makes us subjects of power. We shall investigate some parts of the legacy of this thought later in this book.

Finally, just like we saw Plato begin with the intention of dissolving the existence of the world of perception within the intelligible, we saw Augustine begin with the intention of dissolving the existence of evil within God's goodness. In both cases, their conclusions contradict their intentions, and they come to the realisation that the sensible or evil cannot be restricted, for no other reason than that the fact of embodiment is irreducible.

Additional Readings
Augustine, *On Genesis, Against the Manichees*, Chapter 2
Augustine, *On Free Choice*, Book 3
Augustine, *On the Trinity*
Augustine, Letter 164
Augustine, Letter 166
R. O'Connell, "The Plotinian Fall of the Soul in St. Augustine."
D. G. Hunter, *Augustine on the Body*
Andrea Nightingale, *Once Out of Nature: Augustine on Time and the Body*

Key Ideas

The fact of embodiment involves that the world is divided into the realm
of the actual and the realm of the possible.

The body separates us and gives us access to the possible.

The body is our spatio-temporal localisation.

The body is the possibility of identifying with the spatio-temporal dimension of our person.

This is the possibility of sin ("living according to man").

Embodiment is a structure of being: it separates the world into the realm
of the actual and the realm of the possible.

As a result, it departs from univocal ontology: there is no full sense of
being; the actual is deprived of the potential, and the potential of the
actual.

(In spite of Augustine's best efforts) the body is a positive, fundamental
and irreducible structure of the world as a whole.

Notes

1. See Marenbon (2015), 23–41, and Bettini (2014).

2. Indeed, this is what Augustine argues when he traces the existence of evil to
the fact that God created the world "out of nothing" meaning that the world is made
of nothing. Note that this relies on a reading of the old trope of *creatio ex nihilo* where
nothingness (*nihilo*) is seen as a principle (therefore something that exist somehow),
and brings Augustine dangerously close to Manicheism.

CHAPTER FOUR

~

Descartes and
the Interaction Problem

Readings
René Descartes, *Treatise on Man*, Parts 1 and 2.
René Descartes, *Meditations on First Philosophy*, Meditation 5.
René Descartes, Letter to Mersenne, 24 December 1640.
René Descartes, *Treatise on the Passions*, Part I, Sections 1–40.
Princess Elisabeth of Bohemia and René Descartes, Letters of June–July
  1643.

In the Western philosophical narrative, Descartes is considered a pivotal figure of renewal, and the father of Western philosophical modernity. In a sense, Augustine gives us the tools to see why: Cartesianism is a representative and systematic part of a movement known as humanism, which operates a cultural, philosophical, scientific and political shift towards exactly what Augustine would call living "according to man." Humanism teaches us to do exactly what Augustine warns us about: we must think for ourselves and not accept any external authority for our knowledge or our moral decisions. Rather, man is in charge of positing his own value, thereby living according to his separation from God and from nature. In Greek parlance, humanism is a hubristic moment. In spite of the problems associated with the irreducibility of the sensible (brought out in Plato) and the irreducibility of evil (in Augustine), the convergence of Platonism with early Christian theology had established a worldview that was maintained and enforced by a highly sophisticated philosophical narrative, and when this failed to persuade, propped up by no less sophisticated a legal and penal system, all in the aim of discouraging us from living according to man. This is not to say that ten centuries of medieval thought, with its countless controversies and innovations can be ignored, but its variations remained within a paradigm made of Platonism, Aristotelianism and Christianity which was dramatically left

For it is surely no imperfection in God that he has given me the freedom to assent or not to assent in those cases where he did not endow my intellect with a clear and distinct perception; but it is undoubtedly an imperfection in me to misuse that freedom and make judgements about matters which I do not fully understand. I can see, however, that God could easily have brought it about that without losing my freedom, and despite the limitations in my knowledge, I should nonetheless never make a mistake. He could, for example, have endowed my intellect with a clear and distinct perception of everything about which I was ever likely to deliberate; Or he could simply have impressed it unforgettably on my memory that I should never make a judgement about anything which I did not clearly and distinctly understand. Had God made me this way, then I can easily understand that, considered as a totality, I would have been more perfect than I am now. But I cannot therefore deny that there may in some way be more perfection in the universe as a whole because some of its parts are not immune from error, while others are immune, than there would be if all the parts were exactly alike. . . . The cause of error must surely be the one I have explained; for if, whenever I have to make a judgement, I restrain my will so that it extends to what the intellect clearly and distinctly reveals, and no further, then it is quite impossible for me to go wrong. This is because every clear and distinct perception is undoubtedly something, and hence cannot come from nothing, but must necessarily have God for its author. Its author, I say, is God, who is supremely perfect, and who cannot be a deceiver on pain of contradiction; hence the perception is undoubtedly true. So today I have learned not only what precautions to take to avoid ever going wrong, but also what to do to arrive at the truth. For I shall unquestionably reach the truth, if only I give sufficient attention to all the things which I perfectly understand.—René Descartes, *Meditation 5*.

behind by the humanist movement, of which Descartes constitutes the systematic culmination.

Interestingly, this reversal of Augustine's imperative to live according to God doesn't mean that Descartes represents a clean break with the traditional discussion of the body. In the 1,500 years that separate Plato from Descartes, the body was regarded as whatever poses an obstacle to the soul. The body limits the soul's activities, by confining it to perception and to localisation. Descartes too endorses a form of the view that the soul is primary by founding his philosophy on the first truth of the cogito, which is the encounter of the soul with itself: I think, therefore I am, *cogito sum*. The activity of my soul (which is thinking) makes me aware of the existence of my soul. At the same time, the priority of the cogito carries with it a different connotation than it did in theological philosophy. Although the idea of the cogito is first encountered by Augustine (*City of God*, XI, 25–28), it plays a different role for Descartes because, being discovered by the human subject, it cannot play the foundational role that only a divine insight can. In the Cartesian version, the necessity for the first truth to be given by god has vanished, opening the way for a philosophy grounded in the cogito. The primacy of the soul, therefore, is now presented not as an article of faith (offered to man by the grace of God), but as a discovery (achieved by the sole resources of the human spirit). This has two implications.

First, the soul that is given primacy is the individual soul (each human subject has access to their own individual soul as first truth).

Second, this primacy is epistemic and not metaphysical. What gives the soul priority is that it is the most certain truth, not the first reality. Interestingly, in his discussion of the cogito, Descartes contrasts the certainty of the cogito he has just discovered with the uncertainty of embodiment: we can have dreams about bodies, we can have dreams that we don't have a body; or we can have a dream that our body is made of glass, as he says in the second *Meditation*. We can certainly also have dreams about having someone else's mind, for example. But we cannot have a dream without having a mind. So, the truth about the existence of the mind is more fundamental and primary than any truth involving the body. The cogito is therefore the first *epistemological* truth. In other words, the first thing we find in the order of thinking (Descartes says, in "the order of reasons"), is the soul. That doesn't yet mean that the cogito is the first thing metaphysically (in "the order of causes"). Descartes is therefore confronted with the question of whether and to what extent the epistemological primacy of the soul entails its metaphysical primacy. Let's look at this: Descartes has been called an intellectualist for his doctrine of clear and distinct ideas. He believes that the way our mind is organised reflects the way the world is organised. This harmony between the epistemological and the metaphysical is ensured by "Divine epistemic benevolence." God gave us a mind, God made the world. Because God is "epistemically benevolent" (he doesn't wish to deceive us) the mind he gave us is fit to discover the truth about the world. As a result, Descartes claims that there is a correspondence between the way knowledge works when it works properly, and the way the world is organised.

But all of this depends on our knowledge working properly. What does this mean? Descartes answers that we are using our mind the way God intended when we engage with "clear and distinct ideas." We might think of it a little bit like a car manufacturer. There are two things that can happen with a car accident: the first is human error. Let's say that you crash into a tree, perhaps because you'd had too much to drink. In this scenario, you cannot go the next day to the car manufacturer and say, "this car doesn't work, it drives into trees, give me my money back." In the same way, Descartes would say that when you are misusing your mind, you cannot go to God and say "it's your fault! You gave me a mind that doesn't work!" God, like the car manufacturer, will tell you, "well, it works, if you use it right!" Therefore, Descartes argues, you need a *method*, which is the driving license of the mind. That's why he writes the *Discourse on Method*. The basis of method, Descartes says, is a series of procedures that allow you to keep your imagination at bay (imagination, recall, was the source of error in Augustine, too). Using your mind well means being immune to the influence of imagination, and following the testimony of your understanding. The understanding deals in "clear and distinct ideas." So the basic method tells us that we shall not err if we use our mind the way it has been designed to, and the feeling that we are using our mind the proper way, is a sense of clarity and distinctness: a sense that we know exactly what we're thinking or perceiving. If we do this, if we subject ourselves to the demands of method, then God will take it from there. He will ensure that clear ideas correspond to things in the world and that the distinction between ideas corresponds to the difference that exists between things in the world. Different ideas correspond to different things. So, there are as many basic things in the world as there are basic ideas in the mind. Importantly, as we shall see, the list of clear and distinct ideas is very small, and it contains precisely the idea of body and the idea of mind, two ideas that are clear because we cannot think of them by using other ideas, and distinct because when we think of a body, we don't think of anything mental and when we think of a mind we don't think of anything physical. Let us note from the outset how important the idea of distinction is for Descartes's metaphysics. If it is true that body and mind are two clear and distinct ideas, and if it is true that divine epistemic benevolence ensures that clear and distinct ideas correspond to objective realities, it means that body and mind exist and it means that they are not reducible to anything else, in particular to each other, and are "really" distinct, that is to say, everything that is bodily cannot be mental and vice-versa. This is the step that takes Descartes into the problem of the interaction of body and soul. This problem is, simply put, the following: if it is true that body and soul are "really" separate, then how come they interact? The rest of this chapter will address three moments in Descartes's career. Each of these moments involves him trying a different strategy to deal with the problem of interaction. The first involves rejecting the problem itself by arguing that there is no such interaction, the second involves taking the problem of interaction seriously and the final one involves arguing that the dualistic model has room for interaction.

Descartes' Early Mechanism

The Fiction of "The" World

Descartes's first encounter with the question of the body takes place in the context of his early mechanism. There, the question of the body is seen primarily as the question of the status of matter. In these works, the reflections on matter are aimed at simplifying the science of his time by purging it of unnecessary metaphysical and theological prejudices. In particular, we must rid science of any reliance on phenomena or entities that are not observable. The text called *The World* pursues this project to radical consequences and for this reason, Descartes didn't publish it in his lifetime. We can understand the problems involved with this text by focusing on its title and the use of the word "the." "*The*" is a definite article, and this means that it refers to something specific, something that could be plural (there could be different worlds), but is instead unique, and this is so for both the author and all the readers. The assumption in this article is that we all mean the same thing when we say "the world." This, of course, cannot be assumed unless there has been a previous agreement where the substantive that the article refers to (in this case "world") has been defined. The use of "the" always implies "*the one* I've been talking about," or "*the one* we are talking about." Descartes presents his book as a Treatise-on-*the*-World-that-we-have-been-talking-about. This is important because it involves three important Cartesian points.

The first is that Descartes engages in a little fiction (largely for strategic reasons) whereby he presents his book as saying: "well, let's imagine *a* world that was built absolutely elegantly, beautifully, simply. I'm not saying that it is *the* real world, I'm just saying, let's imagine it." The rest of the treatise will be about this imaginary world. This allows him the deniability of explaining why divine entities are not featured in this story: Descartes' defence would go something like that: "I'm only talking of an imaginary world that looks exactly like this world, but there may be things *in this world* that are invisible and these things I don't describe in my imaginary world." So, let's imagine a world where everything took place the same as in this world, but it had fewer principles, or it had a minimum of principles in it. So, it's a life-scale experiment of Occam's razor. How can we explain everything we see in the world without reference to anything unnecessary? Descartes's conclusion is that the result would be a mechanistic world. The most economical way to account for all events is mechanical, it is to regard all events as guided by physical laws of motion, thereby assuming that bodies are not infused with spirit and will. Not only are occult entities such as God and the soul absent from this story, Descartes also emphatically dismisses any account of the body that would appeal to the union of body and soul: bodies are pieces of matter and nothing more.

Second, this commits Descartes to talking about a model of the real world, but not the real world as such. Rather, the *model-mode* of philosophy addresses not the world we normally experience, but what we are allowed to mean by "world." What happens when we move to the *model* mode of philosophy? One consequence is that we no longer talk about people, we only talk about robots. As Descartes himself mentions in the responses to the *Objections*, we don't talk about the real world where there may be God and angels and things in it, but we talk about the world as it appears without any extrapolation or imagination. We move from *what things are*, to *what we know* about things. In other words, we already build into the account the harmony between the order of causes and the order of reasons, but we do so by reducing the metaphysical realm of what there is to the epistemological realm of what we know.

Third, and importantly, Descartes's description of the world makes it an ontological treatise insofar as it asks about the possible meaning of the word "world": it asks, what do we talk about when we talk about the world? What can we possibly mean by this expression? And he answers that we can only mean about world, the collection of all the things we know about it, namely, that it is a series of objects interacting according to the laws of physics. What this implies is a view of experience whereby we don't experience anything that cannot be accounted for mechanistically. Although this is a view that will be amended and refined greatly through Descartes's career, it serves two important purposes: first, it shows how many objections can be resolved by a strong commitment to mechanism. Second, it allows us to zero in on the objections that cannot be resolved. Interestingly, all of them have to do with the *interaction* between the mind and the body.

The Mechanistic Account of the Body
The mechanistic account emphasises two ideas that inform Descartes's early mechanistic anthropology, the first is the notion of reflex, and the second is mereological reduction.

These men will be composed, as we are, of a soul and a body. And I must describe for you first the body on its own; and then the soul, again on its own; and finally I must show you how these two natures would have to be joined and united so as to constitute men resembling us. I suppose the body to be just a statue or a machine made of earth, which God forms with the explicit intention of making it as much as possible like us. Thus He not only gives its exterior the colours and shapes of all the parts of our body, but also places inside it all the parts needed to make it walk, eat, breathe, and imitate all those functions we have which can be imagined to proceed from matter and to depend solely on the disposition of our organs. We see clocks, artificial fountains, mills, and other similar machines which, even though they are only made by men, have the power to move of their own accord in various ways. . . . As for those parts of the blood that penetrate as far as the brain, they serve not only to nourish and sustain its substance, but above all to produce there a certain very fine wind, or rather a very lively and very pure flame, which is called the 'animal spirits'. For it should be noted that the arteries that carry these from the heart . . . come together again around a certain little gland which lies near the middle of the substance of the brain, just at the entrance to its cavities; and those in this region have a large number of small holes through which the finest parts of the blood can flow into this gland, and these are so narrow that they do not allow the larger ones to get past. . . . Now as these spirits enter the cavities of the brain, they also pass in the same proportions from there into the pores of its substance, and from these pores into the nerves. And depending on which of these nerves they enter, or even merely tend to enter, in varying amounts, they have the power to change the shapes of the muscles into which these nerves are embedded, and in this way to move all the limbs.—René Descartes, *Treatise on Man*, Chapter 1.

For Descartes, all human behaviour is a reflex-arc, where you get as output, just the same amount of energy as you got as input. It is a reflex because it bypasses the mind (or it can be explained without supposing any mind). Using the late Amélie Oksenberg Rorty's example of a human's fear and flight before a charging lion, one could say that when I run away because the lion is running towards me, the energy I'm spending running away is exactly the same as the energy that I'm receiving from the impression of the lion. The lion pushes the air against my eyes, the eyes push the air inside of me. The air is now circulating inside my body in the form of the "animal spirits" which end up pushing the pineal gland, which passes the pressure onto the relevant leg muscles, and I run. This is the famed billiard-ball system: there is no action at a distance. More interesting for us is the implication that we are dealing with a reflex-*arc*. That is to say a movement whose input and output are identical, and both belong to the outside world. This is a process that begins outside (with a lion charging at me) and finishes outside (in my running). First, this suggests that bodies are reducible to their surface, the part of them that is exposed to the laws of physics. Second, what that means is that the only way to feel the body is to feel it in relation to the outside world. This contains, I think, something deep in Descartes's thinking, namely, an emphasis on the fact that the body is our access to the outside world, and the outside world is always the world outside *of the body*. Finally, what that also means, is that in a mechanistic worldview, ideas are just names for physical things. Fear, for example, is really just the name of how much my pineal gland moves and in what direction.

The second basic principle of mechanism is what you might call the principle of mereological reduction. Mereology is the part of philosophy that deals with the relations between parts and wholes. So, for example before *a pile of sand*, a mechanist would say it is the sum of all the grains of sand, and this would probably be acceptable to all of us. But in the case of an organism, or a melody, it becomes harder to say so: should we say that a melody is the sum of all its notes and nothing more? Doesn't, for example, the order of these notes make a difference? Should we say that a living body is simply the sum of all its parts, or as Descartes says "partes extra partes"? This would reduce it to a dead body, which has all the same parts. The question of parts and wholes has been a concern for all philosophers since Plato and especially Aristotle, and we see how Descartes's early mechanism makes a decisive move in favour of the reduction of the whole to the parts. In the case of Descartes, it is very important, because it will lead him into the problem of interaction: what are the parts of the human? The body and the soul. So, if we are not more than body and soul, there's no need to explain the union.

For the union of body and soul is not a third part, but simply the way in which these two parts coexist. But a mechanistic mereology only considers parts. Conversely, if we are more than the body and the soul, more than the sum of our parts, then we need to move beyond this crude version of mechanism. The interaction cannot be explained by the body or by the soul alone or alongside each other.

Although this was not Descartes's intention, the philosophical contribution of the mechanistic experiment is its failure: the discovery of a set of phenomena that resist the mechanistic reduction, and yet remain undeniable. We know that sensible experience played this role in Plato, and sin played this role in Augustine. For Descartes, as we can already foresee, it is the experience of interaction between body and mind.

Letters to Elisabeth and Mersenne

A few years after The World (1636), and on the other side of his *magnum opus*, the *Meditations* (1641), Descartes has systematised his worldview greatly, clarified his discovery of the cogito and in consequence, made some room for internal phenomena, which take place in the soul, relegating more explicitly the externalism of his mechanistic account to biology and medicine alone. As a result, he separated the world into two substances, which he calls the thinking thing (*res cogitans*, the spirit or soul) and the extended thing (*res extensa*, the body, or matter). The resulting dualism is radical because it defines mind and matter as substances, elements that are pure (they contain nothing that belongs to another element), simple (they have no metaphysically separable parts), basic or constitutive (all things that exist are combinations of them), and irreducible (there is nothing more fundamental, in particular, there is no substance that would underlie both and combine them). The result is that their distinction too is "substantial"—that is, irreducible and unbridgeable. Mind and matter are defined as mutually exclusive: nothing can be both material and spiritual. This immediately raises the following question: where does that leave the human? Descartes himself regards the human as the "union" of body and soul, and this is meant to explain why impressions of the soul have physical expressions, or vice versa.

This raises a problem that has already been discussed in two forms. The first is the question of interaction: how can the mind act upon a body, and how can a body act upon a mind? It seems for such interaction to be possible, mind and body would have to be caught in the same causal chain, but on the basis of the Eleatic principle discussed in chapter 2, only consubstantial things can interact. Ideas can move ideas or elicit new ideas, just like physical objects can push each other, but how can an idea push a physical object?

The second is therefore the question about commensurability: what is the link that allows body and mind to "meet" in the sense of "having a causal encounter"? Is such a link conceivable at all? By virtue of the principle of purity this connecting point cannot be physico-spiritual, for two true substances cannot mix. By virtue of the principle of constitutivity mentioned previously, the connecting point cannot belong to any third substance that would be neither physical nor spiritual.

Descartes becomes aware of this difficulty in his exchanges with Father Mersenne. In his letter of 24 December 1640, he refers to the necessity to locate the place of "the common sense, that is to say the sense of thought and consequently of the soul" *in the body*. The expression "common sense" here doesn't imply the "common view" or what we now call "common wisdom." Descartes means "sense" in its connection to perception and skill—just as you would say that a surfer has a sense for balance, for example—and "common" in its connection to community. The common sense is therefore the ability to feel what properly belongs to the other: the ability of the soul to feel the body, and of the body to feel the soul. Descartes attributes this crucial function to the pineal gland, at the top of the spinal cord. And this immediately raises concerns: the pineal gland is a physical gland with a specific place in the brain, and by virtue of Descartes's own dualism, giving it a physical place directly commits him to account for the pineal gland in purely physical terms. So, Descartes is reduced to using the notion of "place" in both the literal and the metaphorical sense.[1] The pineal gland now bears the burden of standing as both a metaphysical and physical place, and what remains to be explained is how anything can belong to both orders. The idea of the pineal gland as common sense will plague Descartes's philosophy until the end as the name of a question, of a mystery, of a problem.[2]

It is for the same reasons that, two years later, Elisabeth of Bohemia expresses her scepticism towards Descartes's dualism: she complains that it doesn't explain interaction. Elisabeth takes the criticism to the next level though, as she points out that all experience is founded on the interaction of mind and body (implicitly this suggests that experience is not reducible to sensations, which are the purview of the body alone, we'll return to this in the next chapter), suggesting that without a satisfactory account of interaction, Descartes leaves us with no account of the world of experience at all. In short, this would make his philosophy abstract in the worst sense of the world: an inapplicable model.

Elisabeth, to Descartes, 10, June 1643: I admit that it would be easier for me to concede matter and extension to the soul than to concede the capacity to move a body and to be moved by it to an immaterial thing. For, if the first is achieved through information, it would be necessary that the spirits, which cause the movements, were intelligent, a capacity you accord to nothing corporeal. And even though, in your *Metaphysical Meditations*, you show the possibility of the second, it is altogether very difficult to understand that a soul, as you have described it, after having had the faculty and the custom of reasoning well, can lose all of this by some vapors, and that, being able to subsist without the body, and having nothing in common with it, the soul is still so governed by it.

 Descartes to Elisabeth, 28th, June 1643: First, then, I notice a great difference between these three sorts of notions. The soul is conceived only by the pure understanding; the body, that is to say, extension, shapes, and motions, can also be known by the understanding alone, but is much better known by the understanding aided by the imagination; and finally, those things which pertain to the union of the soul and the body are known only obscurely by the understanding alone, or even by the understanding aided by the imagination; but they are known very clearly by the senses. From which it follows that those who never philosophize and who use only their senses . . . consider the one and the other as one single thing, that is to say, they conceive of their union. For to conceive of the union between two things is to conceive of them as one single thing. Metaphysical thoughts which exercise the pure understanding serve to render the notion of the soul familiar. The study of mathematics, which exercises principally the imagination in its consideration of shapes and movements, accustoms us to form very distinct notions of body. And lastly, it is in using only life and ordinary conversations and in abstaining from meditating and studying those things which exercise the imagination that we learn to conceive the union of the soul and the body. . . . It does not seem to me that the human mind is capable of conceiving very distinctly, and at the same time, the distinction between the soul and the body and their union, since to do so it is necessary to conceive them as one single thing and at the same time to conceive them as two, which is contradictory.

The exchange of letters between Descartes and Elisabeth in the summer of 1643 stages a fundamental divide in philosophy in general, and it chronicles the way the tensions within Descartes's system come to its pitch of concentration. There are two ways to approach these letters. Depending on whether you focus on what the text *says* or what the text *does*. What Descartes's text says is that his system withstands the objection—that is, that he is right. What the text *does*, however, is undermine Cartesianism. Let us focus on the salient point which is the reference to "the ordinary course of life." Here, Descartes implicitly dismantles the foundations provided by clear and distinct ideas: he implicitly acknowledges that the union of body and soul is real (whether it is a thing, an aspect of a thing, or a phenomenon, is left open) and therefore needs an account. Then he proceeds to say that it is best experienced not via clear and distinct ideas, but via the practice of life. Go to the market, talk to friends, walk your dog: that's how you know you have the union of body and soul. Of course, this misunderstands Elisabeth's question somehow, since she doesn't ask *how* we know that our body and mind are unified, but also *what* this union is. But even keeping to the question of how we know, it is interesting that Descartes suggests that we know about the union of body and soul via the union of body and soul, for the practice of life is exactly the domain in which the union of body and soul is deployed. This amounts to saying that the union of body and soul is self-evident. Interestingly, self-evidence had been, up until now, reserved for the first truth: the cogito. So, in retreating before Elisabeth's objections, Descartes is forced to question the primacy of the cogito. This is not all: here, Descartes assigns to the practice of life an epistemic status—that is, it has the function of allowing us to know the union. It means that everyday life is now an independent cognitive ability, connected to an independent phenomenon that cannot be conceived otherwise. In short, there are truths that elude clear and distinct ideas. So, Descartes needs to expand his epistemology, to one where you don't only have the imagination and the understanding, but where you also have *everyday life*, conceived as a mysterious faculty which must be posited, because the understanding and the imagination are insufficient to account for an experience that we know exists, the experience of interaction.

We can now return to the *what* question. On the basis of the harmony between the epistemic and the metaphysical order, we should conclude that Descartes is also expanding his metaphysics when he adds an epistemic faculty to his theory of mind. There is a certain kind of experience that is irreducible to the others. How do we know it's of a different kind? Because the others are known each in a certain way, and this kind of experience cannot be known in the same ways. This forces Descartes's worldview to move from dualism into some sort of trialism. Not only do we have mind and body, we also have the *union*, which is a third thing. Of course, trialism is no solution; in fact it is double the trouble, because a trialist needs to explain not only how one goes from A (e.g., the body) to C (e.g., the mind), but how you go from A to B (the union) and from B to C. This doubles the interaction problems. Naturally, this is not Descartes's intention. Rather, he wishes to think of the union as something that is not separate from what it unifies, but as we now can see, this is not sustainable either, for it would require a point of contact which would be obscure and confused, or it would imply reducing both body and mind to the union, which would result in monism (this is the way later taken by Spinoza).

The Passions of the *Soul*

Under pressure from Elisabeth's arguments, Descartes focuses his last work, the *Treatise of the Passions of the Soul*, on the question of the interactions between body and mind. Although it provides no metaphysical account of the possibility of interaction, it is intended as a display of how many cases of interactions (passions and affects) can be accounted for by his model, on the condition that we take the union for granted without explaining it. In this sense Descartes inaugurates a strategy that has become very common in the empirically informed strands of philosophy of mind: ignore the explanatory gap that should connect the objectively observable behaviours of the body (let's say, in the brain) to the qualitative experiences that correspond to these events and focus on all the progress that can be achieved without

5. *It is an error to believe that the soul supplies motion and heat to the body.* In this way we shall avoid a very considerable error into which many have fallen, so much so that I believe this is the primary cause that has prevented our being able to explain satisfactorily as yet the passions and other things belonging to the soul. It consists in observing that all dead bodies are deprived of heat and consequently of movement, and in imagining that the absence of soul was what was causing these movements and this heat to stop. Thus, without any justification it was believed that our natural heat and all the movements of our body depend on the soul—while in fact we ought, on the contrary, to believe that the soul quits us in death only because this heat ceases and the organs serving to move the body decay. . . .

12. How external objects act on the sense organs.
We have still to know the causes that prevent the spirits from always flowing into the muscles in the same way—and bring it about that some spirits sometimes flow into certain muscles rather than others. . . . [T]here are three things to consider in the nerves: namely, first, their marrow or interior substance, which extends in the form of little filaments from the brain, from which it originates, to the extremity of the other limbs to which these filaments are attached; secondly, the membranes surrounding them, which, being coterminous with those that cover the brain, form small tubes in which these filaments are enclosed; and finally, the animal spirits, which are carried by these same tubes from the brain to the muscles, and are the reason why these filaments remain perfectly free and extended there, so that the least thing that moves the part of the body to which the extremity of any one of them is attached, causes by that same means the part of the brain from which it proceeds to move—just as when you pull one end of a cord, the other end is made to move.—Rene Descartes, *Treatise of the Passions of the Soul*

having to address that gap. Whether this progress (medical, therapeutic, technological, etc.) is proof of the metaphysical accuracy of the model is left unaddressed.

In the *Treatise of the Passions* therefore, Descartes returns to a model of the type he experimented with in *The World*, a model where we hypothetically abstract from the question of qualitative experience. The question "how does it feel?" is replaced with the question "what is felt?" interestingly, however, unlike in *The World*, Descartes comes to his own contradictions before the fact that it is impossible to bracket qualitative experience itself. If it's true that the life of the human is reducible to a set of physical behaviours, and if it's true that the soul does not provide motion, and motion exists through physical means, then there is no room for the soul. But where does it leave the cogito, which is, indeed, a qualitative experience? This tension is best displayed in the contradictions between paragraph 5, which is aimed at demonstrating that the soul doesn't move the body, and paragraph 12 which has recourse to an Aristotelian account of the soul as a mover. This latter move is made indispensable because otherwise the qualitative experience, the qualitative part of life, cannot be accounted for. And so, in fact, the rest of the text is really Descartes trying to make room for the soul in our behaviour, without leaving the mechanistic model. And, of course, it's bound to fail: as things stand, we are stuck with a view of agency where the soul acts, while supposing at the same time that we can also explain every behaviour in terms of passivity, via something like the reflex arc. Just like we have to decide between body and mind, we now must decide between activity and passivity. This is not accidental, for the body is regarded as the passive element to the soul's active element. The body is passive because it is subjected to the laws of physics—we know that since Augustine. You remember that Augustine told us, "when a soul is in a body, it becomes subjected to the laws of the universe." So, the body is the passive principle. If there is activity, therefore, it must come from the soul. So what fails, here, alongside the failure of the opposition of body and soul, is the opposition of passivity and activity.

And so, is the pineal gland, which connects the body and soul, something that receives or something that initiates motion? Just like we had to call it both a physical and metaphysical "place," we now must see that its relations with passivity and activity are ambivalent too. Remember that the soul has no parts: "The soul is united conjointly to all the parts of the body" (para. 30). "But more particularly . . . to the pineal gland" (para. 31). We know how essential it is for Descartes to maintain the privilege of the pineal gland, but this runs the risk of assigning "parts" to the soul. Descartes suggests that there is more soul in the pineal gland, that the concentration of soul is greater in the pineal gland. How can this be maintained without dividing the soul into parts, because a higher concentration is nothing but a greater number of parts of soul in a smaller area? We know from the *Meditations* that only physical things can be divided into parts, and that by definition the soul cannot. This results in two contradictions. One, the view that the pineal gland is both the unity of the immaterial and of the material, therefore, of partiality and simplicity. Second contradiction, the presumed unity of the active and passive. *Ad contrario*, this already gives us an idea of what it implies to overcome the commensurability problem. It implies overcoming the opposition between activity and passivity *and* the opposition between spatiality and non-spatiality (spirituality).

Conclusion

The interaction problem left unresolved by Descartes is a symptom of the irreducibility of the fact of embodiment. And it suggests, just like Augustine's theodicy problem, and just like the illusion problem in Plato, that the fact of embodiment is fundamental not just to any anthropology but to metaphysics and ontology too. It follows that no thought is valid if it is unable to account for the fact of embodiment. So, the value of reading Descartes, aside from his flawed brilliance, is that it leaves no doubt about the fact that embodiment is irreducible, for if it was reducible, Descartes would have done it. Before his relentless, absolutely creative and desperate attempts at finding a way to reduce the fact of embodiment, we are taught negatively about how good the body is at resisting deflation.

This leads us into an important point to help us map out the history of modern Western philosophy since Descartes, because the problem of interaction in Descartes appears in such a clear and systematic way that it has served as the concentrated challenge that provided the intellectual energy for the rest of the modern age, at least until Kant. After Descartes, philosophers took it as their chief task to respond to this challenge, and their responses to this very challenge became the prominent factor that categorised them as members of this or that tradition. A *priori*, there are three ways of solving the interaction problem. Each of them will constitute the core of one grand tradition.

Before the question of interaction one can say two things. The first and second options involve denying interaction and reverting to monism, and this approach can take two forms depending which side is reduced to the other. Either one claims that the mind is something of the body or that the body is something of the mind. Either everything is mind (the intellectualist position), or everything is body (the realist or materialist position, recently revived in the naturalist branches of neurophilosophy that substitute the brain for the mind).

The third option would find its origins in Descartes's instinctive recourse to the practice of everyday life in the letter to Elisabeth, and presuppose that everything is interaction. This comes with its share of challenges, best formulated in the question: "interactions of what?" which probably explains why it has not been pursued as avidly until the other two options had themselves come to their own exhaustion at the turn of the nineteenth century. I would argue that the interactionist view, however, is what animates the movement known as German idealism, especially Hegel, and its aftermath in Nietzsche and phenomenology, which talks of interaction in terms of intentionality.

So neither the pineal gland nor the practice of everyday life turn out to be sufficient candidates for the transitional instance Descartes is desperate to discover. Philosophically speaking, however, we have a very interesting display of Descartes's instinct: the almost immediate acknowledgement that the practice of life is an indispensable and irreducible form of knowledge, about an object that the mind cannot embrace appropriately and yet is undeniably positive, an object that, just like the sensible world in Plato and sin in Augustine, is irreducible. Just like in their cases, this irreducible resistance, once acknowledged, forces a reversal of the entire system. Although Descartes himself did not make that move, the next step, as we shall see, would consist in acknowledging that the practice of life is in competition with the epistemology of clear and distinct ideas, that neither one of the terms or the union itself is to be primary, and that any account of the union can therefore only presuppose the interaction of body and soul as more fundamental than their separation.

Additional Readings
René Descartes, *Meditations on First Philosophy*, Meditation 3.
René Descartes, *Discourse on Method*, Part 2.
René Descartes, *Dioptrics*.
Baruch Spinoza, *Ethics*, Books III and V.
Nicolas Malebranche, *Dialogue on Metaphysics*.
Amélie Oksenberg Rorty, "Descartes on Thinking with the Body."
Lisa Shapiro, "Princess Elizabeth and Descartes: The Union of Mind and Body and the Practice of Philosophy."

Key Ideas

The body problematises conceptual boundaries (it challenges the correspondence between the structure of the mind and the structure of the world).

Embodiment introduces a kind of phenomena that are irreducible to the body or the mind alone.

The union of body and soul is both a phenomenon and an epistemic instrument.

The problem of interaction testifies to the fact that embodiment is irreducible, primary and fundamental.

Notes

1. You might remember that Augustine had to make use of just such a trick when exploiting the ambiguous meaning of the word "nothingness" as this that doesn't exist and this that exists as restriction, in order to solve the very same problem of trying to account for the interaction of being and nothingness whilst maintaining their distinction.

2. Interestingly, and for the same reasons, the weakest point in Kant's philosophy also relates to the interaction between the spatio-temporal and the transcendental (spiritual), he calls it the "schematism of the imagination" as our ability to *recognise* a resemblance between objects and concepts. He confesses that this must be presupposed but no account of it is forthcoming, it is "an art hidden in the depths of the human soul." Just like the pineal gland is the most threatening point in Descartes' metaphysics (*Critique of Pure Reason* A 137ff.), the schematism of the imagination is the most threatening point in Kant's metaphysics.

PART II

AN EMBODIED WORLD

CHAPTER FIVE

~

Husserl and the Phenomenology of the Lived Body

Reading
Edmund Husserl, *Ideas Pertaining to a Pure Phenomenology and to a Phenomenological Philosophy: Second Book: Studies in the Phenomenology of Constitution*, paragraphs 35–42.

What Is Phenomenology?

So, it seems Descartes leaves us with a task, which is to account for the interaction of body and soul. As we saw, fulfilling this task involves jumping over a number of serious hurdles. Descartes is correct that if we assume the clear and distinct ideas in our minds reflect the real world, then the encounter of body and soul becomes impossible to explain. This is because the idea of mind and the idea of body are indeed clear and distinct. In particular, they are distinct from each other, which would involve that the thing body and the thing mind are really separate from each other too, not just in the mind, but in reality as well. As we saw, this means that experience, which always involves the interaction of body and mind becomes impossible to explain.

Yet, the description of the world as organised in this way is appealing, and Descartes is probably correct in his methodological reluctance to abandon the idea. After all, it accounts for a very important phenomenon: namely that our mind thinks and that it thinks about the world and that events in the world are registered by the mind. It looks like there is indeed some sort of fit between the mind and the world which would be impossible to explain if there wasn't some sort of analogy in their structures. If you look at the keyboard on your computer, you see that the match between the keys and your fingers suggests a certain analogy of relations: for example, the distance between one side of a key and another matches the width of your fingertips, and the way the keys are distributed, mostly horizontally, seems to match the fact that your wrists allow greater sideward mobility than upwards mobility to your fingers. This analogy guarantees a proper or adequate interaction between your fingers and the keyboard. Descartes assumes the same principle: any interaction between mind and world has to involve some sort of common structure between them. If, in addition, this interaction is proper or adequate, it suggests that this analogy of structure is quite precise and adequate. And indeed, there is, it seems, such proper and adequate interaction between man and world, that is, the mind is good at knowing the world. Famously Kant makes the same argument when he sets himself the goal of explaining the facts of knowledge which we find in science, what he calls the *Faktum* of science.

The task that Descartes leaves us with therefore is the task of saving the possibility of experience by rejecting the incommensurability of mind and body while at the same time maintaining the possibility to account for the fact of knowledge. Edmund Husserl's foundation of the phenomenological method in philosophy is entirely animated by this goal: finding a way to explain how we can have both experience and knowledge of the world. For us, who are interested in understanding the body, this is crucial, because it involves asking ourselves what a body is if it stands alongside the mind as one of the two sources of experience. One must now understand how and in what sense the body interacts with the world to offer experiences and how and in what sense it interacts with the mind that extracts knowledge from such experiences. This problem, which Husserl inherits from Descartes via Kant and many others, remains constant in Husserl's work and for the entire phenomenological tradition. At the same time, we shall see that Husserl himself changes his account of it, and that every phenomenologist since Husserl both took up this challenge and dealt with it in their own different ways. As a result, saying general things about phenomenology always runs the risk of excluding an author or a text, and many misunderstandings and oversimplifications may ensue.

One such oversimplification is worth getting out of the way from the start, because it creates much confusion. It is the claim that phenomenology is (1) a *methodology* based upon (2) *description*. We shall see that these two things are incompatible. This is a view very widespread in contemporary circles, and there are two main reasons for it: the first is that many of the canonical phenomenologists (including Husserl himself and later, as we shall see in the next chapter, Merleau-Ponty) do insist that description is crucial to phenomenology. The second is that, for the reasons outlined earlier, any definition of phenomenology must be broad enough as to accommodate a wide variety of thoughts and authors, and this drives us towards the lowest common denominator quite quickly. Description could seem like one such denominator. Now, when the founders of phenomenology insist on description, this always comes with a caveat: what is described is an experience and not an object or a set of objects. As a result, description, for these authors, should not presuppose that there is any existing thing that is being described. This means that any serious description is not about specific objects or even specific experiences but about the structure of experience in general; how do all experiences—in spite of their differences—unfold, and how are they made possible? This is because pure description, if it is to contribute to philosophy, must be combined with explanation: phenomenology begins by describing in order to explain experience. We need to know the experience before we explain it. In fact, if we are to make description part of the definition of phenomenology, we must drop the mention of a method. Phenomenology describes, because it has made a *metaphysical*, not a methodological commitment which is: what there is is what can be described. We see that phenomenology may be viewed as a philosophy which emphasises description, but the result is hardly the clear definition we were hoping for.

Therefore I suggest we take another approach. At bottom, the phenomenological tradition is defined by one problem and two commitments. The problem is the one I have just described as the Cartesian heritage: to account for the coexistence of experience and knowledge. The two commitments are famous, although they are not usually taken together. The first is Husserl's famous slogan: "Back to the things themselves!"; the second is the notion that the thing-in-itself is a contradiction. On the basis of our discussion of description, which suggests that "what there is is what can be described," we can see that these two commitments are not separate. Rather, taking them together allows us to understand what Husserl means when he talks of the "things themselves" and in particular, why this is different from the good old "things-in-themselves."

For Husserl, going back to the things themselves means going back to phenomena. But why going "back"? Were the phenomena once here and are they now gone? According to Husserl, the phenomena have been lost through a process that made us forget that we are dealing with experiences.

Most of us, naively would believe that we experience objects, people, things, etc. In other words our experience of phenomena (what Husserl calls the "things themselves") has been forgotten and covered up by our belief in the "things-in-themselves." And you see that returning to the things themselves is not the same as returning to the things-in-themselves *at all*, because you go back to experience and the thing in itself is precisely the thing outside, before, and beyond experience. So, going back to the things themselves is precisely *not* going back to the things-in-themselves. Things-in-themselves, for Husserl, are misunderstandings of phenomena. They are the result of an act of imagination, where I go, "Oh, because I feel a table, there is a table." This is what Husserl calls the *Weltthesis*, the thesis of the world. It's the kind of judgements you have when you say something that has "there is" in it. You make statements about what there is, and this means that you abstract from your experience of it. So this idea of "going back" is a way of saying: we disable our belief in things-in-themselves, we go back to what is the root of that belief, and what is the root of that belief? Experience. We must remember that we live in a world of experience, not a world of objects.

On this basis, we can see that Husserl's view is correct only if it is indeed true that we should not bother about things-in-themselves. But how can we know that? Surely, we cannot know this through experience, as experience only gives us experiences, not things-in-themselves. So, phenomenology needs to show that things-in-themselves can be disqualified a priori, before any experience. Hence the thesis that the thing-in-itself is a contradiction. It would be one thing to say that the belief in things-in-themselves is wrong, or that it's a mistake, but a contradiction is the kind of mistake that we don't need to look at the world to verify.[1] That's good news, because therefore, we don't need anything external to prove that the thing-in-itself doesn't exist: it doesn't exist because the very idea of a thing in itself is a contradiction. Just like a square circle. You just need to understand what is involved in this idea, to see that it cannot work. The argument goes thus: Can you think of a thing? Any one of the things you're thinking about right now, is either being experienced by you, or it is possibly experienced by you. It seems that what we mean when we say *thing* always refers to the things that we have experienced or can experience. In other words, contained in the notion of *thing*, there is the notion of experience. "Thing" can only be properly understood as "object of experience." Yet, "in-itself" in the expression "thing-in-itself" means: without experience. So, the "thing in itself" strictly speaking, is the object of experience ("thing") without experience ("in-itself"), and that is, indeed, a contradiction. Husserl's is a simple genealogical point: the genealogy of the concept *thing* takes us *back* to the experience of things. We learn to have the concept "thing" by experiencing things. Therefore, thinking of a thing without experience is artificially cutting off the concept of thing from its root, from what makes it alive, from what makes it *about* something.

So, it seems the best way to think of phenomenology is to think of it as the philosophical investigation about the consequences of the rejection of the thing-in-itself. This leaves us with two key questions that drive phenomenology: first, what does the world look like if we remove the thing-in-itself? And second, "how come we have come to believe in things-in-themselves?" The body is crucial to both questions. As Husserl will demonstrate in *Ideas II*, it is the body that plays the role of acquainting us with the world of experience, and it is the body also who teaches us the false belief in the thing-in-itself: In response to the Cartesian concern, therefore, the body turns out to be the unified source of both knowledge and experience.

Ideas I to *Ideas II*: The Radicalisation of Phenomenology

In this chapter, we shall focus on Husserl's phenomenological discovery of the body, which takes place most notably in *Ideas II*, in a very touching analysis of one case, the experience of joining our hands and feeling the surface of our right hand over our left hand and vice versa. I call this Husserl's discovery of the body, not because I wish to say that Husserl didn't know that there were bodies before but rather because he now comes to realise that the body cannot be explained in terms of anything else. In order to understand the importance of this discovery, we need to take a couple of steps back, to Husserl's previous volume, *Ideas I* (1911). It is important to know that although *Ideas II* was not published until 1952, Husserl started writing it in 1912, which is the year after *Ideas I* was published. In other words, and although Husserl revised *Ideas II* many times, until 1928, *Ideas I* and *Ideas II* were almost written at the same time, but strangely they are almost incompatible. Roughly speaking, one could say that *Ideas I* focuses on fulfilling the ambition of "Going back to the things themselves" whereas *Ideas II* adds the second requirement: to do so in the understanding that the thing-in-itself is a contradiction. More concretely, what this suggests is that in *Ideas I*, there remains a commitment to one thing-in-itself (the ego) while in *Ideas II*, this commitment becomes fainter. This has consequences for embodiment because in the process, nothing remains that is beyond the reach of the body.

In *Ideas I*, Husserl applies the principle of going back *to the things themselves* in three ways. They are called the three "reductions." For Husserl, a reduction is the mental removal of any beliefs that are involved in experience, yet, are not otherwise justified. Let's take Descartes's famous example:

I see people outside my window, walking in the street, but this is not strictly what is see: strictly speaking, I see clothes, hair, etc., it may be that even this is an interpretation. Descartes concludes, these could just as well be robots. In other words, our experience brings with it a set of beliefs [in this case the belief that these are people] that are unjustified and that often get in the way of describing what I, in fact, am experiencing. A reduction is the mental process of removing all such unjustified beliefs, to go back to, well, the things themselves: the experience as it is. The three reductions are best defined in terms of what they reduce *to*, what they yield. For Husserl we discover (1) appearances, (2) essences and (3) the transcendental ego.

1. When we discover appearances. What we do is, we say, "oh, I thought I had hands but in fact all I know is I have sensations of hands" or something like that. In short we discover that what we used to take for objects are in fact appearances.

2. If you are reducing your experience to essences, you are reducing it to what makes your experience *that* experience: the essence of an experience. Most of the time it is: what is it that groups a certain set of sensations into one thing? If, for example, if you say, "on Monday I felt stressed about work and on Thursday I felt stressed about work." Although these are very different spatio-temporal instances, you're at least assuming that it is the same thing: stress, in both occasions. You are assuming that there is an essence of stress.

3. In Kantian fashion, the transcendental ego should be seen as the transcendental unity of apperception. What Husserl, and Kant, mean by that, is that if we accounted for our experience only in terms of the impressions or the sensory input coming from the things in the world to our sensitive apparatus, then we would be unable to still explain how these sensations are organised in such a way that they are visible (in the case of visual sensations). Explaining visibility would involve another two phenomena: first, the unification of all the impressions, their grouping into a relevant unity. If I look at a boat on the sea, I have white impressions, coming from the boat, and blue sensations, those of the sea. But my ability to say: "this is a boat on the sea" rather than "there is blue and white," suggests that I am able to group together the impressions that come from the boat and those that come from the sea. For example, I am able to know that the boat is not just a white part of the sea. It seems that in the process of perception, there is a moment where impressions are grouped in such a way that the groups are then recognisable as "boat" (the group of white impres-

sions) and "sea" (the group of blue impressions). Second, it looks like once these impressions are grouped properly, I also need to be seeing all of them *at once*. In other words, I occupy a point of view that grants no priority on any of these impressions. This is a unique point of view over a multiplicity of impressions and this unicity is provided not by the impressions themselves, or by the boat or the sea itself, but by *me*, the fact that I am one thing looking at this "manifold of sensations" in Kant's language. Both unifications—the unification of the perception and the unification of the perceiver—are accounted for by postulating that there is *a transcendental ego* that does the unifying. It is important to point out that this transcendental ego is introduced because experience itself seems to be insufficient to account for itself. In other words, it is introduced precisely as something that is not experienced but rather, which makes experience possible. This is, strictly speaking, the reason why it is called" "transcendental": it is a condition of possibility for experience which *crosses* ("*trans-*") the boundary between experience and those things that are not experienced (i.e., conditions of possibility for experience). Finally, one should add that this third reduction, the reduction to the ego, enjoys a kind of priority over the other two, because the appearances and essences are dependent on the transcendental ego. This means that the transcendental ego becomes the condition for everything else.

Ideas I is committed to this priority of the transcendental ego because it's Husserl's main transcendental idealist work. A transcendental idealist is somebody who thinks that the ego is the subject and the source of all experience. The idea there, is that it precedes—at least in some sense of preceding, maybe logical, maybe ontological, probably not chronological—the experiences that it has. And what that means is that *before*—in some sense of before—it has the experiences, it *is*. This, naturally, makes the transcendental ego look very much like a thing-in-itself, something that exists independently of experience. *Ideas II*, by contrast, is animated by the growing concern to minimise Husserl's reliance on any thing-in-itself. In *Ideas II*, two things happen. First, the fact that those reductions lead us to conclude that there are appearances, essences and ego is becoming less certain. Second, the distinction between those three reductions is becoming less strict, because the distinction between appearances, essences and ego is becoming blurred. In other words, Husserl takes more seriously than he used to the fact that we never have appearances without essences and without ego. Experience always combines those three things, and he takes seriously their ability to combine. One can already see that this suggests that one should abandon the transcendental model: if it is true that all three phenomena co-exist, then it makes no more sense to see the transcendental ego as operating upon the other two. Rather, there is nothing transcendental: all comes as part of the experience and nothing more. This is the model Husserl will explore in *Ideas II*. This turn towards immanence, as opposed to transcendence, involves the return of the body to a central position: the two unifications which once justified the appeal to the transcendental ego, need to now be accounted for by the very perceptual apparatus itself, since they are now taken to coincide with the act of experiencing: in other words, the body is gradually taking the place once assigned to the transcendental ego. Indeed, in *Ideas II*, Husserl uses the exact language he used to reserve to the transcendental ego, to discuss the body, he writes, "the body is now a new sort of unity of apprehension" (163). As a result, one way to think of the overall ambition of *Ideas II* is that it replaces the three reductions I mentioned earlier by a fourth, which you could call maybe a somatic reduction, where what is discovered is the fact of embodiment. But this, of course, suggests that we now must think of the fact of embodiment as a very rich phenomenon: the body is no longer just our sensible apparatus, it is also what carries out the job once assigned to the transcendental ego: it creates experiences. It is an active principle of interpretation of the world.

The key move of *Ideas II* therefore is the shift from explaining the world of experience in terms of the conditions of experience (in particular the transcendental ego) to explaining experience immanently. This involves that there are no conditions of experience that are not part of experience itself, no transcendental conditions. This development is relevant to the theme of embodiment because it pushes Husserl towards an analysis of embodiment as the *only* condition of all experience. The body must now be conceived as the only power behind all experiences, as "the perceptual organ of the perceiving subject" as a whole (para. 56): not only does it provide sensations through the senses, as even Kant acknowledged, but it also *organises* these sensations, and is the source of the additional judgements that are immediately added on to them (i.e., the *Weltthesis* that the reduction was meant to bracket). In short, the way the world appears to us is entirely and solely dependent on our embodiment. In the rest of this chapter and indeed in the following, we shall be investigating how this can be so, how this transforms what we should mean by "body" and what we should mean by "world."

The Touching-Touched

Think of a small child, around one year old, who starts discovering their body. How they intently practice moving one finger without moving the others. This sort of fascination is intriguing for the adult, because it seems that the child is too surprised at their own hands to be aware of the fact that they are hers: she observes them as if they were of another. At the same time, it looks like she is taking a greater interest in them than she would take in say her parents' hands. In fact, when she takes her father's fingers, she stops the game quite quickly, while she could go on for hours when it's her own. This sort of fascination seems to challenge the neat separation of the self and the other: it's more surprising than the self, but more urgent than the other. How come I am discovering something, even if it's me? How come I am different enough from myself that I can be a surprise to myself? Should we say that I am discovering what I already have, what I already know? What kind of discovery is that? What kind of emotion teaches me that I'm still discovering something while I'm actually only discovering something that I know, something that I take for granted—namely me, my body? Husserl tries to go back to that experience by focusing on one case: what happens when my left hand touches my right hand?

Husserl's question has to do with a series of paradoxes regarding touch, and more broadly, perception.

The first has to do with the reciprocity of touch—that is, the simple fact that we only touch things if they touch us back. Husserl calls this experience, of having your hands touching each other, the "touching-touched." This is what the example of the infant playing with their hands illustrates. Touch, in this sense, is an everyday experience that falsifies most of the Western metaphysical presuppositions about the subject and the object and the active and the passive. That is to say, he sees it as a case in which the subject that touches and the object that is touched are hard to distinguish and yet hard to conflate, an experience that questions the usual distinction of the subject and the object and of the passive and the active: my left hand touches my right, this seems to make it active. My left hand is touched by my right, this seems to make it passive. Yet, my right hand touches my left only insofar as—to the exact extent that—my left hand touches my right. Maybe I should say that they touch each other back, reciprocally. And it becomes impossible to tell which is active and which is passive, which is the subject doing the touching and which is the object being touched.

Touching my left hand, I have touch-appearances, that is to say, I do not just sense, but I perceive and have appearances of a soft, smooth hand, with such a form. The indicational sensations of movement and the representational sensations of touch, which are Objectified as features of the thing, "left hand," belong in fact to my right hand. But when I touch the left hand I also find in it, too, series of touch-sensations, which are "localized" in it, though these are not constitutive of properties (such as roughness or smoothness of the hand, of this physical thing). If I speak of the physical thing, "left hand," then I am abstracting from these sensations (a ball of lead has nothing like them and likewise for every "merely" physical thing, everything that is not my Body). If I do include them, then it is not that the physical thing is now richer, but instead it becomes Body, it senses. "Touch" sensations belong to every appearing Objective spatial position on the touched hand, when it is touched precisely at those places. The hand that is touching, which for its part again appears as a thing, likewise has its touch-sensations at the place on its corporeal surface where it touches (or is touched by the other). Similarly, if the hand is pinched, pressed, pushed, stung, etc., touched by external bodies. or touching them, then it has its sensations of contact, of being stung, of pain, etc. And if this happens by means of some other part of one's Body, then the sensation is doubled in the two parts of the Body, since each is then precisely for the other an external thing that is touching and acting upon It, and each *is* at the same time Body. All the sensations thus produced have their localization, i.e., they are distinguished by means of their place on the appearing Corporeality, and they belong phenomenally to it. Hence the Body is originally constituted in a double way.—E. Husserl, *Ideas II*, chapter 3, "The Constitution of Psychic Reality through the Body," paragraph 36.

The second is the paradox related to the question of a limit. If two things touch each other, this means that the distance between them is zero (*Ideas II*, 166). In other words they are both in the same place. Now, if two things are in the same place, either one is hiding the other, or the other is hiding the one, or they are one thing. In other words, the big question for Husserl is, how can I explain that even though my two hands are different, they are in the same place? In a Cartesian context, this would be impossible. As is well-known, Descartes is the one who invented the Cartesian diagram, which precisely decides where and what things are, on the basis of the presupposition that there can only be one thing at any one point on the diagram. Saying that there are two things in one place, as seems to happen in touch, conflicts with Descartes's notion of space and with Descartes's mechanistic notion of the extended thing. And this means that our body lives according to different rules than our mind (for whom there can only be one thing at every point). In other words, what would, for our mind, appear as a contradiction, happens to be the basic mode of life of our body: perception. With Husserl, at least in *Ideas II*, the Cartesian match between the world and the mind becomes undermined. Instead, it is revealed that the order of ideas makes experience mysterious or impossible. We experience things that do not obey the purest form of thinking. We experience two as one, difference and identity, at the same time. In other words, Husserl uses the touching-touched to turn Descartes on his head.

The third paradox has to do with the experience of self-touching. It seems that in the experience of your left hand touching your right hand, you are touching yourself in three senses.

- In the first sense, we have a strict self-touching: my right hand touches itself, because it becomes aware of *itself* by way of touch. But of course, as pointed out earlier, this touch is made possible only by the presence of the other hand. In other words, it looks like the right hand only experiences itself through touch by resisting another, left hand. This returns Husserl to a common theme in German idealism, namely that the self only experiences itself through resistance from the other: we experience ourselves via the other. He writes that there is a "correlative constitution of the Body and external things" (section 37).
- In the second, more straightforward sense, you are touching yourself because a part of you (your left hand) is touching another part of you (your right hand).
- The third sense of self-touching involves the whole of the person: when my left hand touches my right hand, I touch myself because the whole of me is connected internally to my right hand *and* to my left hand. As a result, one should say that the whole of me touches the whole of myself via my hands. This is made necessary by the fact that the consequences of my left hand touching my right seem to involve the rest of my body. I become aware of that touch, of the texture of my palms, and this awareness cannot be properly said to lie in my hands, but rather in my whole being. This is verifiable by the fact that my whole body will respond if for example my left hand feels surprisingly cold: I might start

at the sensation for example. Similarly, if I shake hands with you, your hand will be, physically speaking, the closest of your body parts to my own hand at this point. Yet, it remains farther from me than even the tip of my toes, which are physically much further. Similarly, the back of my right hand touches the back of my left hand via the front of my left hand and the front of my right hand. It's because there is a magical interaction between this part of my hand and that part of my hand that I can say wholeheartedly: my hand is touching my other hand; my hands are touching each other. It would be wrong to say that the palm of my left hand is touching the palm of my right hand. It's true literally, from a physical perspective. If I was a robot it would be true. But for a human it is not true. For a human, my one hand is touching my other hand. Because a robot has no experiential connection between parts of their hands, and parts of their body. As such, the unity between the two hands of the robot, is the same. It's the same kind as the unity between one finger and another finger of the same hand, or between the front and the back of that hand. But such is not the case for us. This involves a departure from Descartes' notion that the body as res extensa is defined as divisibility: a series of parts. On the contrary, there seems to be an internal connection between the parts that belong to the same body which the description of the body in terms of parts fails to account for. As a result, Husserl moves to a view of the body as an organ, that is to say a collection of parts *plus their organisation*.

Husserl's analysis of the touching-touched has consequences for what we call the body. It also has consequences at a more metaphysical level, for what we call the world. Let's turn to the new notion of the body first. The conclusion drawn from the three paradoxes outlined is itself paradoxical: it seems that the body always presents itself to us as a material object *and* as an organic whole. It presents itself as a material thing of the type of Descartes's *res extensa* in two ways. First, because of its commensurability with other physical objects, for example, it enters into contact and plays of resistance with other parts of the body, and with objects in the physical world too. Second, the Cartesian description of *res extensa* as a series of parts remains correct to an extent, for even in the experience of the touching-touched, parts matter: as Husserl points out, when my left hand touches my right, I can localise pretty precisely the sensations involved there on the surface of my skin, and this suggests that the contact in question takes place at some privileged points in my body: some parts are more involved than others in this experience of contact. Second, and although it looks like my touching my right hand with my left coincides exactly with my touching my left hand with my right, Husserl points out that we never confuse the two experiences: we never lose the ability to distinguish the sensations that belong to our left hand and those that belong to our right hand or the ability to distinguish the sensations that my left hand is experiencing about itself and those it experiences about my right hand. So, our body remains to be considered in terms of extension, divisibility, contiguous parts. This is the dimension of the body which Husserl calls *Körper*: the body in the physical sense, the kind of body that dead bodies are made of.

> There exists a material thing, of a certain nature, which is not merely a material thing but is a Body, i.e., a material thing which, as localization field for sensations and for stirrings of feelings, as complex of sense organs, and as phenomenal partner and counter-part of all perceptions of things (along with whatever else could be said about it, based on the above), makes up a fundamental component of the real givenness of the soul and the Ego.—E. Husserl, *Ideas II*, chapter 3, "The Constitution of Psychic Reality through the Body," paragraph 40.

The paradox lies in the fact that the view of the body as *Körper* is unthinkable without the opposite, organic view of the body. Husserl stresses that a body has "non-thingly properties" (section 40, see also section 36). The resulting notion of the body, which differs from the view of body as *Körper*, is referred to as *Leib*. As the name shows, the expression *Leib* is meant to stress that the body is a living thing, and this appeals to the assumption that life emerges from the conjunction of the parts of an organism, but is irreducible to them: a living body is more than the sum of its parts. In this sense, the body as *Leib* is considered as a "concrete unity" (para. 42), contrary to the *Körper* which is considered from the point of view of its parts. It is the body as *Leib* that makes it so that what can be described as my left hand touching my right (from the point of view of body parts), can also be described as me touching myself (from the point of view of *Leib*). The body as *Leib* becomes understood as a sensitive unity throughout which impressions and experiences diffuse themselves. This second, unitary notion of the body, which relies on the intimacy that connects all its parts, presents a direct threat to transcendental idealism, since it finds the unity once provided solely by positing a transcendental ego, in the experience of the body itself. This paradoxical structure of the body as both Leib and Körper leads to the following conclusion: "Hence, the body is originally constituted in a double way: first, it is a physical thing: matter . . . secondly, I find on it, and I sense 'on' and 'in' it warmth on the back of the hand etc."

Now, the paradox must be resolved: if we say that the body is in a way *Körper*, and in a way *Leib*, what are the relations between those two things? And here Husserl is aware of the fact that this needs addressing, for it risks collapsing back into a dualism that sees the *Leib* as the ensouled body and *Körper* as the body simpliciter. However, he only initiates the response rather than address it fully: "On the other hand, the Body appears here at the same time as a 'turning point' where the causal relations are transformed into conditional relations between the external world and the Bodily-psychic subject(s)." What does he mean by "turning point"? He suggests that the body is a turning point because it involves transformation. What is being transformed are causal relations between the world and the subject, and they are transformed into conditional relations by changing direction via embodiment. We had seen that paragraph 37 points out how the body and the material world constitute each other. This mutual conditionality is now dramatised as the relation not just of the body and the world but of the self and the world. This is because, in the meantime, the subject has been recognised as "bodily-psychic." In other words, the mutual constitution of the body and the world is now cashed out as the mutual constitution of the self and the world. Once, the world caused events in the subject, and the subject caused events in the world, but a deeper understanding of the body suggests that in fact the subject and the world are conditions of each other: what we must pursue is a sense of the body as "what is already constituted prior to, or correlative with, material nature" (para. 35). This is why Husserl talks of a transformation that involves reversing directions: what we think of as the influence of the world on the body is immediately seen as the body's influence upon the world. If we return to the example of touch, this makes sense: any experience of resistance is mutual and involves that one experiences themselves via this that resists them. We should not miss Husserl's very self-aware use of the notion of "conditions," which is crucial in the context of transcendental philosophy, for Kant for example. Husserl says that the subject and the world are necessary conditions of each other, that they cannot exist without each other, and this is ensured by the body. But if this is the case, thinking of the body as *Körper*, as reduced to the laws of physical causation, means that we miss its conditional character. So we must rather think of the body as the underlying and unified condition for the existence of self and world, just like the experience of resistance was the condition for the mutual appearance of my two hands. What this suggests is that one cannot explain how the body combines its *Leib*-dimension and its *Körper*-dimension without regarding it as the common condition of existence of the world and the self.

Constitution: The Embodied World

The suggestion that we should be thinking of the body as a condition for the self and the world involves a complete refoundation of Western metaphysics because it defines "the world" no longer on its own terms, but rather as this that is conditioned by the body. The subject and the object, the active and the passive, the parts and the whole and the same and the other, which polarised the Cartesian world, are shown to fail to account for the direct experience of embodiment, which violates them. In the process, the transcendental ego too becomes suspicious, as it seems to be nothing more than a mental presupposition whose validity cannot be traced back to any experience, and we are on our way to replacing it with the "synthetic unity" called the body (section 15b).

Now, all these Cartesian dualities are not rejected offhand. What is rejected, rather, is their foundational character: they are, it seems, not the basis of experience, but its result. They are founded upon embodied experience and rise from it. In short, Husserl remembers the responsibility of phenomenology, which is to account for the mistakes of those views that take flight away from the things themselves: these illusions can only be triggered in and by experience itself since all comes from experience. As a result, a phenomenologist must explain how the false comes out of the true. So, Husserl is asking himself: if the body is the condition of the world and the self, how come Cartesianism is even possible? How come Descartes's misunderstanding is so commonsensical? How come it's even conceivable to look at the world the way Descartes does? This explains why we have these paragraphs 39, 40 and 41 which are intended to explain how *concepts* come out of *physical experience*. Note that this doesn't mean that such false beliefs are accepted, rather, that they need to understood. For Husserl, this means we must explain how they come to be seen as fundamental structures of the world, when in fact, they are misrepresentations of that very structure, which is in truth, experience. These are the passages where Husserl talks about the body as *constitutive*. In phenomenology, constitution is the process whereby non-conceptual phenomena turn into meanings. If we remember the phenomenological attention to the reduction, we can see that constitution is precisely what is to be reduced in order for us to attain the things themselves. Constitution, in the broadest sense, is interpretation: phenomena become interpreted in such a way that they acquire meaning. Think of the most common uses of the terms, for example, the constitution of a country. When a country adopts a constitution, it is hard to pinpoint what has changed: the same people are in the same places, there are no physical or geographical differences in the country between the day of the proclamation and the next day. But a nation has been born. It doesn't mean that the people were not there before, that the land was not there before, that the language was not there before, that the religion was not there before, that the set of beliefs was not there before. All the objective properties remain the same. Simply now, all of that *stands as*, or *counts as* a nation. This expression "standing *as*" is equivalent as "having the meaning *of*." Thanks to a constitution, all of the objective properties of a people, a land and its artefacts now have the meaning: *nation*. So this should allow us to see that what Husserl means by constitution is not so remote from our intuitive understanding of the word. Constitution has always been a key theme for Husserl, but what *Ideas II* contributes, is the idea that it is the body, not the transcendental ego, that is responsible for it. The body if it is to be seen as the condition of the world, should be regarded as an interpretive force, because the world only appears to us interpreted: you see trees and chairs and hands ("perceptions"), you do not see floating particles of colour ("sensings"). This is why, by returning to the touching-touched, Husserl declares: "Touching my left hand, I have touch-appearances, that is to say, I do not just sense, but I perceive and have appearances of a soft, smooth hand, with such a form" (para. 36).

Once we understand what constitution is and why it is so central to a phenomenological account, we can return to the relations of *Leib* and *Körper*. For Husserl, *Leib* and *Körper* do not refer to two different things, but rather they are two different interpretations of the phenomenon of the body as the condition of self and world. In other words, *Leib* and *Körper* are constituted by an experience that precedes them, and which is the experience of the body as the interface of self and world. "Hence, the body is originally constituted in a double way: first, it is a physical thing: matter . . . secondly, I find on it, and I sense 'on' and 'in' it warmth on the back of the hand, etc." In short, *Leib* and *Körper* each correspond to one major option for constitution: objects can be constituted qualitatively, in terms of how they feel. They will be constituted under the regime of *Leib*. They could also be constituted quantitatively, in terms of their objective features. This would constitute them under the regime of *Körper*. Yet, *Leib* and *Körper* as we saw cannot be kept apart because the body is precisely what allows us to both experience things qualitatively and to formalise these experiences in quantitative terms through constitution. This naturally leaves a few questions open which it will fall to Merleau-Ponty to address.

It's impossible to think of the body outside of experience, the body is the subject of experience, and that means that any account of the body, where the body is not the subject of experience, is insufficient and that any account of experience that does not involve the body is false (e.g., the mind for Descartes). Second, the body constitutes the world of meaning. What this means is that any account of the world of meaning that doesn't trace its meaning to the body is wrong. As a result, all the things that Cartesianism used to attribute to the mind, that transcendental idealism used to attribute to the Ego is now attributed to the body. This brings us before a new crossroads for philosophy that I think closes the Cartesian era which was organised around which position you take towards his dualism. With Husserl, this alternative is now overcome. We shall draw the consequences of this shift with Merleau-Ponty.

Further Readings
Edmund Husserl, *Ideas Pertaining to a Pure Phenomenology and to a Phenomenological Philosophy*, vol. 1 (Ideas I).
Maurice Merleau-Ponty, "The Philosopher and His Shadow."
William James, *Principles of Psychology*, chapters 17–22.
James Dodd, *Idealism and Corporeity: An Essay on the Problem of the Body in Husserl's Phenomenology*.
Dan Zahavi, "Husserl's Phenomenology of the Body."

Key Ideas

The everyday experience of the body reveals that:
It is the condition of the appearing of the world.
It precedes and constitutes subjects and objects.
It is bidirectional: by experiencing the world it experiences itself and by constituting the world it constitutes itself.
It is the unity of *Leib* and *Körper*, that is to say, the unity of the qualitative and the quantitative dimensions of experience.

Note

1. In *Ideas I*, 103 and 108, Husserl makes a similar point. He admits that the notion of the thing-in-itself is not a "logical" contradiction (i.e., we need to understand

what it means in order to know it to be a contradiction, as opposed to a formal contradiction such as "A is non-A," which is known to be a contradiction regardless of our understanding of A) but remains "materially counter-sensical" (103). For more on this, see van Mazijk (2020).

CHAPTER SIX

~

Merleau-Ponty
and the Embodied World

Readings
Maurice Merleau-Ponty, *Phenomenology of Perception*, introduction, "Experience and Objective Thought: The Problem of the Body."
Maurice Merleau-Ponty, *Phenomenology of Perception*, chapter 3: "The Spatiality of One's Own Body and Motricity."

"Embodiment changes everything."

Husserl invites us to pursue the consequences of the introduction of the concept of *Leib*. *Leib*, unlike *Körper*, is not a thing, it's not the object of biology or medicine, it's not defined by its contingent or objective features. Most importantly, it is the property of a subject, rather, it *is* the subject. Husserl leaves us with this fact: the body as *Leib* is whatever needs to be posited for the world to appear the way it does. The true sense of a transcendental subject is in the body, not in the ego, and therefore, it violates the distinction between the transcendental and the empirical: the body is both. Additionally, therefore, the body is a principle of commensurability (Merleau-Ponty says that it produces "the intentionality that establishes the natural and pre-predicative unity of the world and of our life," *Phenomenology of Perception*, p. lxxxii) and therefore it transcends once and for all the subject-object opposition inherited from Descartes. This is an invitation taken up most profoundly by Merleau-Ponty.

Merleau-Ponty's interest in the question of the body comes from his interest in the question of perception. The aim of his 1945 *Phenomenology of Perception* is "to seek the essence of perception" (p. lxxx). This is a saving grace because beginning with a focus on perception pushes Merleau-Ponty to look at the body as a perceiving thing, a point of passage between the world and the self, that is to say, as belonging to the world as much as to the subject. As a result, his contribution to the philosophy of the body lies in his focus on the idea that "embodiment changes everything" (from *Sense and Nonsense*). By this declaration, he means four important theses.

- First, that the negative conclusions we've come to via Plato, Augustine and Descartes, are as far-reaching as can be. The inability of these authors to explain away the body infects any possible worldview: the body is central to any possible philosophy, even a philosophy that is not primarily concerned with the body.
- Second, it means that embodiment is a phenomenon which demands not just that we revise our view of the subject alone (as in Husserl, where the subject becomes embodied), but of "everything" that is to say, of the world too. There is an important sense in which *the world, like the subject, is embodied*.
- Third, we must put these two things together: embodiment therefore belongs both to the subject and to the object. The phenomenon of embodiment disables the traditional organisation of the world in terms of subjects and objects. As we shall see, once this is set up, we can see how much "everything" is changed when the fact of embodiment is introduced: the person, the world, history and politics.
- Fourth, if it is true that the body is primary and belongs to both the so-called objective and the so-called subjective worlds, it should be regarded as the very source of the subject and of the world. As a result, the transcendental idealist view of the precedence of the subject is finally overcome. This deepens Husserl's conclusion that the subject doesn't precede the world, neither does the world precede the subject, they both derive from a deeper source, the body, which as such, is neither subjective nor objective.

So, the body and the world are exposed to each other. If you are ill, for example, then you know that you belong to the world. The world made you ill, perhaps by introducing a virus into your body for example. Similarly, consider simply the phenomenon of having a face. When you turn up in someone's field of vision, you don't choose what you turn up *as*. You're exposed. Your body is the public dimension of you. It is the dimension of you that belongs to the others (we will examine in detail in chapters 10, 11 and 12 how this subtends experiences of alienation and oppression). Having a face, having a body in general is the experience of the impossibility to separate what's mine from what belongs to the others. Consider the old domestic cliché, where, in a couple someone gets a haircut and they ask their spouse: "How do you like my new haircut?" And the spouse says, "Well, it's fine if you like it," and then the other says "yes, but you're the one who's going to see it!" The point the first spouse is making is this: "My appearance belongs to you." The other retorts: "No, your appearance belongs to you." And if they had read Merleau-Ponty, they would know that this is not a conversation that you should continue having because they are both right and both wrong. There is no solution to this back-and-forth, because it's wrong to think of belonging to the self and belonging to the other as a mutual incompatibility. There is no such thing as complete self-ownership or complete alienation for the embodied being. By taking embodiment seriously to the degree that he does, Merleau-Ponty allows himself to consider both the subject and the world as embodied. As we shall see, this has three sets of consequences: first, it leads into a new notion of the body; second, it leads into a new notion of the world, and finally, it leads into a new notion of meaning. All of them, as we shall see, are to be understood in terms of their role in structuring possibilities. The body is a principle that precedes the subject and the object. The world is embodied, and this is to be understood in terms of possibilities: the world is best understood as a set of possibilities.

Situatedness

This sounds very abstract and general. Indeed, it seems that it becomes hard to see if Merleau-Ponty has anything like the common idea of embodiment in mind when he says this. Therefore, it is worth noting that Merleau-Ponty draws this conclusion from the most minimal and widely accepted notion of embodiment, which he inherits from the entire tradition, through Plato and Descartes: embodiment means spatiality. We remember that for Plato, to have a body was to be subjected to time and space. For Descartes, it is further reduced to space alone: the body is *res extensa*, a spatial thing. Merleau-Ponty begins there too, adding simply the further determination he inherited from Husserl: the interdiction of the thing-in-itself. Husserl had brought his own transcendental model to the verge of exhaustion because of the implications of the taboo of the thing-in-itself: the ego was now indistinguishable from the body thanks to the new notion of *Leib*. Yet, in the absence of any alternative model under which *Leib* could replace the transcendental ego, he shied away from making the next step, and gave up transcendentalism altogether. It is this next step which Merleau-Ponty makes, and the model that allows him to take that step is based on the notion of *situatedness*.

If it is true that to be embodied means to be in space, then this being in space can possibly be considered objectively, as a place on a map or a diagram, which itself represents the view from nowhere (as in the Cartesian approach). But as Merleau-Ponty notes, this point of view from nowhere relies on the thing-in-itself: to see something from nowhere is to see it as it *is*, not as it is *for anyone*. In addition, it suggests that the body is seen by something that is not embodied, since it is nowhere—that is, since it doesn't exist in space. If one is to respect the ban on the thing-in-itself, they would have to take the alternative option: bodies are in space and now that geometrical space (seen from nowhere) is discounted, what this means is: they are in certain relations with other spatial things (i.e., they are in space from the point of view of other embodied things that they share this space with). The resulting worldview, as we can readily see, involves revising the notion of spatiality into a notion of situatedness: to be in space is to be in a certain position with reference to other spatial things. "Spatiality" minus the thing-in-itself equals "Situatedness." Merleau-Ponty's starting point is to be found here: situatedness is fundamental and philosophy is the analysis of the notion of situatedness.

Situatedness Is *Fundamental*

We are situated; what that means is that we are exposed to the world. We cannot extract ourselves from it, not even a little bit. It is, of course, embodiment which is responsible for making us be somewhere at some time and not everywhere all the time. Situatedness is fundamental, and the body is its condition, therefore, the body is *fundamental*. Now, *fundamental* means that it lies at the ground of everything: everything else depends on it, and it depends on nothing. What this also means is that situatedness does not need to be explained, because in order to explain it, you would have to use something that is clearer and more certain. But situatedness is clearer, more certain, than anything else. Therefore, it cannot be explained, but it *can* explain. Asking for somebody to prove that we are in the world involves a fallacy, a misunderstanding. In other words, when we say situatedness is fundamental, we say that it is easier to explain what we mean by the world in terms of situatedness, than it is to explain situatedness in terms of the world.

The reverse mistake would consist in mistaking this position for scepticism. For in order to regard the view that the embodied experience is situatedness as a sceptical view, one would have to compare it unfavourably to another meaningful sense of being. This means that one would have to commit to the idea that in order for the world to be, it must be *in itself*. But the notion has been repudiated a long time ago as a contradiction.

Situatedness Is Fundamental

A clear understanding of the notion of situatedness would show it to always be reciprocal. When I say I am situated in the world, I say something about me, but I also say something about the world. The world is this that has me in it, I am this that is in the world in a certain way (i.e., in *my* way). In other words, the best way to think of situatedness is as an interaction: the interaction between me and the world. Since situatedness is fundamental, it means that there is no me without the world, and there is no world without me. Because that would cancel the interaction. If I say that the interaction between me and the world is more fundamental than me or the world, this looks like a contradiction. It looks like for there to be interactions between me and the world, there has to be me and the world in the first place. Merleau-Ponty is, of course, deeply aware of this objection. He responds by declaring that "The lesson of the reduction is the impossibility of any absolute reduction." The impossibility of absolute reduction suggests to him that it's easier to reduce the subject or the object—in other words, it is easier to imagine that the subject and the object are not there—than to stop or to remove intentionality, which is their relation. It is intentionality which resists the reduction. This impossibility reveals an obstacle, and this obstacle reveals a deeper underlying, and irreducible phenomenon. What there is, is the fact that there is some directedness. There is intentionality, before there is a subject of intentionality, or an object of intentionality. This analysis of *Leib* as situatedness should suffice to explain why Merleau-Ponty regards the body as a reciprocal phenomenon, one that belongs to both the world and the subject and guarantees their interaction.

The Melody of Embodiment

This leads Merleau-Ponty to the question of the subject: What does the subject look like, if by subject we mean *Leib*? What is it that replaces the transcendental ego? The dominance of transcendental idealism since Kant relied on its ability to reduce all the structures of experience to the transcendental ego. The transcendental ego was single-handedly responsible for the unity of experience (it was synthetic), it disclosed essences (what objects are *for the ego* is what they are essentially), it was given in all acts, it was constitutive of its objects (it guarantees the unity of each object across its different manifestations), it was intentional (its activity was to constitute the world—what it is not). Any competitor to the transcendental ego therefore would have to fulfill all these functions. In order to prevail, it would have to solve the residual weakness of transcendental idealism: namely, that in order to fulfill these functions the ego needed to resemble very much a thing-in-itself.

Merleau-Ponty's proposal is to see all these functions as fulfilled by the intentional body. It too as we shall see, is synthetic (via his concept of the body schema), it too discloses essences (as meaning), it too is given in all acts (since there is no thing-in-itself), and it too is constitutive. It is intentional (in a slightly different sense: it does not *have* intentionality, but it *is* intentionality) (153) and it is behaviour.

We discover in the unity of the body the same structure of implication that we described above with regard to space. The various parts of my body—its visual, tactile, and motor aspects—are not simply coordinated. If I am seated at my desk and want to pick up the telephone, the movement of my hand toward the object, the straightening of my torso, and the contraction of my leg muscles envelop each other; I desire a certain result and the tasks divide themselves up among the segments in question, and the possible combinations of movements are given in advance as equivalent: I could remain leaning back in my chair provided that I extend my arm further, I could lean forward, or I could even partly stand up. All of these movements are available to us through their common signification. This is why, in the very first attempts at grasping, children do not look at their hand, but at the object. The different segments of the body are only known through their functional value and their coordination is not learned. Similarly, when I am seated at my table, I can instantly "visualize" the parts of my body that it conceals from me. As I clench my foot inside my shoe, I can see it. I have this power even for parts of my body that I have never seen.—Maurice Merleau-Ponty, *Phenomenology of Perception*, p. 150.

[The body] is a knot of living significations and not the law of a certain number of covariant terms. A certain tactile experience of the arm signifies a certain tactile experience of the forearm and the shoulder, as well as a certain visual appearance of the same arm. This is not because the different tactile perceptions in themselves, or the different tactile and visual perceptions together, all participate in a single intelligible arm (in the manner that all perspectival views of a cube participate in the idea of the cube), but rather because the arm seen and the arm touched, just like the different segments of the arm itself, together

Finally, the advantage of this embodied account is confirmed, for the body, which is both subject and object, cannot be said to exist independently of the world: it is not a thing-in-itself. Besides this successful avoidance of the thing-in-itself, the main difference between Merleau-Ponty's embodied account and transcendental idealism lies in the fact that essences and constitution are now understood in terms of meanings: the essence of a phenomenon is what it is *for the intentional body* and "to be for X" is always to mean A to X. As a result, to constitute now means to grant (not retrieve) the meaning of the object at hand. As a result, the intentional body must be regarded as *constitutive* of the world and *constituted* by the world at once. This unity of constitutiveness and constitutedness is precisely Merleau-Ponty's definition of the intentional body (169–183) which, because it escapes the traditional divide between the subject (constitutive) and the object (constituted), becomes called a "new type of existence." (102).

The Case of Schneider

This unity of objectivity and subjectivity, Merleau-Ponty argues, shatters the traditional paradigm because it shows the opposition of subject and object (which had been the bread and butter of both intellectualism and empiricism) as secondary. In order to be convinced that the body provides this unitary ground, Merleau-Ponty shows how basic physical phenomena would take place very differently if subjectivity and objectivity were primarily distinct. In fact, his famous analysis of the case of Schneider, a World War I veteran who suffered brain damage, is meant to dramatise what embodiment would look like under the dualistic regime shared by intellectualism and empiricism. What happens with Schneider? Merleau-Ponty uses this case (and Kurt Goldstein's reports about it) to make two points: first, that the normal body is neither active nor passive; second, that the world of *Leib* is a set of possibilities.

The first thing Merleau-Ponty is able to do with the example of Schneider is to distinguish between concrete movement and abstract movement. The fact that concrete movements are so safe, even in the case of Schneider, allows us to see that it looks like just having a body—even a reduced body the way that Schneider has—means being able to respond to real situations. That's what a body is: power to respond. What Schneider is unable to do is to make the world respond to him. In other words, to actively take initiative. As discussed, the body is a power in two senses. In one sense it's a match with the world. And to be a match means to be both subjected to the possibilities that are in the world—you're not able to do things that the world makes impossible. In another sense, it is a power in the sense of something that generates possibilities. For if you didn't bring your possibilities along with your body, nothing in the world would be possible. Schneider responds to the possibilities of the world as if they were demands and only if they are demands. The world makes demands on Schneider, and Schneider responds. If his commanding officer walks into the room, Schneider knows how to perform the salute. He will do it automatically. But if you ask him to show how to do a salute, he doesn't know. The context is not right for it. The context surely offers the *possibility* to do a salute, but it does not *demand* it. And he is unable to supplement this demand with his own initiative: he is unable to *take up* a possibility. By contrast, Merleau-Ponty concludes, this shows us that the normal, able body is just as active as it is passive, or rather, that in the life of the "normal" body, the distinction between passivity and activity is moot.

[Schneider] asked to point to some part of his body, his nose for example, can only manage to do so if he is allowed to take hold of it. . . . Now here, on the other hand, we have to create the concepts necessary to convey the fact that bodily space may be given to me in an intention to take hold without being given in an intention to know. . . . Once more kinetic initiative becomes impossible, the patient must first of all "find" his arm, "find", by the preparatory movements, the gesture called for, and the gesture itself loses the melodic character which it presents in ordinary life, and becomes manifestly a collection of partial movements strung laboriously together.—Maurice Merleau-Ponty, *Phenomenology of Perception*, pp. 104–5 (trans. Smith; for the Landes translation, see pp. 106–7).

For a key, for instance, to appear as such in my tactile experience, a kind of fulness of touch is required, a tactile field in which local impressions may be co-ordinated into a shape just as notes are mere stepping stones in a melody. . . . . Whereas in the normal person every event related to movement or sense of touch causes consciousness to put up a host of intentions which run from the body as the centre of potential action either towards the body itself or towards the object, in the case of the patient, on the other hand, the tactile impression remains opaque and sealed up. It may well draw the grasping hand towards itself, but does not stand in front of the hand in the manner of a thing which can be pointed out. The normal person reckons with the possible, which thus, without shifting from its position as a possibility, acquires a sort of actuality. In the patient's case, however, the field of actuality is limited to what is met with in the shape of a real contact or is related to these data by some explicit process of deduction.—Maurice Merleau-Ponty, *Phenomenology of Perception*, p. 109 (trans. Smith; for the Landes translation, see pp. 111–12).

For these patients the world exists only as one readymade or congealed, whereas for the normal person his projects polarize the world, bringing magically to view a host of signs which guide action, as notices in a museum guide the visitor. This function of "projection" or "summoning" (in the sense in which the medium summons an absent person and causes him to appear) is also what makes abstract movement possible: for, in order to be in possession of my body independently of any urgent task to be performed; in order to enjoy the use of it as the mood takes me, in order to describe in the air a movement formulated only verbally or in terms of moral requirements, I must reverse the natural relationship in which the body stands to its environment, and a human productive power must reveal itself through the density of being.—Maurice Merleau-Ponty, *Phenomenology of Perception*, p. 112 (trans. Smith; for the Landes translation, see p. 115).

What we have discovered through the study of motricity is, in short, a new sense of the word "sense." The strength of intellectualist psychology, as well as of idealist philosophy, comes from the ease with which they show that perception and thought have an intrinsic sense and cannot be explained through an external association of fortuitously assembled contents. The Cogito was the moment of insight into this interiority. And yet, every signification was simultaneously conceived as an act of thought, as the operation of a pure "I"; if intellectualism easily won out over empiricism, it itself remained incapable of accounting for the variety of our experience, for the regions of non-sense in our experience, and for the contingency of its contents. The experience of the body leads us to recognize an imposition of sense that does not come from a universal constituting consciousness, a sense that adheres to certain contents. My body is this meaningful core that behaves as a general function and that nevertheless exists and that is susceptible to illness. In the body we learn to recognize this knotting together of essence and existence that we will again meet up with in perception more generally, and that we will then have to describe more fully.—Maurice Merleau-Ponty, *Phenomenology of Perception*, p. 148.

Second, Merleau-Ponty uses Schneider to argue that the world is a set of possibilities. It begins by rejecting both realism and intellectualism. Schneider is the subject as both realism and intellectualism imagine it: as a form of life that keeps the active and the passive separate. He engages with the world as a passive machine (the way the empiricists would expect) *and not* as an active mind (like the idealists would predict). But for Merleau-Ponty, it is the fact that in the case of Schneider, the active and the passive are so neatly separated that makes it a pathological behaviour. By contrast, Merleau-Ponty seeks to demonstrate that what he calls "normal" embodiment is in fact the life of a body whose mental and physical functions are united "melodically." What he means by melodically, as the text in the box shows, is the way normal gestures are not attributable either to a subject standing before an alien environment (as in intellectualism) or to an environment conspiring through causal means to elicit a certain behaviour on the part of the subject (as in materialism). For Schneider to hold a doorknob, he will have to give his body an order every step of the way: "extend your arm away from your body/stretch your elbow/open your fingers/close your fingers on the doorknob, etc." On the contrary, normal gestures are the result of a harmony between the body and the world, whereby every aspect of the environment and every intention of the subject combine with the features of my body to produce a seamless gesture, grabbing a door handle, say. As we discussed in chapter 3, just like a melody is more than the sum of the notes that are its part, a body is more than the sum of its parts and the inherence of the body in the world is more than a juxtaposition of parts in a greater whole. It is existence itself.

To Merleau-Ponty, the case of Schneider raises the question: How can a physical condition of *Körper*, in this case a brain lesion, transform a person's (non-physical) existence? Merleau-Ponty draws two conclusions. The first one is contrastive. What is missing for Schneider and available to the so-called normal individuals, is the fact that we live with our body in a dialogue *with possibilities*. Note that this is good news if you're trying to say that the body is the replacement for the transcendental ego. For possibility is precisely what defines the transcendental ego: it is the condition of the possibility of experience. The second point is that even Schneider, with his pathology, still possesses a world, albeit a diminished one. In other words, there seems to be a proportional relation between the richness of your world and the richness of the experience of your body. Schneider's body lives in a very limited variety of ways. And Schneider's world is proportionately smaller for that reason. This links up nicely with Merleau-Ponty's focus on the notion of possibility, for possibilities have the same kind of bi-directionality as we find here in the correspondence between the extent of our embodiment and the extent of our world. As we shall see in more detail with Gibson, if we talk of possibilities, we always talk of a certain *match* between an organism and the world. And this match is always about *both* of the two things that match. In other words, the language of possibility is a good way to overcome the opposition of subject and object. Because a set of possibilities does not belong entirely either to the subject or to the object.

The Phantom Limb

This leads Merleau-Ponty to his very famous analysis of the phantom limb. In such pathologies as the case of the phantom limb, which affect some amputees, *Leib* has four limbs, but *Körper* has three. Merleau-Ponty's handling of this long-standing paradigmatic example of philosophy begins by disqualifying previous attempts to explain it. The general way to handle such cases there is to regard the phantom limb as a malfunction of the *subject* (along the dualistic lines inherited from Descartes): we think of our body in ways that don't match how our body really is. Thanks to an analysis of the details of reports about patients suffering from such conditions, Merleau-Ponty disqualifies such attempts. In fact, what is off-kilter in the experience of the phantom limb is not the mismatch between our view of ourselves and our objective state, but rather it is the discrepancy between the possibilities we perceive the world to contain and those that we can fulfill: in short, although

The Phantom Limb
[I]f the emotion is put back within being in the world, then we can understand how emotion can be at the origin of the phantom limb. To be emotional is to find oneself engaged in a situation that one is unable to cope with and yet from which one does not want to escape. Rather than accepting failure or retracing his steps, the subject abolishes the objective world that blocks his path in this existential dilemma and seeks a symbolic satisfaction in magical acts. The ruins of the objective world, the renunciation of genuine action, and the flight into autism are favourable conditions for the illusion that amputees have insofar as it too presupposes the obliteration of reality. If memory and emotion can make the phantom limb appear, . . . it is because one existential attitude motivates another and because memory, emotion, and the phantom limb are equivalent with regard to being in the world.—Maurice Merleau-Ponty, *Phenomenology of Perception*, p. 88.

my left arm is missing, the cup on the table by my left appears as something I could grab. This, not what I think of my body, is the true discrepancy. The conclusion, for Merleau-Ponty, is that the "normal" experience of the body in the world is an experience of *match*, a melodic experience in the same way as the normal experience of embodiment (as illustrated *a contrario* by the case of Schneider) is melodic. The experience of the phantom limb is the experience of possibilities in-themselves: the possibilities presented by the world are recognised as possibilities regardless of my ability to take them up. The pathological dimension of the experience, for Merleau-Ponty, is therefore that of committing to objectivism: the patient recognises possibilities that are not his own. A *contrario*, what this teaches us is that the normal experiences of possibilities are experiences of *our own possibilities in the world*: we do not experiences the world in terms of an "it is possible" but as an "I can." The phantom limb, Merleau-Ponty concludes, is an impairment of our being-in-the-world.

The cases of Schneider and of the phantom limb therefore both lead Merleau-Ponty to the same two conclusions.

First, as regards the body: the mode of life of the embodied self is "motor signification." Although the body is a perceiver, it is not a theoretical observer. Although it is an agent, it is not a pure physical force. Rather, "motor signification" suggests that the body *acts in* ("motor") and *understands* the world ("signification") in one movement. There is a common ground for "sensitivity" and "signification" (like Kant's schematism) which is deeper than either of them (unlike Kant's schematism) (136). As a result, "motricity is original intentionality" and the body is best understood as an "intentional arc," that is the "unity of the senses, the unity of the senses with intelligence, and the unity of sensitivity and motricity" (137). Conversely, the definition of the body as an "I can" suggests that the world that the body lives in must now be reconsidered: it exists as the unity of meaning and polarity. Things in the world both mean and polarise my body for action. We now must talk of the "structure world with its double moment of sedimentation and spontaneity" (13). Finally, we see how the resulting insights regarding the body and those regarding the world can hardly be contained within their own bounds: body and world are best understood under the same category: possibility becomes the principle of commensurability made to overcome the opposition of body and soul.

Additional Readings
Maurice Merleau-Ponty, *The Incarnate Subject: Malebranche, Biran, and Bergson on the Union of Body and Soul.*

Key Ideas

The body as *Leib* precedes the division of the world into the objective and the subjective realm.
The resulting notion of the world is the world as a set of possibilities.
The resulting notion of the body is the body as a set of possibilities.
Possibilities are expressions of a certain match between the body and the world, hence their relation precedes them.
Leib is the harmonious relation of the body and the world.

~

CHAPTER SEVEN

Merleau-Ponty and the "Unmotivated Springing Forth of the World"

Reading
Maurice Merleau-Ponty, *Phenomenology of Perception*, Preface.

With Merleau-Ponty, the body becomes the central question of ontology: any account of being, of the essence of the world, will be informed by the fact that the world must be defined as what the body engages with, that the body is the counterpart of the world, and that nothing exists if it's not caught in this interaction. In other words, not only must we think of the subject as embodied, we must make the next step and think of the *world* as embodied too.

"The problem of a genuine in-itself for us."

If the world of experience, the world of everyday life, of people, bus stops, tables and chairs, books and animals and leaves on the ground is to be traced back to a living body, one must immediately confront the following objections: non-philosophers, who live in this world, experience it as if it was indeed a collection of objects that exist before and after they interact with them. These objects exist, in short, in themselves. Merleau-Ponty himself gives voice to this objection. He writes: "The fact remains that the thing presents itself to the person who perceives it as a thing-in-itself, and thus poses the problem of a genuine in-itself-for-us" (*Phenomenology of Perception*, 336). Merleau-Ponty addresses this question in the introduction to part one of the *Phenomenology of Perception*, titled "The Body." The title of the introduction is "Experience and Objective Thought: The Problem of the Body." The title itself already indicates how Merleau-Ponty doesn't regard the body as anything else than the answer to the question: "How does the objective world turn up in experience?" Taking the conjunctive *and* in the phrase "experience and objective thought" seriously can explain how we come to a "problem," namely the one that he refers to (following Sartre) as the problem of "an in-itself for us" that is to say, "the problem of the body." The identity between the problem of the "in-itself for us" and the problem of the body immediately presupposes the reduction of the ego to the body: it is the body that interprets the world in terms of objective entities: the body, that is, is an interpretive force.

Objective Thought

The positing of the object, therefore makes us go beyond the limits of our actual experience which is brought up against and halted by an alien being, with the result that finally experience believes that it extracts all its own teaching from the object. It is this ek-stase of experience which causes all perception to be perception of something. Obsessed with being, and forgetful of the perspectivism of my experience, I henceforth treat it as an object and deduce it from a relationship between objects. I regard my body, which is my point of view upon the world, as one of the objects of that world. My recent awareness of my gaze as a means of knowledge I now repress, and treat my eyes as bits of matter. They then take their place in the same objective space in which I am trying to situate the external object and I believe that I am producing the perceived perspective by the projection of the objects on my retina. In the same way I treat my own perceptual history as a result of my relationships with the objective world; my present, which is my point of view on time, becomes one moment of time among all the others, my duration a reflection or abstract aspect of universal time, as my body is a mode of objective space. In the same way, finally, if the objects which surround the house or which are found in it remained what they are in perceptual experience, that is, acts of seeing conditioned by a certain perspective, the house would not be posited as an autonomous being. Thus the positing of one single object, in the full sense, demands the compositive bringing into being of all these experiences in one act of manifold creation. Therein it exceeds perceptual experience and the synthesis of horizons. . . . I detach myself from my experience and pass to *the idea*. . . . We must discover the origin of the object at the very centre of our experience; we must describe the emergence of being and we must understand how, paradoxically, there is an *in-itself for us*.— Maurice Merleau-Ponty, *Phenomenology of Perception*, pp. 70–71 (trans. Smith; for the Landes translation, see p. 73).

So, the interaction between objective thought and experience is *the problem of the body*. Now, *of* is a very difficult word to use (in the French also). Is it a problem that the body needs to solve? Like when I say, "it is the problem *of* the government to keep the schools funded." Or is it that the body *is* the problem? In other words, is the implication that the body makes it hard to understand things? Merleau-Ponty, as can be expected, appeals to both senses. The fact that the body is a problem is also what allows us to understand the body as the solution to the problem. The fact that we have a body has been a problem. As we saw, it has been a major problem for the tradition, of Plato, Augustine and Descartes, a thorn in their side. We've seen in the previous chapter how thinking of the body in synthetic terms offers a solution to this problem of interaction: the body is precisely the union of what was previously misconceived as body and soul. But if we bear in mind the first sense of "of," we can see that defining the problem as being the problem of the body already points towards a solution: the problem that the body is the solution to is the problem of the in-itself-for-us, and this defines the body as the mechanism that makes experiences look like objects. And so, what Merleau-Ponty says is: if we understand the body, we will therefore be able to explain how experience and objective thought relate to each other.

The Body as Interpreter

The second move that Merleau-Ponty makes is to pursue the consequences of the fact that the world of perception presents itself as a world of possibilities. Perception, as we pointed out earlier, is perception of possibilities. Yet, in order to be perceived, possibilities need to be interpreted. This should give us a better idea of what kind of interpretive power the body is. First, the body interprets the world in terms of objects. Second, the body interprets the world in terms of what it can do, and this introduces meaning in our experience. Merleau-Ponty declares "To sum up, what we have discovered through the study of motility, is in short, a new meaning of the word 'meaning.'"

On the basis of these two interpretive functions of the body, one could be tempted in the first instance to argue that the body has the ability to interpret. However, this remains inexact since this would presuppose that there is a body before such meaning-making takes place. This would be forgetting that the body is not outside of our experience of it, and that this experience is itself interpretive. Instead of saying that the body has the ability of meaning-making we should rather say that it *is* the ability to make meaning, it is, Merleau-Ponty writes, a "meaning-making core."

Although we shall have to return to the idea of the body as a basic ability, an action without an agent, there is no need to go into such abstractions just yet. In the first instance, Merleau-Ponty reconnects with the phenomenological tradition that investigates the coming to visibility of the world: how come the world appears as a series of objects, rather than a series of shapes and colours, or even worse, William James's "bloomin' buzzin' confusion"? In other words, why does the world of experience *make sense*? Here, we see that Merleau-Ponty's notion of the body as interpreter is only an extension of his general project of replacing the transcendental ego (who was previously put in charge of bringing the world to intelligibility) with the body. In moving the interpreting subject from the subjective pole (as it was the case with the transcendental ego) to the shared interaction of world and self which is called the body, Merleau-Ponty exposes himself to another predictable objection: the world does appear as organised into subjects and objects, not as a mass of phenomena that straddle this divide. At heart this objection is an objection from the point of view of diversity: how can the idea that the world and the body are two aspects of one movement called interpretation accommodate the fact that we experience ourselves as different from the world (the diversity of subject and object) and that we experience objects to be distinct from each other, rather than seeing them blend into each other (objective diversity)? Merleau-Ponty therefore must explain how diversity comes about.

Merleau-Ponty begins by acknowledging that indeed the world presents itself in this way. And therefore that, in the process by which the world appears, the separation between the subject and the object must come very quickly, closely followed by the separation between objects. Merleau-Ponty's criticisms of the metaphysics of subject and object that results from the Cartesian paradigm is not a rejection. Strictly speaking, what he finds objectionable, for example in Descartes, is not the dualism but the idea that dualism is fundamental, that it results in everything but results from nothing. Merleau-Ponty's only contribution is to suggest that before the world breaks itself up into subjects and objects (the Cartesian view), it is unified and it is from this unity that duality originates. This unity, Merleau-Ponty insists, is the body as meaning-making process. Note the strategic elegance of this addition: if the body is indeed a meaning-making process (something that has been independently demonstrated via an analysis of pathologies, the phantom limb and the case of Schneider), then it is by essence the process that distributes things in the world in terms of objects and of subjects. For an interpretation is always the recognition of an entity and the attribution of a distinctive essence to this entity: interpretation always results in entities, either subjects or objects. In short, interpretation is always objectification. It is the unified source of the diversified world of objects.

The Body Is Interpretation

This might allow us to return to a more complex point Merleau-Ponty makes about Schneider. Recall that Schneider is most sensitive to the difference between initiative and response. He is unable to salute his commanding officer on demand, to initiate a salute. Similarly, he is unable to initiate sexual intercourse with his wife. However, if his officer walks into the room, he will salute immediately, appropriately and without fail. Similarly, he is fully capable to respond to his wife's approach, when she initiates intercourse. In short, Schneider's life is structured around the incommensurability of the active (initiative) and the passive (he regards his acts as *results* of other circumstances, the entrance of the officer or the prompts from his wife). As Merleau-Ponty shows elsewhere, the illusory opposition of the active and the passive is a form of the opposition of the subject and the object. In short, Schneider is the kind of human we all would be had Cartesianism been correct. The Cartesian mistake was to subject even the body to the division of subject and object, its insight was to recognise how once the body as preceding this divide is accepted, the rest of the world obeys the opposition indeed. This, however, puts some amount of pressure on the initial division between subject and object. If it is true that the stage that precedes the organisation of the world into subject and object is neither subjective (as the transcendental idealists argue) nor objective (as the materialists argue), it means that subject and object must appear exactly simultaneously.

Merleau-Ponty's analysis of perception offers the resources to address this challenge by returning to Husserl's touching-touched: to perceive, he argues, is always a bi-directional process. In fact, this is required by the fact that perceiving is what the body does and that the body is the bi-directional interchange of self and world. For Merleau-Ponty, any act of perception is two-layered: it perceives the object and the subject of perception at once. One always perceives themselves as they're perceiving something. Merleau-Ponty famously noted that "seeing is always seeing more than one sees." If I look at the wall over there, I see the wall, but I also see that I am a visionary subject. To return to the mixture of passivity and activity which is lost on Schneider, to have perceptual interaction with the world, means that I am part of the world. What that means is that the world is subjected to me, in the sense that *I* see it. But also, I am subjected to it, in the sense that I see it on its own terms, according to its own conditions. For example, according to the laws of physics. This initial reciprocity of perception, therefore, contains all the resources to explain the world of objects without collapsing into dualism or materialism. Thanks to perception, the world becomes clear. The clearer I am to myself, the more the world comes into view. This is evident in early childhood development: as the child becomes acquainted with their own body, as they become able to differentiate themselves from their environment and then their mother, the colours, the contrasts and the outlines of objects become clearer for them because all of these things—colours, contrasts, and outlines, to keep to the visual vocabulary—are just possibilities being activated as the child's abilities become activated too: mostly, they allow recognition of objects as what the child can do with them. The world becomes richer as agency becomes richer: the possibilities of the world become clearer as what I am becomes clearer.

Now, if we must therefore conclude that the body as an interpreting force *precedes* the world which it constitutes, doesn't this make the body a sort of thing-in-itself? How would preceding the existence of the world of perception not suggest that the body exists independently of experience? If we are to take seriously the interdiction of the thing-in-itself, we must also admit that "precedence" should be meant in a very weak sense here. For Merleau-Ponty, the result of taking seriously the interdiction of the thing-in-itself leads to regarding the body only as a process which he describes as the "unmotivated springing forth of the world." He writes: "we must—precisely in order to see the world and to grasp it as a paradox—rupture our familiarity with it, and this rupture can teach us nothing except the unmotivated springing forth of the world" (lxxvii). Let us focus on this phrase. The world turns up ("springs forth"), and it is "unmotivated" because there is no possible event, fact, object or phenomenon (including the transcendental ego) that could be there before the world turns up: therefore nothing to motivate it. In other words, this surging up doesn't precede the constitution of objects in the sense that it exists independently from them: for their constitution is its mode of being. Without them it is nothing. There is no such surging up without objects, without a world. But this doesn't mean that they exist before it, rather, their coming to existence is its existence. This surging up, as we shall see, is none other than the body.

So the first truth is that the world shows up. But of course, this means that we must analyse what turning up for the world means. First, it means becoming visible, appearing. So Merleau-Ponty asks himself under which condition things appear. The first point he establishes, with reference to the psychological analysis of forms (Gestalt) is that for the world to turn up, we must have differences, delineations and contrast. In other words and as we noted earlier, nothing turns up if all is mixed together. So, turning up and being identifiable seem to be equivalent. But of course being identifiable involves a reference to meaning: to identify something you must recognize it, that is to say, you must attribute it some meaning. To mean something always involves definition and distinction. That's how things are meaningful. Even in the most basic sense, for example, a sentence is meaningful to you if you can recognise the implicit definitions of some of the words in it, maybe all of them, and if you can distinguish those meanings from others. But it's also true in basic perception. You identify objects by distinguishing them from each other and that's how they mean something to you. In other words, phenomenology is a genealogy of definition and distinction. This suggests that the unmotivated springing forth of the world is the coming to meaningfulness of the world. Indeed, Merleau-Ponty defines the body as the simultaneous positing of beings and meanings. The mode of being of the body is the positing of being and meaning at the same time. You see that this is only possible if we are serious about *Leib* being the source of the world as it appears. It's only when we place the body as the source of the world that we understand how experience is even possible.

So, the body's mode of being is interpretation, and Merleau-Ponty defines it as a "meaning-making core." This citation, in the text, is followed by this meaningful statement: "In the body we learn to recognize this knotting together of essence and existence." Without going into unnecessary detail, existence refers to meaning (something exists if it means something), and essence to being (something's essence is its being). In other words, the body should be understood as combining an experience of the world as being and an experience of the world as meaning. This doesn't contradict the idea of the body as meaning-making core, for this notion never involved any move away from essential analysis. Rather, it details what meaning-making is: the act of allowing the world to appear as meaning and object at the same time.

This is confirmed in everyday experience. When I interpret something, I grant it meaning and at the same time affirm it as an object independent from myself. When we experience the world, we experience it in terms of its essence, for example, when we talk about what this world means to us, and in terms of its essence, when we talk about it as "how the world works" or when we talk about "the real world." There is a sense in which this world is your world, but there is another sense in which it's *the* world. When we think of it as *the* world, we experience it in terms of its difference and independence from us. And this independence is best experienced when the world resists, refuses to yield to our projects. Now, Merleau-Ponty thinks that this experience, the experience of resistance which Merleau-Ponty generalises as the experience of "adversity" induces the false belief that there is a world in itself, outside of our experience, out there.

To turn up therefore means at least to organise itself along certain lines which differentiate different objects and identify them. These lines are the body. It is in this strong sense that we must think of the body as a structure: a set of rules according to which the world becomes understandable. Yet, as you recall, the interdiction of the thing-in-itself has led Merleau-Ponty to the conclusion that there is no such thing as determinate objects. This allows us one more point about the resulting world of experience: for the world to turn up, it needs to present itself as a series of objects, which it isn't, and we need to interpret it as such: to perceive is to interpret and to present oneself is to misrepresent oneself. This leads us to an answer to the question of the "in itself-for-us."

Essence and Existence

This means that for Merleau-Ponty, the essence of the body is to produce the illusion of the in-itself. This illusion is the price we pay for having a meaningful world. This process of meaning-attribution and therefore this process of solidification of illusion is what Merleau-Ponty calls constitution (after Husserl) and later, sedimentation. This is a crucial theme if we are to understand the ontological consequences of embodiment—that is, why the world is embodied.

Merleau-Ponty makes use of everyday examples to illustrate how at its most basic, experience is involved with illusions. When you look at the façade of a house, for example, you also seem to see the house behind the façade. Most of us would not say "I am looking at the façade of a house" but rather "I am looking at a house." This is so even though it could of course be that only the façade is standing and the house behind it is being rebuilt, like is the case with old houses. In fact, the house behind the façade is doubtful yet taken for granted, an illusion. The house behind the facade is constituted in the very act of perception. You see the front of a house, but you see a whole house. That is constitution. There are in fact, mental illnesses where, unlike the normal cases in which "we see more than we see," we only see what we see, and by contrast such pathological cases show that we cannot function in the world that way. You cannot function as if the façade of the house only registers as the front of a house without any related assumptions about what is behind it. If you only perceived the façade, you would not know you could enter. The idea here is that to perceive something is to attribute things to it, and that's the constitutive part.

This notion of constitution underlies how meaning-making includes a moment of crystallisation: interpretation has a way of usurping claims of truth, or as I said previously, of producing illusions. Merleau-Ponty claims: "our perception ends in objects." He means this in the two senses of "ends." First, our perception *leads into* objects. Like one would say, "my trip ends in Paris." In this sense of "end," perception carries one all the way to the object. Second, it also means, that the perception is a process that *stops happening* when an object appears. And that's another sense of "end." He even says that the full determinacy of even one object is "the death of consciousness." In other words when the production of objects is over, so is the experience of the world. The process of perception is a process of constructing an object, and therefore, when the object is constructed, perception ends. In this second sense of ending, perception ends in objects, in other words, perception is a process of constitution as the "determination of an eidos [essence]."

If I interpret a set of phenomena as a house, I will tend to forget that this phenomenon *means* "house" and take it to *be* a house. In short, Merleau-Ponty shows, we *forget* it's a perception, and that's because I *believe* it's a house. These two moments, one of *forgetting*, and one of *believing*, are in fact two sides of the same coin. "I believe it's a house" is the same as "I forget I interpret this as a house." And so, the big question in the text: "Why is there an itself for us?" is the question of: "Why the for itself is always interpreted as the in itself?" This moment of constitution results, Merleau-Ponty writes, in objects that "appear as the reason for all the experiences of it which we have had or could have." Embodied perception leads to the appearing of something as the reason for the experiences that we have of them. To perceive something is to have the belief that our perception of it is the *result* of its existence. The "unmotivated springing forth of the world" therefore relies on the very structure of perception, which is "Obsessed with being and forgetful of the perspectivism of my experience."

History

But the world is more than the series of objects I encounter in it. Indeed, it contains certain rules for interpreting them, we call them cultural rules, and these rules themselves are grounded in history. This is true for the written word, but also for evocations (as in art) symbols and the entire fabric of our meaningful world. If it is true to say that the world is a series of objects plus history, we must also ask how history emerges from the body as an interpretive force. Precisely, Merleau-Ponty points out that perception relies on the structure of history. At even the most microscopic level, there is an element of time at work when we talk about constitution or coming to clarity. A teacher may have known you three years, and you're becoming clearer and clearer in their mind each time they meet you, because they know more and more things about you every day they see you, or every day they hear about you. That is what human relations are all about. But that's also what other relations are about. For example, the building in which I'm writing this book: every day that I go into this building, I know more about this building. It means more to me. It is also the building that I did stuff in yesterday, which was not the case the day before because I had a free day, and so on. In other words, there is a dynamic where every object comes to greater definition, greater distinction, greater clarity, it becomes harder for me to confuse this building with another one, for example. This process of constitution leads into Merleau-Ponty's idea of history.

History is the milieu in which constitution functions. What does intentionality do? It explores me and the world. What happens when you're at the museum and you're looking at something like a Malevich for example? You look at a nice white square on a black background. Why do you spend hours in front of it? Because in this gazing, things are happening. It is slowly coming to clarity. You know it's a white square on black background since the start. But it's acquiring meaning. That's why people spend time in front of paintings, but that's why people spend time in front of each other also. There something to discover. It's never over, either because you discover a new meaning, or because you flesh out the initial meaning you had. And that's actually what you do when you interpret a painting. No one, especially not Merleau-Ponty, is committed to the idea that this process takes us towards the truth. But we obtain a richer and clearer meaning. And that's what history is. First, you already see a bit of history there, because it takes some time, and at the end things are irreversible. You can never make it so that you haven't had this experience with the Malevich painting. You've been transformed by it, the painting has done its job, and the like. And that's what happens in history. But this individual experience of time is not just an analogy for history. History is rigorously of the same type: a process whereby the way the world is presents itself in a sequence, the world unfolds before our understanding across epochs. All the possibilities of the world are possibilities of history. And some of them become opened up, before some others. This is why some events precede others.

Conclusion

I promised to deliver an account of an embodied world. Since the introduction of Merleau-Ponty's ideas in the previous chapter, it was clear how the world and the body were dependent on each other, suggesting indeed that there was a sense in which the world was affected by embodiment. We can now propose a stronger sense in which the world can be said to be embodied: the world is generated and informed by the intentional activity of the body. How does it affect the way we must think of it? The foregoing suggests first, that the world, as a collection of objects, is falsely determined. Rather we should think of each object as dynamic in the sense that it can always be further determined, and indeed, experience is this endless process of determination. Second, the world is a historical movement of determination that, although endless, tends towards determination, and therefore towards objectification (this will have consequences for the political chapters). Third, the world, both at the individual and cultural level, relies on forgetfulness (the forgetfulness of indeterminacy, the forgetfulness that the world is merely an interpretation), and coincidentally, with belief. This suggests that belief is not justified by experience, but rather constitutive of it (Merleau-Ponty will later talk of a "perceptual faith"). Finally, the world, as an illusion arising from constitution is best conceived as a collection of facts (units of meaning, in context) rather than objects.

Retroactively, this description of the world reflects onto one of its most particular members, the body.

1. In this context, the body becomes understood as the constitutive source of the world (as a substitute for and upgrade upon the transcendental ego) and therefore no longer as a constituted object (*Körper*) but as a constitutive *force*, whose structure itself leads into an illusion about itself: it is the nature of the intentional body to (falsely) regard itself as *Körper*. Earlier, we noted that Merleau-Ponty concludes from the stalemate of modern philosophy that as long as you begin with the mind or the body you will have the problem of interaction. Beginning

in the middle, although it's very difficult, is the only way you can account for interaction, and you must account for interaction because interaction is experience, and no one can deny that there is experience. You can have all sorts of debates about what is doing the experiencing, and what the experiencing is of. Is it experience of dreams? Is it the experience of truth? Is it the experience of reality? Is it the experience of the world? Is it the experience of yourself? What is undeniable is that there are experiences. We also just noted that this means beginning with *Leib* as an intermediary category that stands between two things-in-themselves: the ego and *Körper*. When we say *Leib* is the middle ground between *Körper* and ego, we also mean *Leib* is there *before Körper* and ego, which are results of a process of constitution which "ends" in illusions called "objects" (one of them is *Körper*, another ego). As we noted as well, *Leib* is not something that constitutes, like a postman is someone who distributes the mail. Why? Because the postman exists even when they don't distribute the mail. *Leib* is not something outside of the action of constituting the world as a series of objects, including *Körper*, and as ego. So *Leib* is the constitution of *Körper* as *Körper* and ego as ego. So the essence of *Leib*, is what it *does* and it is defined not as a subject but as a process: constitution.

2. To conclude, let's confront the more radical implications of this view of the world and of the body. If the body is indeed the "unmotivated springing forth of the world" we are effectively saying that the body itself is a *process*. What's left of embodiment? Remember how we started with an analysis of what situatedness implied. This is the only thread that we have followed all the way into such abstract considerations: the situated body is in a vital circuit with the world (a consideration of the pathologies of Schneider and the phantom limbs demonstrate this *a contrario*), therefore leading into the understanding of the world and self as a series of matching possibilities. We see how once the world is reduced to possibilities, the next analysis will have to focus on how possibilities are recognised. The result is that we must posit the unmotivated springing forth of the world as the basic structure that makes situatedness possible: admit that situatedness is intentional and you'll have to admit that the body is a mere force. The picture on the cover of this book doesn't portray any one's body, or any single body, rather, it invites us to think of embodiment as a movement which brings with it its outlines, its range of possibilities and impossibilities, but remains situated in an environment which structures its infinitely possible action. The body is the force that constitutes itself, the subject and the world.

Further Readings
Maurice Merleau-Ponty, *Eye and Mind*.
Maurice Merleau-Ponty *The Visible and the Invisible*, Chapter 2.
Wolfgang Kohler, *The Task of Gestalt Psychology*.

Key Ideas

The body is not an object but a process.
The body is what brings the world to understanding.
It informs and structures the world.
The nature of this process is to produce the illusion of objectivity.
The resulting world is:
- a world of meanings and not objects
- a world of meanings mistaken as objects
- a constant process towards infinite determination

History is the grand scale process by which the world appears to the understanding.
The body as interpretive force is the source of the two false views of the ego as subject and the body as object (*Körper*).

CHAPTER EIGHT

~

Embodied Cognition
From the Ecological Approach to Enactivism

Readings

James Gibson, "The Theory of Affordances" in *The Ecological Approach to Perception*.

Susan Hurley, "Perception and Action: Alternative Views," *Synthese*.

Alva Noë, *Action in Perception*, chapters 1 and 6.

With Merleau-Ponty clear in our minds, we are now prepared to move into an Anglo-American tradition that never took itself to be an heir to Merleau-Ponty. However, it has recently been retrieving some of his insights (e.g., that the body is a perceptual force, that perception and action are one, that the dualism of body and mind is abstract, that the world is a set of possibilities) and retroactively re-discovering its reliance on his thought. This tradition has now developed into a number of partly overlapping lines of research. As Embodied cognition, it emphasises the view that *bodies think*. This means, on that view, that cognition (i.e., knowing or believing facts about the world) is impossible without the body and that conversely, being embodied is impossible without having some cognitive states. As Ecological approach (which will be the first focus of the present chapter), it emphasises the idea that the embodied world should "be thought of as an environment," that is to say, as the correlate of an embodied subject best conceived as an "organism." A third line, which brings the other two together, shall be discussed in the second part of the chapter as the enactivist account of perception. The latter are accounts that have built upon the ecological and the embodied views to emphasise that perception doesn't exist without action and vice versa, in other words: perception and action constitute each other.

Hence, the views that are put forward that we should rethink objectivity: objects of perception, as members of an environment, should not be considered as things-in-themselves somehow retrieved through perception, but rather, they are objects *of perception*. Being perceptual is their rightful mode of being: there is nothing more to them than being perceptual. Finally, such philosophers make the next step, to claim that all that in any relevant sense *is*, is in an environment. This leads to the conclusion that to be is to *mean*, to *stand for*, and to *count as*. Meaning (including value) is the basic mode of being, the basic way that things are. In opposition to Cartesianism, all these views make the pragmatist move that presupposes that things are exhausted by what they *count as* in a practical context. Indeed, it is in this context that we can trace their long prehistory and how they articulate with the traditions we've been tracing so far. Nietzsche, for example, who also rebelled against the modern dualist paradigm inherited from Descartes, declared: "Being and appearance, psychologically considered, yield no 'being in-itself,' no criterion of 'reality,' but only grades of appearance measured by the strength of the interest we show in an appearance" (Nietzsche, 1967, section 588). Wittgenstein, in another context, comes to the same intuition.

> Children do not learn that books exist, that armchairs exist, etc., etc.—they learn to fetch books, sit in armchairs, etc., etc. Later, questions about the existence of things do of course arise, "Is there such a thing as a unicorn?" and so on. But such a question is possible only because as a rule no corresponding question presents itself. For how does one know how to set about satisfying oneself of the existence of unicorns? How did one learn the method for determining whether something exists or not? (Wittgenstein, 1969, 476)

Finally, Heidegger famously accounts for the world as environment as a "workshop" in which things exist in the mode of the "ready-to-hand." In the workshop, things *stand as* tools, that is to say, they exist in terms of what they can allow us to do, or to speak the language of the ecological theories, they exist as *affordances*.

The Ecological View

The idea that crystallised this general move and reinvigorated such discussions in the Anglo-American world was psychologist John Gibson's concept of affordance. Gibson read and annotated Merleau-Ponty's *Phenomenology of Perception* in the early 1970s.[1] He was one of Merleau-Ponty's few Anglo-Saxon readers at the time. Like Merleau-Ponty, he understood that if we are to account for the intimate *experience* of reality, any appeal to the thing-in-itself would be a mere distraction. Experience, not truth, was haunting humans and organising their lives. He also agreed with Merleau-Ponty that in experience, perception (of objects and people) preceded sensation (of so-called sense-data, like patches of colour or pixels). This meant that no mental process needed to be added to perception in order to explain how the world turns up for us the way it does—that is, as a collection of recognisable objects. This led Gibson to the thesis of *direct perception*: we perceive the world directly and transparently. Although the ecological approach yields further insights, all of them can be regarded as resulting from an analysis of what it means for the world to be a collection of "recognisable objects."

Let's begin with the word ecological. Just like in current everyday language, "ecological" is synonymous with "environmental." The ecological view regards the world of experience as an environment. This substitution between ecology and environment allows Gibson to point out the inseparability of the world of experience from a *subject* of experience. For what is specific to "environments," as opposed to "areas," "spaces," etc., is that they are always the environment *of and for an organism*. Without an organism to be an environment for, an environment is just a place. In this sense, environment is a bidirectional concept: it invokes both the set of objects in a certain space and the organism that these objects are organised around. So the ecological view speaks in one unified manner of the environment and of the organism, and of their reciprocal relations: the environment depends on the organism and vice versa. This seems to conflict with our usual view about perception. In that common view, there is an object, and there is a perceiver, and when the object enters the perceptual field of the perceiver, it becomes perceived. In the ecological picture on the other hand, the hypothesis rather is that the world and the perceiver appear at one and the same time, and they *result from* their interaction. The question that must be asked therefore is not so much the question of what this environment or what this organism *is*, but rather how can the world as a collection of recognisable objects result from the relations between an organism and an environment? The answer unfolds via Gibson's analysis of surfaces as affordances.

Surfaces

The first thesis Gibson puts forward is that what we have so far been calling an organism and an environment can entirely be cashed out as "surfaces" and

I have described the environment as the surfaces that separate substances from the medium in which the animals live. But I have also described what the environment *affords* animals, mentioning the terrain, shelters, water, fire, objects, tools, other animals, and human displays. How do we go from surfaces to affordances? . . . Perhaps the composition and layout of surfaces constitute what they afford. If so, to perceive them is to perceive what they afford. This is a radical hypothesis, for it implies that the "values" and "meanings" of things in the environment can be directly perceived. Moreover, it would explain the sense in which values and meanings are external to the perceiver.

The *affordances* of the environment are what it *offers* the animal, what it *provides* or *furnishes*, either for good or ill. The verb to *afford* is found in the dictionary, but the noun affordance is not. I have made it up. I mean by it something that refers to both the environment and the animal in a way that no existing term does. It implies the complementarity of the animal and the environment. The antecedents of the term and the history of the concept will be treated later; for the present, let us consider examples of an affordance.

If a terrestrial surface is nearly horizontal (instead of slanted), nearly flat (instead of convex or concave), and sufficiently extended (relative to the size of the animal) and if its substance is rigid (relative to the weight of the animal), then the surface *affords support*. It is a surface of support, and we call it a substratum, ground, or floor. It is stand-on-able, permitting an upright posture for quadrupeds and bipeds. It is therefore walk-on-able and run-over-able. It is not sink-into-able like a surface of water or a swamp, that is, not for heavy terrestrial animals. Support for water bugs is different.

Note that the four properties listed—horizontal, flat, extended, and rigid—would be *physical* properties of a surface if they were measured with the scales and standard units used in physics. As an affordance of support for a species of animal, however, they have to be measured *relative to the animal*. They are unique for that animal. They are not just abstract physical properties. They have unity relative to the posture and behaviour of the animal being considered. So an affordance cannot be measured as we measure in physics.—James Gibson, "The Theory of Affordances," p. 127.

"interfaces" (127). That is simply because perception is always the perception of something external, which the perceiver is accessing via their surface, their "public" side. Surfaces are what we perceive as per the definition of perception. This means that to perceive is always to perceive a surface and to be a surface is always to be perceptible. However, we would be wrong to restrict this notion of surface to the everyday use of the word and so for two reasons. First, in the everyday sense, surfaces are recognised as such independently of affordances (or so we think). They are seen as a certain area of an object (which is presumed to be known independently). What makes them surfaces is the part they play in the object (they are their outer limit). This means that the common view grants undue importance to what is behind or between the surfaces (the object's "insides"). For Gibson however, we do not know the object independently of the surfaces, and this means that for all intents and purposes, the object *is* only the surfaces and any talk of "insides" is absurd. Second, and correlatedly, this means that Gibson regards as surfaces things we wouldn't normally call surfaces. These may include emotions, internal organs, or proprioception, for insofar as they are felt, they are accessed via (and as) their surface.

Affordances

Once the equivalence between perceptual object and surfaces is established, Gibson adds that surfaces are *affordances*: "to perceive [the surfaces] is to perceive what they afford." (127) In other words, we perceive surfaces and their qualities in terms of what *we can do with them.* For example, an open door affords closing, a closed door affords opening, a key affords sliding into the keyhole. More primarily, the floor affords stepping, and more primarily still, a colour affords matching with another colour (think of your choice of scarf or necktie in the morning). These examples themselves suggest three further insights: first, as the example of the floor shows, it seems that affordances are dependent on what and who they afford *to*. Gibson writes that affordances "are measured *relative to the animal.*" (127) In this case, the floor affords walking on for some (say, those who weigh an average human weight), but not others (say, an African elephant). Second, this means that affordances are not self-contained and objective, they involve a *match*: the door frame affords entrance if its affordances match the affordances that this human possesses, these affordances are in this case, called "dimensions." Gibson writes that they "imply the complementarity of the animal and the environment." (127) Third, as the example of colour suggests, the regression into more primary perceptual features is not infinite. In our example, we stopped with the most basic recognisable perceptual feature: colour. But anything beyond this—

that is, any microphenomenon that affords nothing, is not perceptual. This includes, in most circumstances, a transparent particle, an infra-red or ultra-violet for (unequipped) humans, etc. This already suggests that affordances are *relative* (ultra-sounds afford or do not afford depending on whether you are a dolphin or an unequipped human), *reciprocal* (the affordances of the door frame and the person are mutually dependent), and *holistic* or mereologically primary (surfaces are not infinitely divisible).

Although the notion that objects appear as affordances involves the coinage of the new term "affordance," it shouldn't look too strange. In fact, it is already contained in the very traditional notion of an environment as an ensemble of conditions that apply to the life and behaviours of an organism. This notion of conditions, after all, says the same thing as that of affordances: things are part of my environment to the extent that they have a bearing on what I can and cannot do. When we worry about the destruction of the environment, we worry that it will no longer support the forms of life (including ourselves) that we are attached to. In short, we worry that it will no longer *afford* them life.

There is also another way of explaining why Gibson is so confident in his ability to affirm that all perception is perception of affordances. After all, for a surface to be perceived, it must afford, at least, perceiving. Just like the example of the lock and key, perceiving only takes place as a match between the sensory affordances of an organism and the perceptual affordances of an object. This doesn't cancel the fact that perceptual objects afford other things than perception (a chair affords seeing *and* it affords sitting), but it shows how everything about them can be reduced to affordances without any steep costs.

The fact that affordances coincide with their being perceived suggests that if the organism and the object are merely matched, their affordances might never come forth, and they might remain like ships in the night. On top of a *match*, we need an *encounter*. For this encounter, Gibson takes over the notion of organism inherited from ethologists and biologists, vitalist philosophers and phenomenologists: the organism is organised by a certain dynamic principle (instinct, will, or intentionality, etc.) which polarises it (for example, in terms of life and death, 143). In other words, the body (the "organism") must be defined as *interested*. If there was nothing looking for things to do, then things could not afford anything, and that thing looking for things to do is indeed the intentional body. This amounts to stating that the way the organism perceives the world is interested, and that there is no disinterested perception. An organism is an instance of choice in a certain environment. It approaches the environment as a context for a potential behaviour.

Let us think of the kind of body that an environment—defined as a set of affordances—presupposes. Gibson tells us that the body is an organism, and that organisms are correlates of an environment. He also says that an environment is a set of affordances. As a result, the body is the correlate of a set of affordances. But, as we mentioned earlier, only a set of affordances can be the correlate of a set of affordances. As a consequence, the body exists only as the correlate of the world and therefore it is of the same nature as the world. If the world is a set of affordances, so is the body. But as Susan Hurley (2001, 19) and others have pointed out, we need more clarity about the relations between affordances, organism (the body) and environment. Do affordances appear *on the basis of* the relations between environment and organism (Bermúdez, 1995, 157)? Or do environment and organism *result* from the affordances? Or should we finally simply say that affordances *are the same as* (constitute) the relations between environment and organism? Given that affordances are only picked up by an interested organism, if Gibson's answer were to agree with the first proposal, this would return us to some kind of transcendental idealism: the organism seeks the environment and when it finds it, the affordances of the environment appear. This places the initiative on the subjective pole in transcendental idealist ways. We remember that confronted with the same problem, Merleau-Ponty appealed to the "unmotivated springing forth of the world" for a way out of transcendental idealism: the process by which the world organises itself in terms of subject and object is spontaneous, and therefore neither subjects nor objects are primary. This is of course a highly abstract and speculative move, and it would be out of character for a psychologist, even one as bent on theory as Gibson. As a result, his position about priorities seems unclear. He declares that affordances are bi-directional because they "refer to both the environment and the animal." (127) He adds, in ways reminiscent of Merleau-Ponty's de-subjectified account, that "[affordances] are not bestowed upon an object by the need of the observer observing it" and they are "equally a fact of the environment and a fact of behaviour." (138) "An affordance," he concludes, "*points* both ways, to the environment and to the observer" (129) (see also Bermúdez, 1995, 155).

But what does this bi-directionality mean? For example, how does this fit with his declaration that affordances are "measured *relative to the animal*"? So, Hurley asks: is the bi-directionality *instrumental* or *constitutive*? That is to say: is it a fact about affordances that they aim at the organism and the environment, or is this bi-directionality the *source* of the organism and the environment? If it is instrumental, this tells us nothing about priorities, and the transcendental idealist (or, closer to Hurley's own concerns, the cognitivist) option remains open. If it is constitutive (see Bermúdez, 1995, 155), we must somehow make the Merleau-Pontian de-subjectified account palatable for empirical cognitive scientists, psychologists, and naturalistically minded philosophers. Let us take stock of how abstract the constitutivist option is: it implies that the body is not only as I pointed out earlier, an interested body, it is interest: a general principle of directedness that generates bi-directional affordances. The body is not in quest of possibilities, it is the quest for possibilities.

On the basis of the influence of *Gestalttheorie* and Merleau-Ponty on Gibson in the 1970s, there are historical reasons to read Gibson as choosing the constitutive route nonetheless. Gibson takes over Merleau-Ponty's move which is to say that the subject-object distinction is a secondary distinction. In other words, that the binarity exists secondary to something else. It is the result, not the start, of a process. For Merleau-Ponty, this process is "the unmotivated springing forth of the world" and it results in the constitution of subjects and objects. In Gibson's language, this amounts to saying that the experience of affordances is a fundamental and primary process that results in the constitution of organisms and environments. Let's respond to Hurley, therefore, by privileging the hypothesis that the perception of affordances is primary: affordances are constitutive of the subject and of the environment, not aspects of them.

In a recent book, Alva Noë asks himself "how come we see so much?" (*Strange Tools*, 2015, xi) in the context of his conversation with a painter (his own father), who responded to him that the question should instead be "how come we see so little." For Noë, seeing is to be understood in terms of what it *does* for us, and on this basis, it is hard to explain many of the things we see, for example, so-called irrelevant details (perhaps even colours). The implication being that since we see more than we need to see, we must ask how come we do see so much? This in turn presupposes pre-existing, and independently established interests, most often evolutionarily ones. The painter, on the other hand, presupposes that seeing is first and foremost contemplative and disinterested, and only later interested. It is there to see what there is, and on this basis, it is true that our vision is lacking. On an ecological constitutivist account, affordances coincide with perception by definition and thereby they constitute the objects and the subject of perception. In this case therefore, both views are wrong because they give priority either to the state of the organism, or to the state of the world, both seen in-themselves.

Constitutivism on the contrary, argues that there is an exact fit between what we see and what we need to see, not due to any sort of pre-established harmony, but simply by virtue of the definition of affordances: "the object affords what it does because the object is what it is."

Therefore, a constitutive reading of Gibson's theory allows us to enjoy some preliminary yield of the theory of affordances: First, it allows us to think of the organism and the environment under the same metaphysical category, that of affordances. This solves the commensurability problem which had plagued Descartes and Husserl. Second, it also solves the other Cartesian problem which is that just as difference can be too radical as to lead into incommensurability, so can identity. As you remember, identity makes it impossible to understand how perception, which involves difference, occurs. Affordance is a unified category but not a unified substance, for things always afford *to other things*. When I perceive an affordance, I perceive the difference between the thing that affords, and the thing to whom it is afforded (me). This perceiving is all one experience, however, it's a unified experience of difference. Affordances, Gibson claims, are "neither an objective property nor a subjective property; or it is both if you like." It allows us to "understand the inadequacy" of the "dichotomy of subjective-objective." So, Gibson shows that each perception comes with an interest, possible or actual, but his constitutivist commitments prevent him from making the extra step of saying that the interested organism comes first. Rather, the appearance and the interest are two aspects of the same process, which he leaves unexplained, but which Merleau-Ponty would surely call "unmotivated." What is certain is that one should not look for a priority, either of the subject or of the object, over affordances.

So, if attributing the constitutive view to Gibson is indeed correct, this leads us to the next question, which is to explain how, assuming that the world in general and the self in particular are just affordances, it so happens that our best understanding of the world is that it is a collection of objects, of organisms and environments. Just like Merleau-Ponty was confronted to the problem, we must ask about the notion of the "in-itself for us."

Gestalt
The answer to this question will be important for two reasons. First, it will help dispel suspicions that the constitutive thesis is unworkable. Second, it will allow us to understand more precisely what Gibson means when he points out that affordances are cashed out as "meanings" and "values." Although this is a further step in the analysis of the notion of affordances, it is only making explicit something that was implicit all along. If objects

appear as affordances, then they appear as something I can do. Recognising something as something I can do involves some sort of understanding. This suggests necessarily that to perceive without understanding (for example, the kind of thing a CCTV camera does) cannot count as perception, and since understanding means dealing with meanings, the conclusion should therefore be that to *afford* is to *mean*.

Second, this meaning appears in the context of a project, which is provided by the intentional body. It means that if something affords something to me, it will appear in terms of its relation to my project. The door appears as openable if I may or I do wish to come in. This introduces some normativity: if it helps me achieve my project, it is good, if it is an obstacle, it is bad, and all the shades in between. So we should not make the mistake of assuming that in Gibson's mind, some affordances are "meaning" and some are "values." Rather, we should think of affordances as the concept that covers both meaning and values (or perhaps, the concept that overcomes the false distinction between them). This is because both meaning and value, in this view, arise from an encounter with a project, which provides both readability (the chair *means* "I can sit on it") and value (the chair has a positive "value" because I'm tired of standing). As all theories of meaning agree, meaning implies context. Since affordances have only one context, which is the project of the organism, and since interest involves value, the ecological view merges meaning and value.

Gibson was aware that the unification of perception and interpretation, the idea that perception yields meanings, was established by *Gestalttheorie*. His contribution rather was to cash out such interpretations as affordances and to merge meaning and value. According to Gestalt psychology, as I suggested earlier, perception doesn't get caught in an infinite regress. Rather any meaningless unit (say, sensations, or sense-data) cannot be the object of any perception. This shows the commitment of Gestalt psychology to a form of holism: only complex units (wholes) can have meaning, and their meanings result from the relations between their parts, each of which is in itself meaningless. Building on *Gestalttheorie* therefore, Gibson claims that meaning is "directly" perceived and that it is not the result of a mental process (vs. Hurley, 2001, 19), but of perception itself. Indeed, meanings and values are in fact not properly speaking "subjective" or "mental" (1979/1986, 129, 130). Rather, they are the primary given of perception: "the meaning is observed before the substance and the surface." As a result, meanings involve interpretations, which are the source of illusions such as the belief in "substance," in objects, and in the organism as object. Gibson concludes that perception, because it involves interpretation, is infinite and "economical" (1979/1986,

135). It is infinite because since objects only appear through interpretation, they are—just like these interpretations—revisable: there is no final interpretation. Economical, because well before any such final interpretation comes forth, the organism knows how to respond to the affordances available in their environment: in other words, a minimal amount of perceptual information is sufficient to motivate behaviours adequately. Organisms tend to act *as if* a given affordance is before them. Here, we find Gibson's answer to the question of an in-itself for us: perception interprets, and in doing so, it takes affordances to reveal the existence of independent objects.

One question that should remain open at this stage has to do with the possibility of the existence of non-perceptual objects. What about emotions, memories and imaginings? Should we say that they too have surfaces somehow? Should we say that they too appear as affordances? In short, even if it is true that all affordances are meanings, does it mean all meanings are affordances?

In a sense, the economical and infinite character of the perception of affordances should send us on the path to a response. Taken together, this economical and infinite character suggests that time changes the perception of affordances: that values and meanings are context-sensitive. In short, affordances have a history. Take the example of a butter wire. One of the things it afforded all along was cutting butter and choking someone. Once one of these affordances, say, choking, is actualised however, it acquires certain affordances (as exhibit at a trial, for example, it affords conviction) and perhaps loses some others (it no longer affords preparing your lunch, due to regulations concerning tampering with evidence). This should be enough to recognise that objects have an affordential history. Even further, it could be that the first time someone used such a wire to choke someone, the fact that these affordances have been activated—creatively if maleficently—by that individual, has now become a *cultural* fact. It may be that such wires will no longer afford taking in a carry-on luggage as some restrictions will be placed on them. This suggests that, at least in a certain sense, the evolution of culture is the ability for new affordances to appear and old affordances to recede. Combine this ability for renewal with the emotional substratum already built in the characterisation of the body as interested, and you may be able to do justice to Gibson's dictum that "behaviour affords behaviour, and the whole subject matter of psychology and the social sciences can be thought of as an elaboration of this basic fact" (1979/1986, 135). In short, Gibson sees the source of the realm of culture and of the realm of emotions and thoughts in this basic primary fact, namely, that affordances are never fully closed up and determinate once and for all.

Gibson's proposal allows us to move further into the intuition that "embodiment changes everything"—that is, that the world, too, is embodied. We have now succeeded in defining the world and the body in reciprocal terms, under the unified heading of "affordances."

Noë and Enactivism

In the wake of Gibson's radical proposals, much of the Anglo-American tradition of the philosophy of the body has been focused on a critical process

The main idea of this book is that perceiving is a way of acting. Perception is not something that happens to us, or in us. It is something we do. Think of a blind person tap tapping his or her way around a cluttered space, perceiving that space by touch, not all at once, but through time, by skilful probing and movement. This is, or at least ought to be, our paradigm of what perceiving is. The world makes itself available to the perceiver through physical movement and interaction. In this book I argue that all perception is touch-like in this way: Perceptual experience acquires content thanks to our possession of bodily skills. What we perceive is determined by what we do (or what we know how to do); it is determined by what we are ready to do. In ways I try to make precise, we enact our perceptual experience; we act it out. To be a perceiver is to understand, implicitly, the effects of movement on sensory stimulation. Examples are ready to hand. An object looms larger in the visual field as we approach it, and its profile deforms as we move about it. A sound grows louder as we move nearer to its source. Movements of the hand over the surface of an object give rise to shifting sensations. As perceivers we are masters of this sort of pattern of sensorimotor dependence. This mastery shows itself in the thoughtless automaticity with which we move our eyes, head and body in taking in what is around us. We spontaneously crane our necks, peer, squint, reach for our glasses, or draw near to get a better look (or better to handle, sniff, lick or listen to what interests us). The central claim of what I call the enactive approach is that our ability to perceive not only depends on, but is constituted by, our possession of this sort of sensorimotor knowledge.—Alva Noë, *Action in Perception*, pp. 1–2.

of refinement of the ecological view. The so-called enactive approach to perception in particular is deeply informed by the ecological approach. The discussion in that movement focuses on three issues.

1. Does Gibson's emphasis on embodiment as the mode of being of the organism and the environment conflict with the emphasis on the body as an object of empirical study?
2. In what sense can we truly say that meanings and values are *directly* perceived?
3. If such values and meanings are directly perceived, how come the same experiences are liable to being interpreted differently?

In regards to the first question, the gesture of enactivism stresses the distinction between attention to the body and attention to embodiment, which expresses itself in terms of an opposition between the empirical sciences and the philosophy of perception. The empirical sciences take the body extremely seriously. Their job is to account for almost everything through empirically observed physical processes. But, enactivism claims, they don't take embodiment seriously at all because embodiment requires the idea that the body is animated. If the body as an object of empirical enquiry is given precedence, so goes the implicit argument, then what is really given primary status is the observer of that body, who is, by definition, disembodied. This means that embodiment can only be understood as a certain conditioning of the mind, which is determined not by its bodily dimension in general but by the contingencies of actual specific human bodies. As Merleau-Ponty argues: "humanity is not produced as the effect of our articulations or by the way our eyes are implanted in us. . . . These contingencies and others like them, without which mankind would not exist, do not by simple summation bring it about that there is a single man" (*Eye and Mind* in Johnson, 2007, 125). As we can see, the focus in cognitivist reductionism is in showing that the kinds of bodies we have determined our lives in certain ways.[2] They show quite well, for example, that human thought would be different if humans didn't have the bodies they have (think of the infamous opposable thumbs). They may even, via thought experiments like the famous brain-in-the-vat scenario, show that thought cannot be without a body. But they leave open the question of whether this means that the mind must be *completed* by a body, or whether in any possible sense, the body is indeed the relevant subject of thought. This is quite different from showing that being embodied transforms any possible meanings of the words "to be," "to perceive," "to know," etc. In particular, it is quite different from the ambition of accounting for the general structures that apply to all bodies not because of their specific contingencies, but as bodies in general. In other words, so goes the criticism, empirically informed philosophies of the body, by forgetting embodiment, revive a focus on *Körper* to the detriment of *Leib*. This, of course, doesn't mean that the contribution of science is to be rejected, but rather, that it can only be of indirect value to the investigation of embodiment as the mode of being of subjects and of the world. Yet, the historical positioning of enactivism, as part of an Anglo-American paradigm of philosophy that is resolute in taking the sciences seriously, means that it shall take into account the empirical theories (even if indirectly), and that it feeds on the perceived failure of those theories to address the more general questions. In this context, Alva Noë's early *Out of Our Heads* (2010), subtitled *Why You Are Not Your Brain*, drives home the point that even the empirical sciences cannot hold on to their implicit commitments to the view of a mind *in* a body, and will have to admit to a mind *as* body. We shall return to this, but for now, let us turn to questions 2 and 3.

Noë's enactivist account takes up where Gibson left off. In fact, it could be understood as a response to two questions that Susan Hurley (2001) originally addressed to Gibson.

Hurley's first question concerns *partial perception* (question 2). She asks what it means to say that we perceive meanings "directly." If it is true that meanings are wholes, can it not be that in everyday life, we access only *some* of their parts, and if so, should we say we don't "see" the other parts? This would suggest the other parts are not perceived directly, and that meanings which are holistic, are not perceived directly, but only once the parts are somehow assembled. Imagine I am looking at a tree trunk from very close up. All that appears to me is a blur, perhaps a blur of brown. As I walk back, I begin to make out the outline of the tree until I can determine that what I am dealing with here is a tree trunk. Should we say that I was seeing nothing until I was seeing a meaningful whole: the tree? Should we say that I was indeed seeing something, and that it was meaningful, let's say, as a blur? Should we rather say, like Kant for example, that when I recognise the tree, what I do is that I transition from sensing to perceiving, and that the moment of transition coincides with the moment of recognition? In short, Hurley asks: how can meanings and values be perceived without any processing taking place? Shouldn't we assume that we are doing something to the sensations we have gathered in order to make them meaningful? This question suggests that we might, in the end, retain an element of sensationalism in our account: we must maintain that perception derives from sensations. But if so, those meanings are indeed not directly perceived, and Gibson, the Gestalt theorists, and Merleau-Ponty should have some explaining to do.

Hurley's second question concerns the closeness problem (question 3). How do we know the difference between two sets of sensations in different contexts? It seems that what she calls the "input" (the passively retrieved sensations) cannot be enough to suggest an interpretation, or the assignment of any meaning. They are not self-explanatory. If this were the case, one wouldn't know the difference between a distant but loud sound and a quiet but close sound, or between a big object in the distance and a smaller one close up. The input might be the same, and if the input was all there is to perception, this would result in our interacting with both in the same way. Yet, this is not the case. We see how this closeness problem dovetails with the implicit retention of sensationalism in the first question, for it presupposes that impressions come before meaning-assignment. It does seem, however, that the closeness problem *motivates* rather than *results from* the retention of sensationalism because it suggests precisely that two sets of *identical* sensations can have different meanings assigned to them, suggesting that meaning and sensations are not perceived at once, and therefore, that one of them (probably meaning) is not experienced as "directly" as formerly assumed. In this sense, Hurley suggests implicitly a return to the Kantian model of experience as including both a "receptive" moment (responsible for what Hurley would call "input") and a "spontaneous" moment (responsible for processing).

"Perceiving Is Something We Do": What Are Sensori-Motor Skills?

Alva Noë and the enactivist movement inherit from Gibson the insight that the organism directs itself spontaneously in the environment in ways that suggest that it deals with meanings directly. From Hurley, he inherits the necessity to nuance the direct character of the perception of meaning. How can these insights be reconciled?

The solution Noë puts forth involves overcoming the sensation-perception divide by referring to the notion of action. It is true after all that in skilful activity, say, in riding a bicycle, it is impossible to pinpoint the difference between sensing and understanding. For example, an experienced cyclist will immediately handle or cope with a trembling in a pedal appropriately. This appropriateness suggests understanding, but it would also seem abstract to suggest that the sensation manifested itself before the understanding. In action, so goes the intuition, they're all one. Noë declares: "what informs you of the shape of what you feel or hold is not the intrinsic character of your sensations, but rather your implicit understanding of the organization or structure of your sensations . . . it seems plausible that feeling alone is not sufficient to enable you to learn or discover the properties of objects or layouts around you" (2015, 15).

Let's dig deeper: in this example a skilled cyclist may offer a case of the unification of sensation and perception, but this is only so because indeed, they are skilled, or as I said above "experienced," in other words this situation results form a learning process. This offers Noë an angle to work towards a solution. This solution will rely on the notion of sensory-motor *skill*. The main idea is that perception is something we do because we've *learned* to do it. *Once learned*, it is direct in ways that satisfy Gibson, while at the same time enabling us to account for the cases where this skill fails (partial perception and closeness problems) by pointing to imperfect skill acquisition: if I take a loud remote noise to be a nearby quiet noise, Noë can now respond, it is that I haven't learned to perceive noises appropriately. It is now the learning process that plays the role of what Hurley calls *processing* (note that this saves us from a Kantian-style processing model, which would return us to the problems associated with the transcendental ego). It is in this sense that perception is now seen as a skill, something that has been learned. In this context, Noë introduces his mantra: "perception is something we do."

There is a trivial sense to this claim: at least grammatically speaking, to perceive indeed, is something we do, it has a doer; "to perceive" is an active verb. What makes Noë's claim original becomes visible if we bear in mind that the "doing" in question is the kind of doing that one *learns* to do. It is skilful doing, based on a skill that has been learned. Noë writes: "Think of a blind person tap-tapping his or her way around a cluttered space, perceiving that space by touch, not all at once, but through time, by skilful probing and movement."[3] It allows Noë to return to what Merleau-Ponty called the "prospective activity of perception." Perception is a seeking out of an encounter with the word. The perceiving body is directed towards the world and perception *looks* for stuff to perceive. Second, this introduces a notion of development through time which will be crucial in addressing Hurley's challenges: there is indeed a progressive gathering of information which nuances Gibson's claim that meanings are "directly" perceived. Whatever "directly" means, Noë suggests, it cannot mean "all at once." This is why we perceive "not all at once, but through time" he writes. The temporal element, of course, is provided by the idea of movement that the blind person's stick illustrates so well: this probing takes place in time because it depends on motion. In fact, Noë multiplies the examples that show that sensory blindness (either visual or otherwise) occurs every time movement is impaired (including, but not restricted to the movement of the sensory organs like the eyes, the fingers, etc., but also the legs, etc.). And so, movement is essential to perception. The relation between moving and perceiving is not only instrumental, it is *constitutive*. Moving, Noë declares, "is not for acting or for guiding action" and all of perception is a kind of action, not *for* action (193). It is in the space allowed for this progressive probing that skill becomes deployed: we use "skilful probing and movement." In other words, the body of the perceiver, in this case, the blind person, is questioning the world. He is asking: "What are you made of?" "Where am I?" She does this through movement so that the process of addressing these questions "takes place through time."

"This is," Noë concludes, "or at least ought to be, our paradigm of what perceiving is." In other words, the case of the blind person is not a special, unusual case of perception in which a blind person is using a certain tool to do something like perceiving that a non-blind person would do "naturally." Rather it only brings out what "normal" perception is in more readable ways. The appeal to the tool-mediated perception is meant to bring out the tool-like character of *all* perception. And a tool is something that works only if you use it right, a tool appeals to skills. Think for example of a person who *became* blind, and the process of learning to use a stick that they must be going through. Any non-blind person who's tried it will tell you how difficult it is, how skilful one must be in order to use a blind person's stick to good effect. The paradigm of the blind person and their stick organises the entirety of Noë's argument. It suggests two points:

- First, there are two kinds of learning at play here, namely learning to use our bodies (learning to use our "tool") *and* learning to read the world.
- Second, there is an implicit definition of the body as a set of sensorimotor skills. This skilfulness shall come to be seen not only as an attribute of the body, but as its very essence and definition. Let's take these two points in turn.

Two Kinds of Learning

Learning to Use Our Bodies

The first skill involves learning to use our bodies. In order to perceive correctly, we must move our eyes correctly, learn to crane our necks in the right way, to press on textures in the right way, and the like. Observing small children learning to touch a surface for example should be enough to convince us that this doesn't go without learning. A newborn doesn't know how to reach properly and a toddler will most likely pat instead of stroke, for example. In fact, the view that the difference between perceiving and sensing involves skill seems to have common language on its side. We use the verb "to savour" for example, to refer to "skilful tasting." Savouring is the skill adequate to the sense of taste. And there is no doubt that savouring is a learned skill.

There is more: using our body properly means moving properly for perception to take place adequately. It is a skilful movement of a different kind than say, throwing a good pitch in baseball. Rather, the criterion of the skill is success in *perception*. It is in order to capture this combination of movement and of perception that Noë uses the phrase "sensori-motor skills." To perceive, he writes, is "to understand implicitly the effects of movement on sensory stimulation." For example, it involves being able to correlate the fact that we're moving away from the source of a noise and the fading out of that noise. It is both understanding and using our body, at once. Recall the common experience of sitting on a train at standstill in a train station. The train next to yours pulls out of the station while yours remains still. For a second, your skills (in this context, your ability to implicitly understand that it is not your train, but the other train that is moving) are caught short; you feel and think that your train is moving. In fact, such cases, cases where things go wrong, allow us to realise that it takes skill for things to go right. Because it is not your sensory apparatus that fails, rather, it is the sense you make of it. This example too, as you might note, involves temporal development and learning: after a few times in this situation, you are already developing the skill and you become less easily deceived. And most likely, an experienced train conductor would not have this experience anymore. This serves to illustrate Noë's notion of an "implicit understanding." The movement of the train has caused certain stimulations that led you to the wrong conclusion, to the wrong understanding. Now, the way Noë cashes this out is to say: this is not only a practice about trains. It would be wrong to think that the reason why the train conductor is no longer subject to this illusion is that she knows more about trains. It is, rather interestingly, that she is better at understanding her body. But of course, this means she is better at understanding her body *in this situation*. In short, skill about perception is bi-directional: it concerns our use of the body and of the world at once.

This leads us to Noë's implicit definition of the body. This is where Noë's theory of perception becomes a theory of embodiment (he opens his book by citing Merleau-Ponty's dictum to the effect that a theory of perception is already a theory of the body). The question that Noë addresses now is the following: what is the body so that to understand our *bodies* better means to understand *situations* better? We've already mentioned that to do something with your body means to move. So the first hint at the nature of the body is that your body is a set of abilities for motion, both negative and positive. Negative affordances, because it is your body that prevents you from doing certain movements. For example, your elbow doesn't afford bending backwards; positive, because your elbow does afford bending forwards. There are a lot of things you can do, and a lot of things you cannot do because of the way your body is. But every doing will be movement. This leads us to a first, preliminary definition of the body: the body is a certain set of possible and impossible movements in a situation.

Second, in keeping with the paradigm of the blind person and their stick, Noë seems to claim that the relevant sense of the body must be an extended sense. In this case: "natural body" + stick = body. There is a continuity between the natural, the artificial or the technological. This is because the blind person perceives through their stick. The difference between the natural body and the extended body, and Noë's preference for the second as his best candidate for the title of "body proper" suggests that he makes it a necessary condition of being a body that its abilities coincide with the extent of possible perception. Noë's notion of the body is co-extensive with his notion of perception: whatever perceives is the body; whatever is the body perceives. It is only in this view that the stick can be regarded as part of the body: it is because it takes part in perception that it is part of the body. If this point—namely that to be a body is to be a perceiver—obtains then we should also say that to be a body is to be a set of sensorimotor skills. Sensorimotor skills are what our embodiment is made of, and accordingly, they have a body's dynamic process of mastering the skills necessary to activate all the possibilities of our body and of the world. This is why it is strictly accurate to say that the body can fluctuate as we acquire (and sometimes lose) the skills appropriate to use it, or as it acquires and loses the skills appropriate to certain situations. A different set of sensori-motor skills is a different body. If it was true for Merleau-Ponty that Schneider's brain injury meant that he lived in a smaller world (a world with less possible meanings to interact with), it is also true, for Noë, that we may live in a smaller body. Although it is true to say that a baby doesn't, strictly speaking, acquire a body, but is born with it, we must still recognise that the process of appropriation of that body is gradual and corresponds to the process of acquiring the right skills to make use of this body in world-situations. As I mentioned earlier, it takes several months for a newborn to take full possession of their own body. In other words, the body as *Körper* may be there since birth, but it remains beyond our reach until the right sensori-motor skills are developed. The acquisition of sensori-motor skills coincides with the appropriation of one's body.

This indicates that there is something very intuitive about what Noë is talking about: to have a body is to come to recognise a certain body as ours, and this is achieved through recognising the possibilities of this body as our possibilities. This is a view that can allow us to make sense of a number of everyday occurrences, take the case of acrobats or high-level athletes. Barring injuries or disabilities, they have more or less the same body as us. But they have developed their skills, so that everything their (and our) body can possibly do, *they* can actually do. Think also of experiences of dissonance between our objective body and our body schema, such as sex misassignment or racialisation. Noë's insight is that we always begin with a discrepancy between what our body can do and what we are skilled to do with our body. The body is something we acquire, and it is through the process of acquiring *it*, that the world acquires affordances. It is as our body grows that our world grows.

The second skill involves reading the world, or how to grasp "contents." It is best understood as a talent for "reading off" the world. Noë writes, "to be a perceiver is to understand." This makes perception look a lot like reading. What is the object of understanding normally? To understand is to interact with meanings. That's what happens when someone says "I understand"; they mean "I understand what it means," "I am catching the meaning of this." So, Noë follows in Merleau-Ponty and Gibson's footsteps in claiming that to perceive is to have a certain relationship with meaning. Gibson would call this directly perceiving values and meanings, and Noë says "acquiring contents." Noë concludes his example of the blind person's stick by saying: "in this book, I argue that all perception is touch-like in this way: perceptual experience acquires content thanks to our possession of bodily skills." In other words, being-touch-like in the way that defines the use of the stick and perception in general means *acquiring contents*. "To perceive you must have sensory stimulation that you understand" (Noë, 2015, 183). "The enactive view insists that mere feeling is not sufficient for perceptual experience" (2015, 16, see also 27, 30), says Noë in ways very reminiscent of Gestalt theorie: there is no perception without understanding, or rather: sensation + understanding = perception. This provides the foundation to Noë's response to Hurley's challenges.

Indeed, it is this interpretive skill that we appeal to when it is a matter of addressing the closeness objection, concerned with how we "know" when a noise is close and another is far. Young children are unable to tell the difference between a distant loud noise and a nearby quieter noise, and anyone

/

who has spent much time with them will notice their distressed faces looking around the room when a thunderbolt is heard in what to the adult is obviously "in the distance." For the newborn the difference is simply that a noise is loud and a noise is weak. But for the adult it immediately means closeness and distance. If, for example, a family with a small child moves to an area where there is traffic noise at night, the first nights the child will not sleep. The child will be awakened every five minutes because there is a truck backing up, or a car shifting gears. And then they learn the sensorimotor skills to *make sense* of that noise. In this context, this making-sense means: they establish a stable, liveable and productive relation between these noises and their sleep; they recognise that these noises are irrelevant to their sleep. In other words, these noises take their proper place in the child's worldview. In fact, we should reframe the closeness objection: it is not so much that we know near from far, it is rather that we know relevant from irrelevant. For such small children, all noises sound the same because they are not yet distinguished in terms of their meaning. Adults, on the other hand, hear loudly what makes sense to them, and ignore a lot of things: they have developed a selective, hierarchical skill, the skill of directing their attention in appropriate ways, that allows them to tell foreground from background in the ways that have been canonically investigated by *Gestalt theorie*. That's what sensori-motor skills are: the ability to construct a world out of impressions, to contextualise them, to calibrate them. To give them meaning.

Noë's emphasis on the notion of skills allows him to reach a relatively stable position which does justice to both Gibson and Hurley's insights. For skills, as we have seen, are a unitary and synthetic concept which falsifies the distinction of sensation and meaning. Rather, the analysis of skill shows that the fit between a body and their environment can be explained without referring to a moment of input and a moment of output or to the distinction of sensation and perception, and the reference to any processing. Rather, by describing our embodied life as skilful, Noë allows us to see how body and world co-constitute each other in such a way that it is impossible to think of them independently from each other. By repudiating this mutual independence, Noë also repudiates the idea of a subjective processing of objective input. This placates the transcendentalism implied in Hurley's objections.

Yet, the notion of skills, because it relies on skill acquisition, a temporal and slow process, does justice to Hurley's partial immediacy thesis: the world is only encountered partly directly because it is encountered thanks to skills that are themselves not immediately present, but rather, slowly acquired. The processing, that is to say, doesn't take place in perception, but in skill acquisition.

Further Readings

Francisco Varela, Evan Thompson and Eleanor Rosch, *The Embodied Mind*.

Hubert Dreyfus, *Skillful Coping: Essays on the Phenomenology of Everyday Perception and Action*.

Shaun Gallagher, "Philosophical Antecedents of Situated Cognition."

Key Ideas

The body and the world are mutually constitutive.

The body's essence is to interact with meanings and values.

The body is a transient set of sensori-motor skills.

To perceive is to have the skill to live in one's body.

To perceive is to have the skill to live in the world.

These two skills are two sides of the same coin.

Notes

1. Mace (2015).

2. See, for example, Gallagher (2005).

3. This is an example that has haunted modern philosophy since Descartes's *Dioptrics* and Merleau-Ponty's *Phenomenology of Perception*.

PART III

POLITICAL BODIES

CHAPTER NINE

The Body Politic

Readings

Aristotle, *Politics*, Book 3, sections 1–6.

Jean-Jacques Rousseau, *On the Social Contract*, Book 1, sections 3 and 7, Book 2, sections 1–3.

Sigmund Freud, *Totem and Taboo*, chapter 2, section 3, "The Taboo of Rulers."

Ernst Kantorowicz, *The King's Two Bodies: A Study in Mediaeval Political Theology*, chapter 1, and chapter 7, "The King Never Dies," section 2.

From Metaphysics to Politics

The previous two parts have established the following four general points, which have come to function as the coordinates for any discussion of embodiment in the Western tradition.

The first point has to do with the irreducibility of imperfection. Both Plato and Augustine can be read as illustrating the failure of any attempts at explaining imperfection away, as well as connecting conceptually this notion of imperfection with the notion of embodiment defined as limitation.

The second point regards the ambiguous relations between the notions of body and soul. It seems like any account of embodiment must explain the inherence of the soul to the body, and yet, that any such inherence contradicts any pure notion of the body and of the soul. As a result, a synthetic notion has become necessary. It finds its most stable point in the phenomenological concept of *Leib*.

The third point is mereological. Just like it is impossible to think of the body and the soul as parts of the person, Descartes presupposes that our body is matter and matter is divisible, and therefore, he cannot account for the experienced *unity* of the body. "Having parts" means something different for bodies than it does for souls, and it becomes unclear what sense this may have when it comes to a "person" whose "parts" are, precisely, body and soul. In short, it seems like the correct notion of the body as *Leib* resists analysis: it is not explained by breaking it down to the conceptual units that would account for it. In fact, it doesn't obey the conceptual distinctions that Cartesianism regarded as basic for both thinking and being. For example, we still encounter the Cartesian impulse that seeks to retroactively account for unitary phenomena in terms of their parts in the debate about the place of processing in perception: are parts processed into wholes or should we say, with *Gestalttheorie*, that meaningful wholes are directly perceived? In short, the body, if understood properly, should be viewed as *more than the sum of its parts*—as an organic unity.

The fourth point has to do with reciprocity. Husserl reinvigorated the question of the body by emphasising the reciprocity contained in the special case of the touching-touched. Merleau-Ponty takes this reciprocity further: it is more than a property of the body, but rather, the mode of existence of the embodied world. In other words, having a body influences both how we should think of the self, and how we should think of the world, because the body is both part of the self and part of the world. Therefore, it's both subject and object, passive and active, receptive and productive, vulnerable and sovereign and the world itself should be regarded as embodied.

Sovereignty

You will note that these four points, although arrived at in different ways, all converge around the idea of the impossibility of subjecting the experience of embodiment to any pure conceptual category: as embodied, there is no pure self (no transcendental Ego) no pure object (no thing-in-itself, no purely physical body as *Körper*). Rather, the body is always part of an interaction which it constitutes and yet exceeds and overwhelms it. The body questions the conceptual notion of transcendence (the notion of a part of the world— say, the ego—which still dominates the world) and therefore, it questions the metaphysics of independence. The ego is no longer an independent and withdrawn entity that magically has access to the world (it constitutes it) without the world having any access to it. The insistence on reciprocity does away with such fantasies. To be, rather, is to be embodied, and to be embodied is to be, at least partly, subjected to the world. Now, if we move to the political domain, this rejection of the metaphysics of independence has tectonic consequences.

In the political context, this fantastical ability to act upon the world without *being acted upon by the world* is called "sovereignty": a kind of power that is not vulnerable, pure agency without resistance. In this third part of the book, we will look at the history of political theory as a history of the ways in which the fantasy of sovereignty was established, maintained, criticised and finally defeated. Unsurprisingly, this development parallels almost exactly the fate of another fantasy of sovereignty, the metaphysical fantasy of a subject unimpaired by their body, which was the focus of the first two parts. Let's examine the *prima facie* analogies that obtain between the political and metaphysical orders before fleshing out in more detail how and why these analogies—or at least a few of them—are more than coincidence. I see four such significant analogies.

First, we note an analogy between the metaphysical and political treatments of imperfection. Just like Plato and Augustine (alongside the entire theodicy tradition) lamented the irreducibility of imperfection and just like the subsequent tradition tried to take stock of it, the Western tradition in political thought too takes its starting point with the imperfection of human existence. Following Augustine, who in *The City of God* explicitly regarded "living according to man" as a political problem, this imperfection is usually regarded as "freedom." Freedom is both the cause and the sign of imperfection. The human is free and this includes free to misbehave, and this is why political structures are necessary. For freedom must be matched by coercion if states are to protect *themselves* from the unpredictability that comes with free agents and *their subjects* from each other's freedom and from themselves. Additionally, it is precisely because human life—unlike natural life—is imperfect that it has room for freedom. It is the human's imperfection which supports human indeterminacy, and in turn, it is this indeterminacy which means that we are free to stray.

The second analogy lies in the concept of legitimacy, which is central both in the metaphysical and political realms. As just noted, the problem of state authority is immediately connected to freedom as a reciprocal notion: your and my freedom interact with each other. It leads to the founding presupposition of political thought according to which freedom must be kept in check. Naturally, this gives rise to all sorts of questions about the "right" ways that this check can be enforced—that is, questions of legitimacy. Interestingly, again, we find deep-running structural analogies between the political question of legitimacy, and the metaphysical question concerning the relations of body and soul. Following Plato who regards the soul as the source of the meaning and value of the body and entrusts it with the task of guiding it, the Western political tradition considers that legitimacy gives meaning and value to the physical force that constitutes and maintains the state (i.e., the police and the military). The state, as the saying goes, has "the monopoly of the legitimate use of force" (Bodin, 1955; Hobbes, 1996; Weber, 2004). The question of the body and soul is a question about two kinds of forces. The body has physical force. The soul has spiritual force. And politics, especially modern politics since Hobbes, is the question of how these two things, the "forces of war" and the "will of the people" can legitimately interact.

The third analogy concerns the mereological problem. The metaphysical question inherited from Cartesianism concerned the possibility to conceive appropriately of the body without the soul and of the soul without the body. What is the relevant entity? Descartes is torn: if the relevant entity is the substance, this presents the advantage of allowing all souls to communicate with each other as part of the substance called res cogitans and to understand the physical world as one entity called res extensa. But of course, this denies the relevance of individuality, of difference, of the fact that you and I are different. The more recent form of this problem in the political realm is the well-known clash between utilitarianism and political liberalism, in particular as articulated by Rawls (1971). For the utilitarian, so goes the argument, utility is not affected by difference, whereas a liberal considers that the distribution of advantages has intrinsic value, thereby placing individuality at the centre of political ethics. We traced how the tradition gradually came to reject this hypothesis. In a more general sense, one could say that the debate in political philosophy has largely focused on such mereological questions. The question here is whether we should think of collectives as sums of individuals or inversely of individuals as parts of communities. In particular: are communities here for the sake of the individuals or are individuals there for the sake of the community? As we can see, this question is directly connected to the problem of freedom, for it determines in what way the aim of protecting subjects from each other's freedom can justify subjecting them all to the freedom of the state.

The last analogy between the metaphysical and political treatments of the body has to do with the question of reciprocity. In the metaphysical context, reciprocity involved the mutual constitution of the subject and the world by way of embodiment. This issue becomes equally crucial in the political context, under the heading of "power." As we shall discuss in chapter 10, the notion of power is the name of an interaction between two agents, neither of which is absolutely dominant, and neither of which is absolutely stripped of freedom. In short, power involves resistance, and resistance is the basic model for reciprocity (indeed, Husserl's notion of the touching-touched itself appeals to the notion of resistance).

Although this overview is hasty, I hope it shows that there are strong lines that connect the political issue to the metaphysical treatment of the body, and that these are more than prima facie or simply semantic. Not only do we talk of freedom, legitimacy, mereology and resistance in metaphysics and in politics, but we do so *in the same sense of the terms*. The structural analogy between the order of the metaphysical and the order of the political suggests that there is something about the body that is crucial to politics too. However, it remains only an analogy as long as the notion of the body isn't shown to be central in politics too. It is such a demonstration that this chapter is attempting to initiate. As it is becoming obvious, the rejection of the notion of sovereignty, which is the common core of the four metaphysical problems of the body, seems to be the common core of the four, corresponding, problems of political philosophy too: just like metaphysics has moved from a transcendence-based model to the recognition of the impossibility of transcendence, politics has moved from a transcendence-based account of authority to become the art of making the most of the impossibility of sovereignty.

Two Notions of the Body Politic

The starting problem of politics lies in the tension between the fact of embodiment and the need for sovereignty. Embodiment threatens the political order because whatever threatens the political order does so with their body; political disobedience is always something we do with our body, be it a protest, armed insurrection, or running a red light. Indeed, political order has traditionally distinguished itself from religious authority insofar as it regulates behaviours and not thoughts. Additionally, whoever can resist that order (e.g., the People) do so because they have control over their own body to do so. For causally at least, you are the only thing that moves your body. And therefore, the relation between you and your body is a relation of freedom. This is made even more blatant by way of purely metaphysical reflections after Merleau-Ponty's reduction of the body to a power. The body is the power to do some things and one's ability to use our body is irreducible. In short, having a body means having some freedom, the kind of freedom which threatens order, social peace and the established authorities. The kind of freedom politics is there to address. So, when politics is haunted by the irreducibility of freedom, it is really haunted by embodiment, which is the home of that irreducible freedom. Conversely, the political authority is in the business of maintaining orderly behaviour, and it needs a body to do so. Yet, as we saw, any talk of embodiment brings a principle of reciprocity with it: whatever has a body, is vulnerable. Without a body, you are no authority, but with a body, you are exposed to contestation. But this has momentous consequences: it exposes that sovereignty is a contradictory notion. Without a body, an institution is impotent if unassailable. With one, it is potent, but assailable. Sovereignty is the fantasy of the combination of unassailability and power and the fact of embodiment exposes its contradictions. Politics begins with the fact that freedom is ineradicable, because freedom is the freedom to use your body and this key fact breaks down any claim to sovereignty. It is embodiment, therefore, that challenges any idea of sovereignty. As a result, it is only natural that the project of modern political philosophy is to tame bodies. Because its project is to tame freedom and freedom is the freedom to use your bodies. We shall examine two cases illustrating such attempts in chapter 11 and 12.

If the state cannot be entirely composed of good men, and yet each citizen is expected to do his own business well, and must therefore have virtue, still inasmuch as all the citizens cannot be alike, the virtue of the citizen and of the good man cannot coincide. All must have the virtue of the good citizen—thus, and thus only, can the state be perfect; but they will not have the virtue of a good man, unless we assume that in the good state all the citizens must be good. Again, the state, as composed of unlikes, may be compared to the living being: as the first elements into which a living being is resolved are soul and body, as soul is made up of rational principle and appetite, the family of husband and wife, property of master and slave, so of all these, as well as other dissimilar elements, the state is composed; and, therefore, the virtue of all the citizens cannot possibly be the same, any more than the excellence of the leader of a chorus is the same as that of the performer who stands by his side. I have said enough to show why the two kinds of virtue cannot be absolutely and always the same.—Aristotle, *Politics*, III, 4.

This should provide us with a starting point to examine the intuition illustrated in the expression "body politic." It is an expression that is common both in everyday language, in political language and in philosophical parlance too.

How seriously should we take this reference of the body? Could it be that the insistence with which the Western political tradition has used this expression reveals some deep connection between embodiment and politics?

Just like it was the case in metaphysics, which spent the two millennia between Plato and Descartes repressing the ambiguity involved with the notion of embodiment, the tradition of the body politic was not animated by the will to affirm the importance of embodiment for politics. Rather, it was an attempt at bracketing embodiment from the field of the political or at least, at mitigating it. Just like embodiment introduced imperfection into metaphysics, it introduces disorder into politics. It was a phenomenon that political orders had to protect themselves from. This has been done along two notions of the body politic, each of which insists on one aspect of embodiment in particular. The first line uses the expression "body politic" to refer to the authority (the King). The second, to refer to the subject of the state (the People).

The foregoing chapters have pointed out that bodies are individualising and localising (to have a body is to be me and not you, here and not there) *and* that they are caught up in reciprocal relations. Let's call this "the phenomenological insight," namely, the conjunctive claim that embodiment involves *both* the principle of reciprocity *and* the principle of individuation. It is this conjunctive claim that shows that "sovereign power" is a contradiction. For (a) any power must give access to the world for its implementation; (b) by virtue of the phenomenological insight, access of the power to the world coincides with access of the world to the power (vulnerability); and (c) sovereignty excludes vulnerability. To have a body, so goes the phenomenological insight, means to be able to act upon the world to the exact extent that we are susceptible to be acted upon by the world and the others. This is why, as we traced the development of this insight from Husserl to Noë, we came to realise that the body is a concept that unifies passivity and activity as well as subjectivity and objectivity. If no active entity can be assigned, no sovereignty can be assigned either. For the body, if it's understood carefully, is two-sided: it acts upon the world and the world acts upon it. The last point we made was that the body was a structure of possibilities *and* of impossibilities *at once*. Possibilities are on the side of sovereignty; impossibilities are on the side of subjection. This suggests that insofar as a body is involved with politics, it will always be a thorn in the side of any theory of sovereignty. The history of Western political thought is animated by a desperate attempt to make sovereignty viable at all costs. It appeals to the notion of the body politic to do so, along two lines, both of which replace the conjunctive view with a different kind of disjunctive view.

The first line admits the localisation principle but rejects the reciprocity principle. It suggests that the individual body is indeed relevant, simply, it is possible to conceive of a sovereign body, a body that is not subjected to resistance. We shall discuss it next. The second line rejects the localisation principle but admits the reciprocity principle: the body politic is a homogenous collective (thanks to the commensurability ensured by the reciprocity principle). On this basis, it does not admit of any otherness: it is not engaged in relations with any external entities, for there is no relevant externality that obtains between two members of the same collective (e.g., Rousseau, 2018, II, 5), and belonging to another collective simply means being incommensurable with it, just like the collectives called *res extensa* and *res cogitans* are incommensurable (this, of course places international relations in a conceptual limbo). In such views, the body politic is one great universal collective, as evidenced in Enlightenment universalist rationalism for example.

Historically, the first line provided the template for the second. It will be the focus of this section. In this view, the expression "body politic" applies not to the community but to the King insofar as he possesses divine attributes, in particular, the ability to be active without suffering resistance. It is a line of thought that was developed as an attempt to prop up the notion of sovereignty: what distinguishes the body politic of the King from his body natural is that, unlike the body natural, which is subjected to the laws of nature (including the constraints imposed on it by other body naturals, such as people and viruses), the body politic is immune to the action of others or other forces. For example, it is not subject to immaturity in youth, senility in old age, illness and even death, for the body politic of one King becomes transferred into the next King in an uninterrupted manner: "The king is dead, long live the King." In other words, the body politic is not subjected to the vagaries of physical events. At the risk of anachronism, one could say that at the general level this theme of the body politic was meant as a response to (an implicit grasp of) the phenomenological insight. The more specific problem dealt with here is related to debates that have been raging in theological circles from Augustine (if not Aristotle) to Aquinas: if god is almighty, can he possess contradictory powers? If he doesn't, does it mean there are powers he doesn't possess? Similarly, if the Sovereign King possesses all political powers, how can we resolve the apparent contradictions that seem to obtain between some of them, in particular, the power to act and the power to avoid being acted upon? As I mentioned earlier, to have a body involves both power and an exposure to power. Losing your body means losing power, but possessing it means losing invulnerability. Although embodiment makes one susceptible to the actions of external objects, forces and people, it is also indispensable for ruling. In other words, it shows that sovereignty is a self-contradiction. So, the order is tall: how does one keep the body that can *do*, without keeping the body that can *be done to*?

The solution to this double bind, as is often the case in politics, lies in the production of a series of myths and legal fictions, namely, the myth of a sovereign body, called the body politic. As we shall see, this has taken several expressions, including the taboos analysed by Freud through Frazer and the myth about angels and the legal distinctions between body politic and body natural analysed by Kantorowicz. All of them however have the same object: to prop up the myth whereby the active side and the passive side of the body can be distinguished, or distinguishable. Interestingly, the two main sources we shall examine here refer to widely different historical epochs and geographical locations. They combine history and anthropology with philosophy in ways that make it difficult to trace what conclusions are supported by the data, or by the author's own thinking. They do suffice, however, in showing how the anxiety concerning the contradictory foundations of political sovereignty has informed all sorts of political systems, and how this contradiction was always instinctively recognised as lying in the ambiguity of embodiment.

Freud

The core idea that one can distil from Freud's analysis of the "Taboo of Rulers" in *Totem and Taboo* is that there is a deep intuitive understanding of the phenomenological insight in so-called tribal societies. These societies are organised according to the insight that bodies can touch *only to the extent* that they can be touched. That bodies are active only to the extent that they are passive. As a sign of this awareness and of the corresponding anxiety about political stability, Freud analyses their whole, very complex and rich technology of symbols, laws and taboos, designed to neatly (if fictionally) separate the passive and the active. Freud presents this system in terms of paradoxes, which is, as we saw, also the language used by Husserl and Merleau-Ponty. In particular, he insists on the following paradox: rulers must both be guarded (because they are vulnerable) and be guarded against (because they are powerful). The "paradox" of course comes from the fact that we think of power as sovereignty and therefore, that we think that to have power means that to the extent that you have power, you are invulnerable. In this logic of sovereignty, one would rather expect that if you are to be guarded against, you are *not* to be guarded. If you're to be guarded against, it means you have power. To the extent that you have power, you don't need protection. But

The attitude of primitive peoples to their chiefs, kings and priests is governed by two basic principles which seem to be complementary rather than contradictory. A ruler 'must not only be guarded, he must also be guarded against'.

Both of these ends are secured by innumerable taboo observances. We know already why it is that rulers must be guarded against. It is because they are vehicles of the mysterious and dangerous magical power which is transmitted by contact like an electric charge and which brings death and ruin to anyone who is not protected by a similar charge. Any immediate or indirect contact with this dangerous sacred entity is therefore avoided; and, if it cannot be avoided, some ceremonial is devised to avert the dreaded consequences. The Nubas of East Africa, for instance, "believe that they would die if they entered the house of their priestly king; however they can evade the penalty of their intrusion by baring the left shoulder and getting the king to lay his hand on it." Here we are met by the remarkable fact that contact with the king is a remedy and protection against the dangers provoked by contact with the king. No doubt, however, there is a contrast to be drawn between the remedial power of a touch made deliberately by the king and the danger which arises if he is touched—a contrast between a passive and an active relation to the king (pp. 48–49). . . .

Frazer attributes to these circumstances the fact that in the course of history there eventually came about a division of the original priestly kingship into a spiritual and a temporal power. Weighed down by the burden of their sacred office, kings became unable to exert their dominance in real affairs and these were left in the hands of inferior but practical persons, who were ready to renounce the honours of kingship. These, then, became the temporal rulers, while spiritual supremacy, deprived of any practical significance, was left to the former taboo kings. It is familiar knowledge how far this hypothesis finds confirmation in the history of old Japan.—Sigmund Freud, *Totem and Taboo*, p. 55.

the phenomenological insight says that to the extent that you have power, you have passivity. To the extent that you can touch, you can be touched. And so, this double concern for guarding and guarding against comes out of one unitary phenomenon, which is the body. Their separation therefore can only be enacted abstractly, in this case, with appeal to taboos.

By "guarded and guarded against," Freud means that the Kings must be kept from being touched (guarded) and kept from touching (guarded against). The taboo stipulates that touching the King leads to death, and being touched by the king can (depending on circumstances) lead to death too, although it may be healing too. Indeed, the same king, when touched, can bring death and when touching, can bring healing. But of course, where is the touching that is not touched? Only in thought can we distinguish the active and the passive in the experience of touch, and taboos must now be understood as a ritual that imposes conceptual distinctions onto a reality that doesn't abide by them. The taboos of the rules are procedures that separate the active from the passive *symbolically* even as they are inseparable *concretely*.

Every touch is reciprocal, but taboos allow us to artificially determine some touches as active and some touches as passive. Since the structure of touch makes this separation impossible, tradition supplements it by setting rituals that enable the interpretation of one occurrence of touch as the occurrence of A touching B rather than the other way around. These rituals are called taboos. Although in modern language, we talk of taboos as interdiction, it is important to recall that they are originally interdictions only in a *derived* sense. The originary sense of a taboo is as an interpretive technology: a taboo determines in which circumstances a touch between a King and a subject *counts as* the King touching the subject or the subject touching the King. It is only as a result, that taboos count as a legal interdiction. They outlaw any behaviour that makes use of the touchability of the King. For remember that the touchability of the King is the weakest point in any society, it is the ineradicable exposure of order to chaos: the possibility of resistance and therefore the possibility of the collapse of society. In other words, like all human laws, taboos correct and complete the laws of nature: although the laws of nature allow for touching the king, they need to be supplemented by human laws that make this *physical* possibility *legally* impossible. The true object of the taboo, Freud shows, is therefore the ineradicable threat presented by the possibility that one pledge allegiance to nature rather than to society. Eminently, what is taboo (in all legal systems including ours) is to confuse "can" (natural possibility) and "may" (legal possibility). We shall see how this becomes worked out as allegiance to the body natural or to the body politic. This is why Freud and Frazer are at pains to show that what is at stake in these taboos is not just the integrity of the body of the King or Chieftain, but it is the very survival of the polity. Breaking these taboos means breaking the society itself, which can only maintain itself if it dominates nature.

But like the body, taboos too are two-sided. This is not surprising since their role is to take the two-sidedness of the body and operate the separation between the two sides. This separation will therefore in turn be two-sided itself, suggesting already that this two-sidedness cannot be overcome. As a result, taboos apply not only to the subject who mustn't touch the king, but on the other side, they apply to the King themselves, whose touch is so powerful that it exceeds their control. As Frazer points out, the body of the king is perceived as so dangerous that the king paradoxically becomes the ultimate pariah, excluded from social interactions, and burdened with so many responsibilities that his or her every move must be controlled. As a result, the quest for sovereignty undermines itself because any full sovereignty can only be dangerous to the community at large: "Rulers are allowed great privileges, which coincide exactly with the taboo prohibitions imposed on other people." Invulnerability, which was protected for the sake of sovereignty, ends up turning against power, and the king becomes impotent. By wanting to preserve the sovereignty of the king, we annihilate the sovereignty of the King. The king becomes caged up in an avalanche of taboos, and Frazer reports that young men have to be physically forced to accept kingship, for nobody wants the job (there is a faint echo of this phenomenon in the nomination process of Chairs in academic departments these days). So, paradoxically, the attempt to separate power from subjection via the introduction of taboos *recreates* the unity of power and subjection suggesting that those two things cannot be separated.

Interestingly, this separation appeals to the supernatural as a justification and ultimate guarantee: the greater force that dominates both nature and the state and justifies the taboos is a supernatural force which is itself sovereign. It is up to the divinity to make the taboo-breaker ill, or dead. And of course, this divinity is disembodied. And this reiterates the problem of the impotent invulnerability of the disembodied. The body of the king's sovereignty is only dependent on a higher sovereign force. The sovereignty of the king or the chieftain seems to require a higher legitimate and sovereign force that makes the legitimacy and sovereignty of the king redundant. Invulnerability brings impotence; sovereign power requires supernatural forces. Taboo-based power is bound to one or the other of these two contradictions. This seems enough to give us the *ad absurdum* argument we were looking for: power comes with vulnerability. Invulnerable power is a contradiction.

The politics of taboo, which Freud, after Frazer, sees most evident in ancient tribal societies, provide a model for all kinds of social orders (including modern, highly institutionalised ones like Western democracies). For they are all organised by the tension inherent to the concept of sovereignty: sovereignty is dangerous but the absence of sovereignty is dangerous too. Sovereignty is impossible and yet it is necessary for the survival of the community. As a result we can read the hyper ritualisation of the body in politics as an intuitive recognition of the phenomenological insight. Yet, it regards this insight as its chief enemy, a devil to be thrown back into the box, a problem to be resolved fictionally. The subjects of the king should never come to realise the vulnerability that comes with the king's power.

The King and His Two Bodies

This leads us to a later analysis of the body politic in an entirely different context. No longer Oceanian and African tribal societies but late medieval and early modern England. There too the question of the body politic is crucial, there too it motivates a desperate appeal to fiction to prop up an untenable notion of sovereignty, and there too, it collapses under the weight of its own contradictions, demonstrating negatively that the reciprocity of embodiment cannot be overcome.

Body Vulnerable and Body Invulnerable

Ernst Kantorowicz presents the legal problem of the body politic under the Plantagenets and the Tudors as a way to address the weakness of the human body and its inability to maintain political stability. In particular, the core concern in that historical context involves a temporal problem: kings die, raising the problem of succession from one king to his successor. In such times of transition, the weaknesses of sovereignty are even more visible than usual, because in the absence of the ruler, there is no longer a reason to be ruled. This is solved, Kantorowicz shows, by suggesting that the ruler is never absent. For the absence in question is the absence of the body natural of the king, but not of his body politic, which is immortal, and therefore remains until a new king ascends to the throne, and acquires the pre-existing body politic, thereby ensuring stability in transition.

As is already visible, this solution to the problem of transition of power leads to a host of complications: in particular, in what sense is the body politic truly a body if it needs to incarnate itself in the body natural of a new king? Or conversely, in what sense does the individual king supplement the body politic with his body natural, if the right to rule depends on the body politic alone? Although we'll discuss it shortly, we can already note that this is the problem that was solved by democratic theorists such as Rousseau, who cut the middle man and moved to a model where the body politic (the general will) rules alone, without the help of any individual body natural

(Kantorowicz, 1997, 364 ff). As Kantorowicz points out, this democratic instinct which consisted of conceiving "the Crown as something disconnected
from the King" (364), was already present in the pre-modern age. However,
it encountered fierce resistance, which all but delayed the democratic transformation. Although it is admittedly true that thinking of the body politic
and the body natural as entirely separate is a more intelligible view, and although many of the physical duties of the king can be performed by the body
politic without a body natural (via the police and the military for example),
it fails to account for the necessity for power to lie within the owner of a body
natural: the body must be an enforcer of the will, it must present and stage
itself as the incarnate presence of the law, and finally, some of the duties of
the king involve some sort of passivity, which is best achieved by the body
natural: a king must have "eyes, ears, hands and feet" (367). He must act via
his men, but he must also perceive. As power for action, the king must have
a body that acts without resistance; as power of surveillance, he must be an
invisible and passive observer. In both cases, so went the medieval reasoning,
he needs a body natural alongside his body politic.

The Body Sovereign: The King

The problem of the body politic emerges as a political problem in two ways
therefore: first, it must maintain the notion of sovereignty, of a body that can
do but cannot be done anything to. Second, it introduces the connection between sovereignty and legitimacy (since between the death of one king and
the ascent to the throne of the next king, the population must remain orderly
because the body politic retains legitimate authority) (365). The body natural is insufficient but indispensable: it is vulnerable but offers a way into the
world. The body politic likewise: it offers invulnerability to the contingencies of life, but no action. Sovereignty is the fantasy that seeks to get the good
of both without the bad of either. Therefore, it must begin by examining to
what extent the good in each can be kept without the bad. These political
requirements involve some complicated metaphysical gymnastics: we must
find an account of what it is to *have* a body (through which action can be
carried out) without *being* a body (so that hurting or forcing our body would
not register as hurting or forcing us). In short, we must resolve the question
of the relations between the embodied self and the transcendental ego. Just
like we saw in Freud, the answer lies in mythical dissociation. Unsurprisingly
in the context of monarchy by divine right, the figure of the king is modelled
after the figure of the Angel: like the Angel, the king is the representative

The *cause célébre* concerning the Duchy of Lancaster, which the Lancastrian Kings had owned as private property and not as property of the Crown, was tried—not for the first time, to be sure—in the fourth year of Queen Elizabeth. Edward VI, the Queen's predecessor, had made, while not yet of age, a lease of certain lands of the Duchy. Thereupon the crown lawyers, assembled at Serjeant's Inn, all agreed:

"[T]hat by the Common Law no Act which the King does as King, shall be defeated by his Nonage. For the King has in him two Bodies, viz., a Body natural, and a Body politic. His Body natural (if it be considered in itself) is a Body mortal, subject to all Infirmities that come by Nature or Accident, to the Imbecility of Infancy or old Age, and to the like Defects that happen to the natural Bodies of other People. But his Body politic is a Body that cannot be seen or handled, consisting of Policy and Government, and constituted for the Direction of the People, and the Management of the public weal, and this Body is utterly void of Infancy, and old Age, and other natural Defects and Imbecilities, which the Body natural is subject to, and for this Cause, what the King does in his Body politic, cannot be invalidated or frustrated by any Disability in his natural Body."

It may be mentioned immediately that the pattern after which the King's body politic—"void of Infancy and old Age, and other natural Defects and Imbecilities"—has been modelled, can be gathered readily from Sir John Fortescue's tractate on The Governance of England, where he writes: "it is no poiar to mowe synne, and to do ylle, or to mowe to be seke, wex olde, or that a man may hurte hym self. For all thes poiars comen of impotencie . . . wherefore the holy sprites and angels that mey not synne, wex old, be seke, or hurte ham selff, have more poiar than we, that mey harme owre selff with all thes defautes. So is the kynges power more."

What matters is that John Fortescue's passage shows how closely the legal speculations were related to . . . the mediaeval concept of the king's *character angelicus*. The body politic of kingship appears as a likeness of the "holy sprites and angels," because it represents, like the angels, the Immutable within Time.—Ernst Kantorowicz, *The King's Two Bodies*, pp. 7–8.

of god on earth. In the figure of the Angel as presented by Fortescue and discussed by Kantorowicz, we see a concentrate of this dissociative intention.

In traditional theology, an angel is an intermediary figure between God and the world. They are also a messenger, an intermediary figure between the sender and the receiver. Why does God or the gods have any need for such an intermediary figure? Because for a deity to present him or herself to the real world, for them to *appear*, they need to take on some sort of bodily shape. In other words, the notion of an angel, or of a messenger (including prophets and monarchs of divine right) already presupposes that some powers *require* being physical, either for the sake of visibility, or of action. It therefore presupposes that god is limited by his lack of embodiment. Recall how this problem, namely that since the spatio-temporal world is to be ordered by virtue, it means that it is irreducible, became the core problem for the later Plato and for Augustine. At the same time, for a God to become embodied, they become subjected to the laws of physics (including to other bodies), and this infringes on their sovereignty. In order to maintain the divine sovereignty, theology appeals to angels. The angel therefore is the paradigmatic expression of the fantasy of sovereignty: it is the being that has a body that can do, without a body that can be done to. This fictional proposal is meant to solve, artificially, the challenges to sovereignty presented by the phenomenological insight and therefore to satisfy the fantasy of a one-sided body. The angel is only active, not passive. The angel does but you can't do anything back to the angel. This ability to do without being done to, to be embodied without compromising its sovereignty is what Fortescue refers to as the "caracter angelicus" of the body politic.

Universality

In spite of all its supposedly pre-modern theological contortions, this view animates the modern democratic tradition of thinking about the body politic. This is a tradition that takes the second line of thought about the body politic. It regards the body politic as the body of the community. Although it is a view that precedes the debates discussed by Kantorowicz, it becomes reactivated in the modern era. But all began with Aristotle. Aristotle, at the very birth of political theory in the West already uses the organic model. He initiates the notion of the body politic, which he understands in terms of parts and wholes: citizens and city. Just like an organism is more than the collection of its parts, so is a city more than the collection of its members: it involves an *organisation* which gives to each their place and function. The core problem for such a project of a cohesive city has to do with personal freedom.

In organisms, a leg doesn't have either the mental or the physical freedom to pursue its own interests in neglect of the rest of the body. Not so in the case of cities: individuals can stand up to the collective out of their own free will. In other words, in Aristotle already, the notion of the body politic is wishful, a social catechism, a noble lie. It is by telling men that their fate is one like the parts of a body that one might hope to make it so. Remember Augustine's answer to the question: what is evil? It's when you forget that you are part of God. What is a bad citizen for Aristotle? It is someone who forgets that they are only a part of the biological unit called the city. As a result, the body politic is only one when it is, Aristotle says, "sovereign": Every sovereign act of the state is the result of a balance between sovereignty and subjection *within* the state. Every citizen must subject their individual freedom in order for them *as a body politic* to undertake free actions.

For when any number of men have, by the consent of every individual, made a community, they have thereby made that community one body, with a power to act as one body, which is only by the will and determination of the majority: for that which acts any community, being only the consent of the individuals of it, and it being necessary to that which is one body to move one way; it is necessary the body should move that way whither the greater force carries it, which is the consent of the majority: or else it is impossible it should act or continue one body.—John Locke, *Two Treatises of Government*, Second Treatise, chapter VIII, section 96.

This view runs from Aristotle to Hobbes, Locke, Rousseau and Kant. Locke insists, for example, on the necessity for the owner of an individual body to regard themselves as parts of a greater body, and therefore as only second-hand possessors of freedom. This is a model meant to suppress individual freedom and replace it with political freedom, mediated by the community as a whole: on this new view, I am free only because I am a member of a collective body which is free. This of course, preempts any personal use of freedom, which would then be regarded as a breach of the integrity of the body politic, just like it would be a breach of the integrity of your own body if your thumb went rogue and started acting on its own accord. In other words, sovereignty can only come from the organic unity of all those who have natural freedom: only the community as a whole can be sovereign. Any smaller entity (say, a class, or a caste, or an institution or interest group) will always have their power threatened by the ability to resist that lies in everyone's relation to their body: those not included in this unit will have no reason to subject their individual freedom to that external body. In short, for there to be sovereignty, there has to be legitimacy: I must believe that the balance between my sacrificing my individual freedom for collective freedom is positive. So, modern thinkers, for example Rousseau, understand, in their constant struggle against individual interests, that to every body should correspond a will, and that therefore the body politic too, should have a will, which Rousseau calls the "general will." Only this will, Rousseau tells us, is sovereign, because it is general, and as such it has no boundaries, and nothing is external to it. As a result, nothing is in any position to oppose it and it is therefore unchallenged. In short, the body politic as body of the community is a body without outside, a fully sovereign body, yes, but is it a body at all anymore, or are we returning to another fantasy of a now disqualified sense of sovereignty? More on this in the next chapter.

Conclusion

What unifies the universal and the personal notions of the body politic, is that it is the correlate to the theory of sovereignty. The body politic is a fiction which is implemented in a variety of ways (ritual, legal, fictional, mythical) but is always meant to address the tension between the need for embodiment and the need for sovereignty. They should be read as strategies to prop up the notion of sovereignty. In this context, we can see how political thinking is haunted by the thought of bodies as free, as dangerous, as vulnerable, and as necessary. It is also, and since long before the rise of phenomenology, haunted by the phenomenological insights that bodies are two-sided and therefore falsify any logic of sovereignty and subjectivation.

A final point, therefore. If it is true that this tension can only be resolved mythically, and if it is true that sovereignty is necessary for society, we must conclude that societies are only as strong as their myth of the body politic. That is to say, societies are always vulnerable. The history of the concept of the body politics is best understood as a process through which societies have become acquainted with the fact that they suffer from the precarity of their fictions.

Additional Readings
John of Salisbury, *Policratius*.
John Fortescue, *The Governance of England*.
William Shakespeare, *Coriolanus*.
Thomas Hobbes, *Leviathan*.
Thomas Hobbes, *De Corpore*.
John Locke, *Two Treatises of Government*.
Giorgio Agamben, *Homo Sacer, Volume I*.
Claude Lefort, *The Political Forms of Modern Society: Bureaucracy, Democracy, Totalitarianism*.

Key Ideas

The theme of the body politic should be taken literally.

The question of the body is essentially connected to the development of Western political theory.

The fact of embodiment appears as the proof that sovereignty is an untenable concept.

The body of the people is a permanent threat to political sovereignty.

CHAPTER TEN

~

Alienation and Micro-Power

Readings
Karl Marx, *The Economic and Philosophical Manuscripts of 1844*, pp. 30–35.
Michel Foucault, *The History of Sexuality*, volume 1, part 5: "Right of Death and Power over Life."

The previous chapter examined how the fact that politics is always involved with bodies—the body of the king, the body of the constituents, and the body of society as a whole—means that political sovereignty is impossible. The language of body in politics is a desperate acknowledgement of the impossibility of sovereignty. Let us reiterate one more time the double bind: to have a body is to be exposed to other bodies: no sovereignty. To not have a body is not a solution, however, because without a body, no *power* and therefore, no sovereignty either. This means that one must choose between *power* (provided by embodiment) and *invulnerability* (provided by disembodiment). Sovereignty is meant as the unity of power and invulnerability, and it is untenable. Political theory is now forced to choose between its two darlings: power and invulnerability.

We saw how until the classical age, sovereignty was the holy grail of politics. First, it was invested in the figure of the king. But this model had to fail: resistance was everywhere, rulers were always threatened, political orders could change from one day to the next. Let's call this the Machiavellian moment, where the precarity of power becomes obvious, the dikes set up by taboos, rituals and the Theologico-mythico-legal rhetoric of the body politic of the king exhausted itself. This led into the second attempt at propping up sovereignty, which relies on defining the body politic as the people. There too the problem becomes reiterated under the realisation that each individual was bound to deviate from their functional role in the organic whole of the body politic: as long as members of a society have a personal body which responds to their own individual freedom, the cohesion of the body politic will be threatened. This marks the exhaustion of the ideal of sovereignty in Western political theory. Interestingly, this corresponds almost exactly to the exhaustion of the dualistic model which we observed in Plato, Augustine and Descartes. It is no surprise therefore that critics of the democratic model, which is committed to the second sense of the body politic, operated a shift analogous to the phenomenological shift in metaphysics. At the very moment where, in the wake of the failure of Cartesian dualism, the metaphysics of the body moved towards a non-dualistic model of *Leib* emphasising the body-mind union rather than the separation, we witness, in the political field a new model which also emphasises the union of body and soul over their separation. Freedom is never fully destroyed because it is co-extensive with the intimate bond that links a subject's will (which is part of the soul) with their body. Remember how the undeniable responsiveness of one's body to their will was the paradigmatic anomaly that allowed Elisabeth to turn Cartesianism on its head. The union of the body and the will is the obstacle to sovereignty. The new model developed on the ruins of the notion of sovereignty takes as its starting point the discovery that individual freedom was beyond the reach of the authorities: the ruling of bodies and of their behaviours, therefore, cannot be achieved without the *collaboration* of those who own these bodies. We move from a notion of authority as domination to one of authority as collaboration.

Power is no longer regarded as the repression, denial or elision of freedom. On the contrary, Foucault claims that power relies on freedom: power exists only if it triggers free obedience. Power is therefore defined as the management of freedom, that is the management of the indissoluble union of the body and the soul. The very union of body and soul now becomes the central concern of politics. The works of Marx and Foucault illustrate this shift towards a model of soft power. They analyse how political authorities have come to regard it as their job to interfere in the union of body and soul so as to enlist individual freedom for their own purposes. How can the authorities ensure that my will's privileged access to my body will not translate into disobedience, resistance and rebellion? How do authorities persuade (since they cannot coerce) other bodies to relinquish their own freedom? How does one use their own body to enforce the will of another?

Marx and Alienation

Marx's hugely famous account of alienation in the factory worker can be read as an analysis of the shift from the politics of sovereignty to politics as the interference in the relations of body and mind. He calls such interference alienation. Literally, "alienation" means the breaking of a bond. *Un lien*, in French, is a bond. Alienation is *unlinking*. For all intents and purposes, whenever the notion of alienation does any work, what is at stake is an institutional interference in the body-soul bond. It is only on the basis of this basic form of alienation that alienation of the will or of freedom (which are the politically operative forms of alienation) can come about. Alienation, Marx argues, delivers power to the dominant structures by disrupting the people's relation to their body, thereby disrupting their ability to exercise freedom. He claims that this intervention has been achieved by a material economic structure called capitalism, within which the use that a worker can make of their body is largely subjected to legal structures of employment. It is worth noting that this shift to capitalistic domination involves no longer the exclusion, but rather the co-option of the worker's freedom.

The theory of alienation presented by Marx is grounded in a description of the everyday life of the worker. Since the Greek ethicists, the body has been regarded as a way into the soul and vice versa. This gave rise to a host of ascetic techniques that were meant to exploit this link. In many of their forms, these techniques relied on the union of body and soul in order to overcome it; that is, in order for the soul to liberate itself from the body. Such practices relied on the insight that the union of body and soul allowed one to access their own or another's soul via their body, or vice versa. In other words, we have here a new extension of the fact that embodiment undermines invulnerability: the body is not just an access through which harm can be done to me, but it also is a way into my soul, it is a zone of exposure of what was traditionally taken to be one's "innermost." Marx sees the same development in the history of capitalism, but by contrast to the ascetics, he shows that this access to the worker's "inside" via a body may bring about not enlightenment but alienation. One could say that Marx regards mechanical labour as a reverse *askèsis*. It is mechanical labour, Marx contends, that leads to exhaustion, depression, alcoholism in the working classes. These, he points out, are all mental and spiritual phenomena, but they arise exclusively from what the worker has been doing with their body, on the factory floor. Marx traces carefully how the mind-numbing and dehumanising character of labour leads into the impossibility to have a healthy family life, the impossibility to create friendships, and therefore the impossibility to foster self-esteem and how this results in the destruction of the human dimension in a worker's life. In capitalism, the embodied nature of the worker leads to the separation of body and soul. For Marx the union of body and soul is in fact the very definition of the human, and any separation between them (any alienation) constitutes dehumanisation. Let's examine how capitalism achieves this dehumanisation.

For Marx, the working life in capitalist, industrial societies, leads to four kinds of alienations. They each involve a sort of dehumanisation and they each are experienced to varying degrees by every worker.

We proceed from an actual economic fact. The worker becomes all the poorer the more wealth he produces, the more his production increases in power and range. The worker becomes an ever cheaper commodity the more commodities he creates. With the increasing value of the world of things proceeds in direct proportion the devaluation of the world of men. Labour produces not only commodities: it produces itself and the worker as a commodity—and does so in the proportion in which it produces commodities generally. This fact expresses merely that the object which labour produces—labour's product—confronts it as something alien, as a power independent of the producer. The product of labour is labour which has been congealed in an object, which has become material: it is the objectification of labour. Labour's realisation is its objectification. In the conditions dealt with by political economy this realisation of labour appears as loss of reality for the workers; objectification as loss of the object and object-bondage; appropriation as estrangement, as alienation.... What, then, constitutes the alienation of labour? First, the fact that labour is external to the worker, i.e., it does not belong to his essential being; that in his work, therefore, he does not affirm himself but denies himself, does not feel content but unhappy, does not develop freely his physical and mental energy but mortifies his body and ruins his mind. The worker therefore only feels himself outside his work, and in his work feels outside himself. He is at home when he is not working, and when he is working he is not at home. His labour is therefore not voluntary, but coerced; it is forced labour. It is therefore not the satisfaction of a need; it is merely a means to satisfy needs external to it. Its alien character emerges clearly in the fact that as soon as no physical or other compulsion exists, labour is shunned like the plague. External labour, labour in which man alienates himself, is a labour of self-sacrifice, of mortification. . . . We have yet a third aspect of estranged labour to deduce from the two already considered. . . . In estranging from man (1) nature, and (2) himself, his own active functions, his life-activity, estranged labour estranges the species from man. It turns for him the life of the species into a means of individual life. First it estranges the life of the species and individual life, and secondly it makes individual life in its abstract form the purpose of the life of the species, likewise in its abstract and estranged form. For in the first place labour, life-activity, productive life itself, appears to man merely as a means of satisfying a need—the need to maintain the physical existence. Yet the productive life is the life of the species. It is life-engendering life. The whole character of a species—its species character—is contained in the character of its life-activity; and free, conscious activity is man's species character. Life itself appears only as a means to life.—Karl Marx, *The Economic and Philosophical Manuscripts of 1844*, pp. 30–32.

1. The first relation that capitalism severs is the worker's relationship to themselves, their self-ownership. This alienation is achieved in two ways that are two sides of the same coin. First, it is achieved through the *objectification* of the worker. The worker's social standing relies exclusively on their being the owner of their physical body and its energy. The worker's insertion into society (i.e., capitalistic society) is provided by their profession and their profession is defined by their ability to interact with machines, that is to say, to be a machine among machines. The body of the worker lives alongside physical objects (i.e., primary materials, artefacts and machines). As a result, the worker's body becomes a good for the worker himself, who begins to value himself only as this body that works. Not only is the worker socially reduced to his mechanical existence, he is also consciously reduced to it: he considers himself to be a *Körper* only and their relationship to their body becomes instrumental: my body is not who I am, it is merely my means of subsistence.

   Second, alienation takes place through *universalisation*. In this context, where the worker is reduced to a "force of production," they become identifiable according to universal, impersonal and objective criteria. This interacts in momentous ways with the monetary structure of capitalism: this force of production (how much of what the worker's body produces), once measured, can be matched with a market value, and this match is reflected in their wages. As a result, all human workers are interchangeable and their value has become a currency, immediately matched to wages paid in monetary currency. Universalisation thus becomes cashed out as interchangeability, demonstrating how self-alienation involves the alienation from the personal: the individual determinations of the worker (their tastes, their emotions, their appearances, their attachments, etc.) become irrelevant to all the areas of their conscious and social life.

2. The second kind of alienation at work here is the worker's alienation from the object of their labour: according to the logic of interchangeability just described, the spiritual connection that develops between the worker and the object of their labour (say, between a textile factory worker and the clothes they create) cannot be accounted for. This is because manufactured objects are also defined only in terms of their market value, which refers to the universal currency (money) rather than their particular determinations (e.g., who built it, and with how much care and attention). The worker is therefore no longer allowed to see himself reflected in the object of their work (for example, by regarding themselves as the "author" of the object, or by being proud of the object as their achievement). Rather, objects exist in the neutral public sphere, under the regime of a fantasy whereby the fact that these objects have an artefactual history (i.e., that they've been made by somebody) is deliberately disqualified and ignored. Marx refers to this fantasy as "fetishism."

3. The third relation that becomes severed in capitalism is man's relation to nature. Marx makes the implicit point (later developed explicitly by critical philosophers) that capitalism has a deep connection with Cartesianism. In this Cartesian framework the worker, once reduced to their body, is part of nature. Since the first reduction, that of the individual to their body, is an instance of alienation, the second only extends the worker's alienation from himself to the whole of nature: by losing access to their own body, the worker loses access to nature. This creates a sense of estrangement from the whole of creation, a sense of isolation, as well as the impossibility to experience the spiritual relief and satisfaction that comes from admiring nature.

4. Finally, and consequently the worker is alienated from those around him and from his community: since social integration is dependent on work, it is conditional on the reduction of the worker to her production value, society becomes a vast field of zombies, clusters of production-value wandering past each other, unable to acknowledge each other in their singularity, and rather, seeing themselves and the other as interchangeable in ways that deny their differences, their identities and therefore their humanity.

Those four forms of alienation give us more insight into reverse asceticism. All four kinds of alienation rely on the fundamental structure of embodiment: they rely on the fact that the worker's body is public and therefore susceptible to being choreographed in ways that inform his physical life and disrupt the relations between her body and her soul. In this sense, it exploits the resources of the causal relations between body and soul: by lording it over the worker's body, the capitalist superstructure weakens the very will of the worker, separates it from her physical behaviour, essentially annulling her freedom to resist. However, it does so, it will be noted, through no coercion whatsoever, but rather, through the worker's own freedom: her free (if admittedly tightly constrained) choice to work. By stripping the worker of her power to act, capitalism turns workers into what Fortescue would regard as reverse angels: no longer those who have a body active without a body passive, but rather the reverse, those who have a body passive (mechanically going through the motions of work and mass culture) without a body active, one that could disrupt the existing order.[1] Through the mechanisation of her movements, through the management of her bodily needs, capitalism turns its victim, the worker, into its ally, in its efforts at controlling his body. The trick of capitalism is therefore to use embodiment against itself. It replaces the *human natural existence* defined as the *immediate* interaction of soul and body with *the existence of the worker* defined as the interaction of the soul with the body *mediated* by relations of production. By enabling the worker to use their body freely, capitalism turns the worker's freedom into its accomplice.

Two results follow from this. The first is human misery, the second is political subjection. Here is Marx's tragic insight: when we are miserable and depressed, when we feel that our life is meaningless, when we feel cut off from each other and from nature, we reinforce the system that makes us miserable and depressed. First, because we don't resist it. Second, because we have no reason to change our own course of life: in order to have aspirations, one would have to still retain a human dimension, one would have to retain self-esteem and a glimmer of inspiration. Rather, the worker will go back to work the next day. In the *Communist Manifesto* (1848) Marx and Engels very famously wrote that in a revolution, the worker has nothing to lose but their chains. This should be understood in two ways. First, as it has mostly been understood, it expresses their belief in the inevitability of revolution: the proletariat has nothing to lose, so they will not object to a revolution. Second, it expresses Marx's uncertainty about the first: perhaps the proletariat will be worried about losing their chains. In short, alienation forces the worker into a contradiction: as humans they wish to live according to the unity of their body and soul, as a healed, complete, natural organic unit. On the other hand, as a historically constructed subject, as a worker, they strive to live according to their alienated state. We shall see in the next two chapters that this model still informs contemporary critical race and gender theories.

Finally, Marx's analysis of alienation is essentially connected to an implicit phenomenology of embodiment. For Marx, body and spirit are distinct and unified. They are distinct in the sense that the outside world can only access the individual's spirit via their body, and not directly. They are connected, because they each have—and provide—access to each other. As we mentioned in the previous chapter, the notion of the body politic involves the separation of the public (which exists in the political mode) and the private (which exists in the natural mode). For Marx however, their separation is an anomaly which he calls alienation. In fact, it is the illusion of their separation (inherited from Cartesianism) that places existing orders in a good position to abuse their union: by pretending that the realm of the public and of the private are entirely distinct, sometimes even by institutionalising this distinction, capitalist societies are able to claim that manipulating a worker's body doesn't violate their freedom of conscience. Yet, it is thanks to the intimate connection between the life of our body and the life of our minds that the established order allows itself to invade the sphere of the private. This moves Marx towards a new model which Foucault later thematises as "biopower" and "micro-power," both of which involve the invasion of the political into the private (Foucault, 1990, 152).

Foucault and Power

Foucault's work could be regarded as a close-up on this last remark: what are, in their great diversity, the subtle, invisible, often minuscule mechanisms through which the body's life is organised, choreographed, regularised, rendered predictable, tamed and appropriated? In Foucault's language, how do we become "normal"? In order to investigate this deeper, Foucault makes two moves. The first is to remove from Marxism the implicit idea that alienation is an impingement on some originary, natural or at least possible state of unity, something like originary authenticity. For Foucault, this would involve an equally ruinous misunderstanding of what bodies are, namely porous interfaces between the subject and the world. If capitalistic subjection via alienation is indeed historically contingent, this doesn't imply that the structure it makes use of—namely the vulnerability of the union of body and soul to outside interference—is also contingent. In other words, the political project of resistance cannot be to preserve the human as she is, or the individual in his or her singularity. Rather, understanding embodiment means understanding that to be human is always open to being artificially and contingently turned into what Foucault calls a subject. Foucault's objection to alienation is not based on a fantasy of authenticity, but rather it exposes the falsity of the claim that the norm being applied to the alienated subject by a dominant order is legitimate.

In concrete terms, starting in the seventeenth century, this power over life evolved in two basic forms; these forms were not antithetical, however; they constituted rather two poles of development linked together by a whole intermediary cluster of relations. One of these poles—the first to be formed, it seems—centered on the body as a machine: its disciplining, the optimization of its capabilities, the extortion of its forces, the parallel increase of its usefulness and its docility, its integration into systems of efficient and economic controls, all this was ensured by the procedures of power that characterized the disciplines: an anatomo-politics of the human body. The second, formed somewhat later, focused on the species body, the body imbued with the mechanics of life and serving as the basis of the biological processes: propagation, births and mortality, the level of health, life expectancy and longevity, with all the conditions that can cause these to vary. Their supervision was effected through an entire series of interventions and regulatory controls: a biopolitics of the population. The disciplines of the body and the regulations of the population constituted the two poles around which the organization of power over life was deployed. The setting up, in the course of the classical age, of this great bipolar technology—anatomic and biological, individualizing and specifying, directed toward the performances of the body, with attention to the processes of life—characterized a power whose highest function was perhaps no longer to kill, but to invest life through and through. . . . Hence there was an explosion of numerous and diverse techniques for achieving the subjugation of bodies and the control of populations, marking the beginning of an era of biopower.—Michel Foucault, *The History of Sexuality*, vol. 1, pp. 139–40.

The law always refers to the sword. But a power whose task is to take charge of life needs continuous regulatory and corrective mechanisms. It is no longer a matter of bringing death into play in the field of sovereignty, but of distributing the living in the domain of value and utility. Such a power has to qualify, measure, appraise, and hierarchize, rather than display itself in its murderous splendor; it does not have to draw the line that separates the enemies of the sovereign from his obedient subjects; it effects distributions around the norm.—Michel Foucault, *The History of Sexuality*, vol. 1, p. 144.

The second idea, which Foucault inherits from Marx this time, is that alienation involves a new understanding of the field of politics. Foucault argues that the field of politics should heretofore be defined as the field of *power*. The politics that takes place within the field of power, Foucault calls "micro-politics." His best approximation of what micro-politics is requires introducing yet another technical term: bio-power. This is an expression meant to emphasise that it is a politics that applies itself to *bodies*. Second, it's a politics that begins with a world that, like life (*bios*) pre-exists it and which it doesn't choose. Life, as you remember, was the definition of the unity of body and soul. And as we have discussed in the previous chapter, the modern political concern is the concern to deal with this irreducible given: that the individual freedom of subjects has a direct access to their bodies. Life, as the unity of body and soul in each of us, is what is given before any political order comes in. In other words, Foucault retrieves from Marx the deep insight that paradoxically, the stronger political position is not that of sovereignty, which distributes freedom and subjection along neat lines, and into homogenous blocks. Such systems are fragile because the fact of embodiment is a constant reminder that they rely on voluntary subjection, on a naïve and precarious belief in the fiction of a sovereign body (the body of the king or of society). On the contrary, the most effective powers, Foucault argues, are those that do not remove the freedom of those they dominate but rather, composes with it, manages and guides it, co-opts and collaborates with it. In the process, of course, we moved to the management model, and managing is always managing what there is, and what there is, is life. As Foucault insists, power cannot give life, and so the power that focuses on life is always the power that *manages* what there is (organisms that have received life through biological processes), but does not *choose* it.

We can see how much of a new model of power this is. It is power that focuses on managing what there is, and what there is, is the constant threat of resistance. It is no longer a matter, Foucault argues, of the power of death, which a sovereign power can visit upon its subjects, but the power of life which the power cannot create, which precedes it, and yet, which the power can co-opt. Foucault claims that life and death are not symmetrical politically. This is because death can be created institutionally (e.g., through the death penalty), whereas life cannot. When it comes to life, the institutional political powers are secondary and reliant on nature. Power over death is the power to bring death about. It is negative, but Foucault calls it "creative" in the sense that it brings about something that previously wasn't there: death. Power over death is a radical power in this sense. But power over life is different for no ruler can bring life about, they can only channel it, cope with it, and manage it. A political order of bio-politics *organises* and "administers life" (138), but it doesn't *create* it. As such, it is impotent before the fact that life exists. Rather, it depends on life for its existence. Power now "fosters" and "disallows"; it no longer enacts or execute. This fostering requires constant and individualised care, and no longer the one-size-fits-all law: life is dynamic and normalising it is constant and detailed work: this is why bio-politics is the work of "micro-power" (145).

This model of management would merely amount to the recognition of a move to so-called soft-power (141) if it didn't emphasise the place of the body in it: the understanding of soft power as bio-power brings with it the recognition that the failure of the old system of sovereignty was caused by embodiment, that embodiment was the political threat, and that a more resilient sort of power would have to manage, rather than repress, deny, or ignore, embodiment. What that means is that any possible organising or political system will have to be the kind of system that organises bodies, because bodies are whatever it is that resisted, that broke the previous system.

What do we get out of this micro-power model? First, we get a very elaborate analysis of all the multiple ways in which power exercises influence over freedom, of how power manages life. Micro-power, Foucault argues, allows us to grasp a further sense of alienation: identity construction. Not only can we understand alienation negatively the way Marx did: that is to say, as the severing of some sort of natural bond, but we must also see it positively as *this that assigns us an identity.* The reason this remains a case of alienation is that the contingent set of circumstances that determine this identity are external and mediated by our body: they are micro-power itself. Race and gender are two axes for identity construction because they both proceed by inducing internalisation. They induce the subject to identify with their public side— that is, their ideologically laden physical appearance. The alienation element at work here is that the public dimension of the individual (their bodily appearance) is reflected into their subjectivity. Alienation in this context is the conquest of the inside by the outside, mediatised by micro-powers. There are more such examples besides gender and race of course: sexual orientation, age, nationality, ethnicity, membership to any sort of community, membership to your family, loyalty to your parents or friends and so on. All of this is identity construction because all of these operate by inducing you to take on an identity which is defined by pre-established ways of categorising your own body.

This notion of soft power, as we see, relies on the subject's willingness to collaborate with the established structures (e.g., through identification or through the normalisation of behaviour). This is far from suggesting that bio-power is a more minimal form of power. Rather, bio-power, although it penalises little, controls more widely, for it is exercised in every area of the most intimate realms of life, the realm traditionally left alone on the grounds that it is "private," the realm of the body. You will recall that for Descartes, the problem of interaction is the problem of the will: how come my will, which is mental, can result in behaviours, which are bodily? In other words, freedom is best understood as the privilege of the interaction of the body and the soul. Foucault follows from this insight: power will be most successful in normalising behaviours if it shapes the will that motivates these behaviours. In order to do this, power must insert itself in the relations of one's soul with their body. From how we sustain our bodies (alimentation, nutrition, lunch breaks, medical examinations, where the sportsground is located, etc.) to how we live in and with our bodies (sexuality, marriage, procreation/child-rearing, demographics, etc.). Foucault focuses on the case of sexuality because he regards it as both a representative example of many such bio-powers (sexuality is involved in the family structure, demographics, health, identity) and also because it provides a clear historical example to illustrate the shift of emphasis from the notion of sovereignty to the notion of micro-power. You shall note how Foucault's intention is precisely to contest the view prevalent in his time according to which sexual liberation involved the contestation of power. It is only if one believes that sexuality is the assertion of the body *as this that escapes power* that one could believe that it challenges power.

This is the background that enables us to understand the importance assumed by sex as a political issue. It was at the pivot of the two axes along which developed the entire political technology of life. On the one hand it was tied to the disciplines of the body: the harnessing, intensification, and distribution of forces, the adjustment and economy of energies. On the other hand, it was applied to the regulation of populations, through all the far-reaching effects of its activity. It fitted in both categories at once, giving rise to infinitesimal surveillances, permanent controls, extremely meticulous orderings of space, indeterminate medical or psychological body. But it gave rise as well to comprehensive measures, statistical assessments, and interventions aimed at the entire social body or at groups taken as a whole. Sex was a means of access both to the life of the body and the life of the species. It was employed as a standard for the disciplines and as a basis for regulations.—Michel Foucault, *The History of Sexuality*, vol. 1, p. 146

[D]oes the analysis of sexuality necessarily imply the elision of the body, anatomy, the biological, the functional? To this question, I think we can reply in the negative. In any case, the purpose of the present study is in fact to show how deployments of power are directly connected to the body—to bodies, functions, physiological processes, sensations, and pleasures; far from the body having to be effaced, what is needed is to make it visible through an analysis in which the biological and the historical are not consecutive to one another, as in the evolutionism of the first sociologists, but are bound together in an increasingly complex fashion in accordance with the development of the modern technologies of power that take life as their objective. Hence I do not envisage a "history of mentalities" that would take account of bodies only through the manner in which they have been perceived and given meaning and value; but a "history of bodies" and the manner in which what is most material and most vital in them has been invested.—Michel Foucault, *The History of Sexuality*, vol. 1, p. 152.

The point, however, is to realise that in a world of biopower, the body is not external to the system of power, but its very focus. Sexual liberation only reinforces micro-power; it doesn't offer liberation, but rather invites control.

There are very powerful ways in which micro-powers control us. But the kind of control they exercise is of a new type, more akin to influence. And, as Foucault argues, if we understand that move from *law*, which is about controlling reliably and completely, to *norm*, which is about nudging and influencing and managing, then we understand why with this move to norms we also have moved to bio-power, micro-power, and normalisation. Think of demographic policy for example. Nobody is deciding how many children you will have. But most states have incentives, tax incentives for example. Some governments have put in place building restrictions, for example, that almost literally architecture our use of our bodies. In 2017, Turkey passed a law that banned the building of studio apartments in the capital city. The result was to drive up the price and rent on studio apartments, thereby discouraging the single life, encouraging marriage and driving up fertility. Nothing was forcible, nobody mandated marriage or the making of more children and freedom was respected. But of course, the statistics were there to prove that the policy had results that lined up with the family and fertility-oriented government.

Picking up where Marx left off, therefore, Foucault chronicles the defeat of the capitalist and democratic cut between public and private by (a) showing how power always invades the private (138), (b) exposing the illusion of the body politic in a renewed way, and (c) demonstrating the systematic and necessary relations between power and control over bodies. The result is nothing short of a paradigm shift, from a system organised around the mutual opposition of sovereignty and freedom to the complementarity of power and freedom; from externality to union, via alienation.

Further Reading
Marcel Mauss, "Techniques of the Body."
Judith Butler, *Bodies That Matter*, chapter 7, "Arguing with the Real."

Key Ideas

The abandonment of a sovereignty-focused political theory led to a management-focused one.

This new form of theory is defined by how it changes the place of the body: the body is now the medium through which power applies its control.

The resulting form of power functions by interfering in the relation of body and soul in the political subjects.

Power is a relation to freedom, not to constraint: it relies on each agent's ability to control their own bodies while influencing this control.

Note

1. Aristotle discusses slaves in similar terms: they can understand orders but not think for themselves (*Politics*, I, 5).

CHAPTER ELEVEN

~

Race, Visibility and Power

Readings
Linda Martín Alcoff, "Towards a Phenomenology of Racial Embodiment."
Frantz Fanon, *Black Skin, White Masks*, chapter 5, "The Lived Experience of the Black Man."

Marx and Foucault introduced three ideas that have been foundational for the subsequent understanding of race:

1. First, the body grants the external world and the others access to our innermost. Having a hold on my body is having a hold on *me*. As a result, by considering ourselves as fundamentally embodied, we are also saying that we are fundamentally vulnerable. This raises a further two points: first, we see how this meshes well with the defeat of the notion of sovereignty, for sovereignty assumes an absolute subject. And sovereignty, therefore, is undermined at the moment the absolute subject or the idea of a radical subjectivity is undermined also. This undermining is provided by the analysis of *Leib*. Second, we see more clearly how the undermining of sovereignty, if pushed to its natural consequence, involves the irreducibility of alienation: as humans, we are always caught up in alienation (of some form and some degree): the

embodied human is an alienable being. With this alienation comes not only the defeat of sovereignty, but the defeat of authenticity as well. For Foucault, for example, the fantasy of authenticity fails alongside the fantasy of sovereignty.

2. The second idea, mostly from Foucault, is that this transfers us into a new system of power, that is no longer best understood in terms of a monopoly of force or domination. Instead, we must think of power as an interaction between mutually contesting freedoms, and of the resulting order as a collaboration between unequal yet free partners. We get a very elaborate analysis of all the multiple ways in which power exercises influence over freedom, of how power manages life. Foucault's umbrella term for the most effective area of application of power is subject-formation: power construction is the result of both external constraints and our own agency, while at the same time, it results in reliable and predictable agents whose behaviour no longer needs to be controlled because they are already designed to "act normal." In fact, the permeability of the individual to ideologies and behaviour architecture opens up a space for pre-subjective normalisation: micro-power precedes the formation of our subjectivity, and the intimate relations between ourselves and our bodies, thereby influencing and informing them. As a result, and as we shall see, they deliver us with a subjectivity as with an alien burden. Identity construction here results in a certain set of demands and expectations that one freely applies to themselves (through internalisation) on the basis of a certain coding of these facts with certain behaviours. Sexual orientation, age, nationality, ethnicity, membership to any sort of community, membership to your family, loyalty to your parents or friends, all of them and more are factors in our self-image that we permit to determine our behaviour: depending on what we believe a man is, a person of my age is, a philosopher is and so on, I will dress, talk and present myself in such and such ways.

3. The third idea emphasises the body as the privileged medium of micro-power. Foucault and Marx noted that power should be understood as an interference in the relations between the body and the soul. Foucault shows how bio-power invades the private sphere and transforms power. Marx shows how capitalism interferes in our own relations with ourselves. And both agree that these interferences rely on the choreographing of body practices, be it in the factory and the ergonomics of operating machines, or through urban architecture. Similarly, ideologies inform how we live in our bodies, by abusing the public dimension

of the body as a point of passage between the order of objects (forces, including discourses, etc.) and the subjective order (first-person experience). The discovery of those specifically modern technologies of power highlight the possible unity of freedom and subjugation.

These three basic views animate the discussion surrounding the relations between identity, oppression and embodiment. The experiences of gender and race and the way they are mediated by normalising discourses are two paradigmatic, urgent and tragic examples of how micro-power works. Although the next two chapters focus on these two cases, I hope that they provide a framework for analysing other cases, such as disability, sexuality, age, and more broadly, to make more concrete the general argument according to which the way we live in our bodies is not immediate and natural, but rather cultural and ideological, and informed by discourses.

As we shall see, partly under the influence of Foucault and Merleau-Ponty, the analysis of the experience of members of oppressed groups (in this case, victims of racism and of sexism) yields a double insight. The first has come to be known as an "ontological" insight: that is to say, first, following Foucault, an insight about how beings (in this case, subjects) are constructed, and secondly (following Merleau-Ponty), an insight about what it is to *be* (real). Here, the insight is that even though racial and gender reality are historically, ideologically, linguistically and culturally constructed, they are not less *real* for it. Rather, the appropriate meaning of "reality" cannot ignore such factors. The second insight involves an analysis of the resulting subjectivities: namely, oppressive normalisation results in a restricted experience of embodiment and subsequently, in an incomplete sense of belonging.

The Ontological Thesis

Body as Race

Linda Martín Alcoff's first concern is to evade the false alternative of race as either objectively real or an illusion. Calling race objectively real runs the risk of immediately justifying racism or at least, of leading the conversation about racism astray, towards discussions about whether and how racism is proven or disproven by racial differences. Regarding race as an illusion, on the other hand, runs the risk of dismissing the seriousness of racism, or diminishing the experience of suffering racism: race is real because which race you belong to alters your life in very real ways. Race is real because racism is real. Naturally, Alcoff's solution is to examine in what sense race resists both objectification and dismissal: what makes race real is the experience of racism. What makes it unreal is the fact that racism is constructed and contingent. Does it suggest that race is real in some diminished sense? There is a strong intuition that suggests that this is not so. As we saw with Husserl, Merleau-Ponty, Gibson and Noë, embodiment brings with it a new sense of "real." To be real means to be commensurate with *Leib* and to exist in the realm of value and meaning. In this context, race cannot be regarded as less real than anything. It is, Alcoff (1999) claims, "as real as anything else in lived experience, with operative effects on the social world" (17). In this sense, race is real in all the humanly possible sense of real. Race is contingent but real and it will not go away just by being ignored. This is the argument that subtends Alcoff's move to contextualism, that is, her view that the real is dependent on socio-historical context.

Race as Embodied Meaning

This leads to an additional insight: race is real precisely because and insofar as it is embodied. Racialised people are racialised as owners of a racialised body. So, Alcoff (1999) claims that "Race is real, though like witchcraft, its reality is internal to certain schemas of social ontology that are themselves dependent on social practice" (15). But this reliance on "schemas of social ontology" doesn't imply that the reality of race is social as opposed to embodied, rather, it is social *because* it is embodied, because a body is public and visible, because by having a body, one is exposed to the social practices that apply to this body. In short, there is a "third [i.e. social] dimension of the body," and the racialised body belongs to it. There is no conflict between being bodily and being socially determined. In order to understand how racialisation comes about we must recognise that this social dimension of the body is constitutively embodied. Following Gibson, a body is essentially a set of surfaces, including of course skin, and its "epidermal schema" (Alcoff, 1999, 24). That is to say, body as skin shall best be understood as a readable surface, a surface on which race in particular is readable.

Yet, the metaphor of readability should not induce the illusion of an author. On the contrary, the subject, the owner of the skin, is not in control of the text that the other can read off their skin. Their skin does not "express" them, for this skin has no meaning until it is read off of by a gaze that is informed by impersonal "schemas of social ontology." In short, our skin is ours enough that we must take responsibility for the others' experience of it, but not enough that we have any power over that meaning: alienation indeed. The result as we shall see, is a singular influence of the reader (i.e., the other, be it a person or social structure) on my personal body-schema, and subsequently, on my behaviour. "Race is socially constructed, historically malleable, culturally contextual, and produced through learned perceptual practice."

This has ambivalent consequences: considering the body as interpreted suggests that it is constructed and more importantly, that this interpretation is never final, but always revisable. However, interpretation always includes an objectivist moment: I interpret A as B insofar as I believe myself to be retrieving the intrinsic meaning of A in my interpretation B. In short, although interpretations *create* meaning, they take themselves to be *retrieving* meaning. That is to say, they induce the belief in objectivity. As you might remember, it is by appeal to this hermeneutic model that Merleau-Ponty managed to explain the origins of "an in-itself for us." So, the body, once interpreted, tends to present itself as the objective standard of value of this interpretation.

Objectivism

Yet, Alcoff's aim is not to reject objectivism but rather to point to the discrepancy between two elements in racism: the first is the claim that the race of a person is relevant to their value. The other is that race is an objective fact. The fallacy there is in the implication that the latter can support the former: how can a neutral objective fact support a normative judgement? As a result, the role of objective features in racial identity cannot, on its own, exhaust the notion of race. Racism cannot be justified naturalistically in terms of some biological notion of race; it is much richer (if deeply flawed). On the contrary, Alcoff (1999) relies on *Gestalt theorie* to recall that visibility does not precede value judgements, rather, it relies on them (19, 23). This visibility is a function of the habitual body of the perceiver (21). Race relies on the judging habits of the racist. To put it in ecological terms, there is a perverse match between racialised bodies (as perceived) and racist bodies (as perceivers). Racialisation is a form of social affordance (21, 23) and racism is a result of "practices of visibility" (25). In other words, racialisation, and its other side, racism, are meaning-making practices. We need to think of race as a meaning structure, a way to make sense of the world, a way to understand. Racism (like sexism) is built on a certain narrative about what racialised people are (or what women are), and although it is an interpretation whose purpose is not truth but the creation of a liveable world, this narrative has objective pretensions (21). And the closest we come to support these objective claims is by measuring, looking at bodies, calculating skin tone, etc. As a result, Alcoff (1999) declares that the flaw of the "implicit ideologies of race" (16) is to uncritically mix objectivism and interpretation.

The sting in Alcoff's argument is that this *reliance* on objective reality doesn't involve a *priority* of objective reality: for Alcoff, it is true that race is real and visible, but not real because visible or visible because real. On the contrary, reality and visibility refer to each other (Alcoff, 18). This means that on the one hand, we claim that race is real because of the racialised person's visible features (e.g., the colour of their skin), and on the other hand, these features are recognised as racial for constructed reasons: these visible features are *real* and *meaningful* for contingent social reasons. "Visible differences naturalise racial meanings. . . . Locating race in the visible thus produces the experience that racial identity is immutable" (Alcoff, 1999, 23). In other words, racialisation commits to a fallacy: it commits to two different meanings of "real," one as objective (say: skin tone) and the other as culturally constructed (that skin tone registers as race) but it takes them to be unified: here is the implicit logic of the racist: "I say that such features are real in the sense of *objectively* observable, and I also say they are real because they are *significant* and these two things are one thing." The problematic implication there is that by assuming that there is only ever *one* meaning of "real," reality as objective visibility and reality as significance become conflated, and we can use the one to falsely support the other. The upshot is that this disseminates the illusion that these visible features are intrinsically meaningful, that they are intrinsically racial, that interpreting them racially doesn't involve any interpretation, any cultural influence, any ideological interference; that race is not a "social reality" (16). The political upshot is that reality (in a vague sense chaotically combining objectivity and meaningfulness) becomes regarded as a source of legitimacy for racial discourses: the racist takes themselves to merely be "stating the fact" or "telling it like it is," sound familiar? In times of political correctness, racists add to this first fallacy the claim that their view is disqualified only by those, who, enthralled by political correctness, refuse to name reality. We shall see in the next chapter how gender theory has responded to this fallacy by pulling the rug from under it: sex is objective, gender isn't, thus you cannot justify gender assignment with sex, just like you cannot justify racialisation with physical features.

Ideology

The structure whereby interpretation is received and mistaken by individual minds and whole societies as objective truth is exactly the definition of an ideology: an interpretation that takes itself not to be one. With it comes the great normalising fallacy according to which essences, which are abstractions, become the standard according to which we concretely must live and to which we must fit. Because I belong to this race, then I must live according

And then we were given the occasion to confront the white gaze. An unusual weight descended on us. The real world robbed us of our share. In the white world, the man of color encounters difficulties in elaborating his body schema. The image of one's body is solely negating. It's an image in the third person. All around the body reigns an atmosphere of certain uncertainty. I know that if I want to smoke, I shall have to stretch out my right arm and grab the pack of cigarettes lying at the other end of the table. As for the matches, they are in the left drawer, and I shall have to move back a little. And I make all these moves, not out of habit, but by implicit knowledge. A slow construction of my self as a body in a spatial and temporal world—such seems to be the schema. It is not imposed on me; it is rather a definitive structuring of my self and the world—definitive because it creates a genuine dialectic between my body and the world.—Frantz Fanon, *Black Skin White Masks*, pp. 90–91.

to the clichés vehiculated about this race; just like you belong to this race, I will be entitled to expect that you will fit those cliches.

In the case of race, the connection of this objectivism to the problem of the body is most visible. We had noted how Cartesian dualism satisfied the demands of reason by ignoring the demands of experience: the concepts of body and soul are only thinkable separately even though experience can only be understood in terms of their union. As we have seen, this gave rise to two impulses illustrated in the modern era: intellectualist reductionism, of the body to the spirit, or materialist reductionism, of spirit to body. We can see how the two illusions that Alcoff objects to are each connected to one of these two sides, making it all the more understandable how she resolves it along Merleau-Pontian lines. On the one hand, we have those who reduce the subject to their racialised body (racism), and on the other, those who deny the embodied self, thereby ignoring that race is real in its own irreducible way. Both views, as Merleau-Ponty argues, are committed to objectivism, a sense that the truth of the subject is objectively determined. The reduction denounced by Alcoff according to which the existence of objective racial features was enough to make race objectively real should therefore be understood in this context: there are racial features, but racism is a system of interpretation of people, and not of features. Therefore, these objective factors do not warrant racism. It is this fallacy that we see crop up in ideological discourses, thus uncovering another dimension of the political disadvantages of dualism: it is the fantasy that the body is nothing but *Körper* that undergirds oppressive racialisation and sexualisation. In short, racism is a reduction of a subject to their features and of their features to an unquestioned (ideological) meaning (or in Alcoff's language, "coding").

There is a visual registry operating in social relations which is socially constructed, historically evolving, and culturally variegated but nonetheless powerfully determinant over individual experience. And, for that reason, it also powerfully mediates body-image and the postural model of the body. Racial self-awareness has its own habit-body, created by individual responses to racism, to challenges from racial others, and so on. The existence of multiple historico-racial schemas produces a disequilibrium that cannot easily be solved in multi-racial democratic spaces—that is, where no side is completely silenced. Racial identity, then, permeates our being in the world, our being-with-others, and our consciousness of our self as a being-for-others. . . . If racism is manifest at the level of perception itself and in the very domain of visibility, then an amelioration of racism would be apparent in the world we perceive as visible. A reduction of racism will affect perception itself, as well as comportment, body-image, and so on. Toward this, our first task, it seems to me, is to make visible the practices of visibility itself, to outline the background from which our knowledge of others and of ourselves appears in relief. From there we may be able to alter the associated meanings ascribed to visible difference.—Linda Martín Alcoff, "Towards a Phenomenology of Racial Embodiment," p. 25.

Phenomenology of Racial Embodiment

So far, we have examined the structure of racism by indicating its involvement with ontological accounts of what being and what subjectivity are. The idea that race is real was meant as a middle view between those who say that race is *objectively* real and those who say that since it is not objectively real, it is *not real at all*. Alcoff's answer there was to implicitly appeal to the Eleatic principle: things are real if they have real consequences. Race is real because racism has real consequences. It is now time to focus on what those real consequences are. What is it to suffer from racism? There, Alcoff's suggestions follow two lines, first, it is a matter of *describing* the experience of racial embodiment, and by this she means the experience of being exposed to a world organised by racial interpretations. This exposure is called visibility. The second line is analytic: *how come* the subject of the group of fallacies called racism gets affected in their experience of embodiment itself?

Description

The descriptive discussion focuses on four points. First, that the experience of racialisation involves a sort of alienation. Second, that racial concepts filter through all social interactions: if a society has racialised concepts, no social situation in that society will be racially neutral. Third, that although no experience is racially neutral, not all are racialised to the same extent. Fourth, that this asymmetry is a political phenomenon. Let's take them in turn:

First, Alcoff shows how the objectivism of dominant interpretations leads to "double layers of self-awareness" (24): the subject doesn't recognise themselves in the responses they elicit in others and are at the same time robbed of the authority to determine which of the competing interpretations about who they are is more legitimate, that of the other or their own. The first move involves an experience of social alienation, the second an experience of self-alienation. As you will note, both are results of what Fanon, cited by Alcoff, calls a "corporeal malediction"; the visibility of one's body allows others to make a claim on ourselves. In fact, this corporeal malediction is a constant feature of our lives, it is for example what drives you to look in the mirror before stepping out of your house: others have the authority to judge how "good" or "bad" you look (let alone how racialised, gendered, etc.).

Second, based on the analogy of the skin and text sketched out previously, we must understand how the coding of skin and meaning means that skins are always liable to being read. Owning a skin—any skin—means being confined and (on the basis of alienation) self-confined to a specific position in a latent racial mapping network. If anyone is racialised, everyone is racialised. There is no non-racial experience, even for the white man. The difference is in the semantic indexation of race and power, which results in oppression for non-whites and not for whites.

Third, even though racial experience is never overcome, it's also never even. Some members of society are more racialised than others, and racialisation has more or less dire consequences, including, almost everywhere, consequences to do with life and death. Alcoff uses an idiosyncratic reading of a famous text by Jack Kerouac to establish how, as a white man, he is surprised to find himself racialised, which shows three things. First, that no one is ever beyond racialisation. Second that there are circumstances that move the burden of alienation one way or the other, towards one race or another: a white man in a white man's world can afford to forget about race, but this is different from being racially neutral, because it is entirely dependent on shifting contexts (for more, see Mills, 2007). In the case of Kerouac, it depends which neighbourhood he's taking a walk in. Third, that forgetting about race is the privilege of the person who is in their own pre-racialised context. Racelessness is a fantasy of the dominant race. In other words, forgetting race is always forgetting about *my* race and *yours* at once. The privilege of the racially dominant is to forget about their own race, but it is also to forget about the racialised minority's race—that is, it is to forget about racism.

Fourth, point three connects to a further insight namely, that the ability to diminish one's experience of race is eminently a *political* ability: it is by shifting contexts that we can liberate ourselves from having to worry about race. This is what the dominant white establishment has been doing by building racially homogenous neighbourhoods for example. This initiates Alcoff's shift towards the political implications of her phenomenological argument. She concludes that the difference in the levels of racialisation tends to be proportional to the political dominance of the subject in question. Although race is universal, it is not proportional. This has interesting extensions in contemporary standpoint theory, which systematises the view that certain social positions bring with them increased or decreased insight (blind spots about the reality of race can be attributed to racial dominance whereas the ability to see racism may be increased in the victim of racism) into power structures (Harding, 1991, 119–31). Alongside standpoint theory, this is meant to emphasise the fact that the body is the general principle of individualisation. As a result, any view that "trivializes difference" (16) will also repress the subject's ability to live in their body.

Now that we have reconstructed and systematised the ways in which the experience of race spans the entirety of individual experience—from the intimate relations of body and spirit to the political structures of our public lives—we can briefly turn to the basic mechanisms that must be presupposed for this multifarious phenomenon called race to be explained.

Analysis

Alcoff argues that race becomes real via a series of mechanisms of internalisation. The first has to do with Foucault's notion of micro-power as a subjectivity-building force. Here, Alcoff shows that since discourses and concepts are the basic structures of normalisation, race, once embedded in a given culture's conceptual framework, becomes a factor of normalisation among others. In fact, racism "precedes" the acquisition of our body, or rather, the establishment of an intimate relation to our body (we remember from Noë that the acquisition of a body is a learning process) (18). As such, race is *constitutive* of bodily experience, making it even harder for those subjected to racial thought structures to resist them, or even recognise them as alienating: we identify with our race and thus rejecting racial structures is experienced, paradoxically, as a loss of self (17).

The second form of internalisation lies in the very nature of embodiment: being embodied means forfeiting self-ownership. Because my body belongs to the world (as a part of it), I cannot dismiss how the word handles it. Yet, because it belongs to me as well, the handling that the world, including the social world, subjects my body to, naturally makes its way into my psyche and informs my worldview. Being told what race I belong to and what the implications are (i.e., being told racial prejudices about myself) is routinely understood as defining (it tells me who I am) and from here, as normative (as an order). Embodiment means that we cannot disconnect the handling of our appearance by the others from our own handling of ourselves. Thus, it is because racism is embodied that it can make use of micro-power: the way I regard you forces you to regard yourself in a certain way. By interpreting your appearance, I handle your body, by handling your body I handle your soul. Power can move your bodies, and therefore transform your souls.

Further Readings
Charles Mills, "White Ignorance."
Sandra Harding, *Whose Science? Whose Knowledge?: Thinking from Women's Lives*, chapters 8 and 9.
Jean-Paul Sartre, *Saint Genet, Actor and Martyr*, Book II, chapters 1 and 2.

Key Ideas

Race is an extension of the semantic dimension of embodiment.
Racism uses the unity of subjects with their bodies but results in their estrangement from their bodies.
Race is one of the fundamental forms of embodiment.

CHAPTER TWELVE

~

Female Disempowerment

Readings
Iris Marion Young, "Throwing Like a Girl: A Phenomenology of Feminine Body Comportment, Motility and Spatiality."
Elisabeth Grosz, *Volatile Bodies*, chapter 1, "Refiguring Bodies."

We started this third part by exposing the notion of sovereignty as an untenable fantasy. What makes sovereignty impossible is that embodiment ensures individual freedom. Soon, we had to move to a seemingly paradoxical consequence of this fact: freedom is irreducible, and yet, there is oppression everywhere. Foucault's notion of micro-politics shows how freedom itself can become co-opted towards the oppression of the subject. In micro-politics, oppression makes its way into subjectivity through non-confrontational and mostly invisible processes. Micro-politics works by designing subjects. Power normalises, it makes subjects the "right" kind of subjects.

As Foucault points out elsewhere, micro-power is also always individualising: it adjusts to every individual it normalises, and it simultaneously allows the individual to develop an individual identity. In other words, micro-power relies on the general structure of difference which is contained in the phenomenon of embodiment. Understanding that normalisation is always individualised suggests that we should go further into differentiating between kinds of normalisation. The specific suggestion implicit in Young's "Throwing Like a Girl" and made explicit later by Grosz, among others, is that there is an affinity between the metaphysical dualism inherited from Descartes (and which organises the metaphysics of Western culture) and the duality of genders that organises how power flows. An ontology of female embodiment therefore is more than an example of normalisation among others, it is paradigmatic. As discussed earlier, micro-power relies on the unity of body and soul to disrupt this unity. As such, it is staked on Cartesian dualism. If it is true that the male-female divide entertains an affinity with the body-soul divide, then the female condition should be regarded as the paradigm of micro-power.

For Elisabeth Grosz, the paradigmatic meaning-making mechanism that underlies the entirety of Western thought is the complex of the dualities of body and soul and of the male and the female. I call it a complex because it would be wrong to think of this as two distinct dualities, just as it would be wrong to reduce either one to the other. As a complex, Grosz argues, they are responsible for the dualities that characterise Western ideologies: activity-passivity, sovereignty-subjection, public and private, home and world, passionate and rational (Grosz, 13–14). The first term of each of these pairings is to be associated to masculinity, and as a result, "Women are produced as passive and feminine and men as active and masculine" (16). The first concern this raises is that, as we've seen, such duality falsifies lived experience, which always involves the unity of these poles. Gender dualism becomes now coded in ways that effectively exclude the gendered subject from life, which is a principle of unity of activity and passivity. In the case of women, the problem is more acute: not only are they confined to one side of the duality, but they are confined to the passive side.

On top of an ontology of embodiment, this calls for an ontology of femininity. Femininity is not just a social or psychological construct. In fact, in every woman, femininity is encountered as a pre-existing category, one that for all intents and purposes, could be regarded as natural. This may allow us to deepen the point made by Alcoff about race: race is real because racism is real, but real doesn't mean objectively real, she said. Further, femininity is real, not just because sexism is real, but because femininity, just like nature, precedes the female individual: it presents itself to the little girl before she even is anyone for whom this taking on of femininity may or may not correspond. Now "natural" means two things: it means primordial (that it precedes individuality), but it also means objective (i.e., independent, permanent and universal). Gender categories falsify this unity: femininity is natural in the sense of primordial. In the sense of objective, however, it most emphatically isn't. Femininity is primordial because it precedes and informs the woman's experience of herself. "There is a specific positive style of femi-nine body comportment and movement which is learned as the girl comes to understand that she is a girl" (Young, 153). Yet, femininity "makes no claim to universality" (139) This suggests that we need a sense of "primordial" that is not dependent on "natural" (138–39).

The Problem of Female Embodiment

Although she writes before Grosz, Iris Marion Young is contending with this very problem. She begins with the observations of Erwin Straus regarding the difference between the gestures of young boys and young girls. Far from rejecting the popular cliché that girls "throw like girls," she insists we take it seriously: girls are worse at throwing than boys. Young's target is that what is wrong with this cliché is not that the phenomenon of "throwing like a girl" is false, but it is the implication that it has any natural legitimacy. Rather, when a girl throws like a girl, it is not because she's a girl, it is because she experiences femininity as a disability. And that, in turn, is because the only meaning of femininity available in her culture involves disability. This disability, as we shall see, is cashed out in terms of a discrepancy between the demands of life (which require a harmonious relation between motion and intention) and the demands of female identification (which require a disjunction between them). Hence Young's (1980) truly tragic declaration: "Women in sexist societies are physically handicapped" (152).

The girl of five does not make any use of lateral space. She does not stretch her arm sideward; she does not twist her trunk; she does not move her legs, which remain side by side. All she does in prepara-tion for throwing is to lift her right arm forward to the horizontal and to bend the forearm backward in a pronate position. . . . The ball is released without force, speed, or accurate aim. . . . A boy of the same age, when preparing to throw, stretches his right arm sideward and backward; supinates the forearm; twists, turns and bends his trunk; and moves his right foot backward. From this stance, he can support his throwing almost with the full strength of his total motorium. . . . The ball leaves the hand with considerable acceleration; it moves toward its goal in a long flat curve.—Erwin Straus, *The Upright Posture*, pp. 157–58.

Young expands on Straus's description to emphasise the fact that women's movements and gestures are not only constrained (Straus) but also ambivalent. A woman's movement is always self-defeating. For the woman, every time there is movement towards the world, there is also a movement of restraint that undermines this projection towards the world. And therefore, Young (1980) returns to Merleau-Ponty's notion of harmony and melodic movement (146). The intentional life of the female body exhibits a fracture in the body's harmony with the world. This fracture reveals that the deeper, prerequisite harmony between intentions and gesture is broken too. The experience of female embodiment is therefore characterised by reluctance: the reluctance to live in one's body, the reluctance to rely on one's body, to take possession of one's body. It is already visible that this reluctance involves an almost incomprehensible contradiction, namely, a contradiction at a level of experience so deep that it makes the female form of life in principle impossible. How can a form of life be defined by contradiction? Thanks to Foucault the possibility of such deeply contradictory commitments (attachment to one's body and mistrust of one's body) becomes conceivable: this contradiction precedes the formation of subjectivity so that when the subject (in this case the little girl) is constituted and comes to suffer from this tension, it is too late; rejecting the terms of the contradiction becomes impossible: it would amount to the only deeper contradiction possible: rejecting oneself. This shows us *in actu* the depth of Foucault's insight: external powers enrol individuals in their own oppression by hijacking their attachment to themselves and recuperating it. Although Foucault is definitely in the back of Young's mind, she presents this idea in an existentialist context, informed by Beauvoir and Sartre. In their language, the woman's contradictory commitment to life (and harmony) and to her subjectivity (as handicapped) is best expressed as a commitment to being (achieving existence in the world) and nothingness (subjectivity without identity). The first task of the little girl therefore becomes to make someone of herself: to attain being, and this means, fatally, to teach herself to be a woman.

This unavoidable yet deplorable process is achieved through education. In truly Beauvoirian fashion, this presupposes that normalisation takes place before identity becomes formed, as well as after. As Beauvoir shows very well, there is no identity that's genderless: attaining identity, attaining existence, means acquiring a gender. Acquiring a gender in turn, involves subjecting oneself to pre-established gender-norms. To acquire a gender always means to contort oneself into a gender. As Beauvoir famously claims, girls are not born with a gender. Rather, their gender determines their subjectivity, and therefore they are assigned a gender before they have an identity on the basis of which they could choose the modalities of their gender-acquisition. It is this process of gender self-assignment that Young calls the education period. Education for a girl is the process of learning to be yourself and learning to not be yourself at once. The result is a split identity in which the alienating elements cannot be questioned or rejected without questioning the very self that is doing the questioning in the first place. As Foucault suggested, it is in the invisibility of micro-power that lies its effectiveness, and one form of invisibility is the impossibility for the self to recognise micro-power as external. The result is a certain ambivalence of girls and then women towards themselves, one that sometimes expresses itself through self-hatred when one "part" of the psyche rejects the other, surrender when one suppresses itself for the sake of the other, or a whole range of emotions and practices of self-destruction, self-reduction and self-repression.

> Women in sexist society are physically handicapped. Insofar as we learn to live out our existence in accordance with the definition that patriarchal culture assigns to us, we are physically inhibited, confined, positioned, and objectified. As lived bodies we are not open and unambiguous transcendences which move out to master a world that belongs to us, a world constituted by our own intentions and projections. To be sure, there are actual women in contemporary society to whom all or part of the above description does not apply. Where these modalities are not manifest in or determinative of the existence of a particular women, however, they are definitive in a negative mode—as that which she has escaped, through accident or good fortune, or more often, as that which she has had to overcome.—Iris Marion Young, "Throwing Like A Girl," p. 152.

This leads Young to examine the factors of embodiment for little girls and women. She categorises these factors into two. The most determinant corresponds to the phase of subjectivation (identity-formation), which takes place in early childhood. But the fate of women in patriarchal societies is such that female embodiment remains influenced and restricted even in adulthood. The chief factor there is sexual violence. Although Young doesn't deny, of course, that little girls and boys are victims of sexual violence, she suggests that the internalisation of the awareness that one is a potential victim of sexual violence generally comes with early teenage and sexual maturity. In a similar way to Alcoff's description of the owner of a racialised body, who is now made responsible for the racist readings of this body by others, women, as potential victims of sexual violence, train themselves to think of such threats as a circumstance that dictates a set of behaviours upon them (and not upon the potential predators). Here, a new dimension of normalisation appears: although all—men and women alike—are normalised, the responsibility for normalisation is not equally distributed. For it is part of female normalisation that the woman is taught to take responsibility for her objectification by men, whereas male normality doesn't come with any such responsibility. The same applies, as we saw with Alcoff, to the white individual whose whiteness doesn't come with the demand to take responsibility for the racial prejudices of others: the white doesn't have to worry about racial prejudices (even when and if they exist). This is important because it allows us more insight into why a system of micro-power, although it doesn't eradicate freedom, also doesn't eradicate any meaningful notion of oppression. Rather, such oppression is now to be understood in terms of the asymmetrical distribution of responsibility for gender normativity or racial normativity. Sexism is now a question of the social hermeneutic habits that dictate where responsibility lies (the so-called systemic sexism), rather than a question of person-to-person or group-to-group dominance.

The Body and Space

The core problem for Young, therefore, lies in the fact that in the case of female subjectivity-building, the micro-powers at work result into a broken unity. She details it by characterising feminine embodiment as a sort of syndrome that combines two groups of factors. Every woman (or every potential subject of a feminist analysis) experiences (1) a disturbance of the relations between her will and her body as well as (2) a disturbance of her belonging in her spatial environment. In order to assess such disturbances, Young compares them to the account of the body unhindered by gender which she finds in Merleau-Ponty.

1. The disturbance of the woman's relations with her own bodies are analysed along three modalities. First, she notes that female embodiment is characterised by "ambiguous transcendence," "a transcendence which is at the same time laden with immanence" (145). What she means by immanence is objectivity. In the fully empowered embodied subject (possibly the "white male" body is the closest approximation to this), transcendence is not laden with immanence, because the body is

experienced as a force belonging entirely to the subject. This fully sub-jective body is experienced neither as a hindrance or a limitation, nor as the medium through which the order of external objects can access and restrict my own possibilities. "Ambiguous transcendence" means that our ability to project ourselves into the world (transcendence) is tempered by a contrary force (immanence) that constrains the first. This force of immanence infuses the woman's body with inertia, and pushes it towards becoming an object among others. In other words, a woman's experience of embodiment always involves partial objecti-fication and therefore to live in a woman's body is to constantly be at risk of total objectification. This objectification can take many forms, but one of the starkest examples of this surrounds the theme of sexual assault mentioned earlier. The resulting experience of embodiment is not only a certain mistrust of the woman in their own physical abili-ties, but also a mistrust of their bodies as a potential enemy, a conduit for objectification.

2. The second modality of female embodiment in a patriarchal society is "inhibited intentionality," which is a result of the experience of "am-biguous transcendence." "Inhibited intentionality" involves that any intentional act towards the world on the part of the woman *coincides* with an experience of repression, a certain holding back which betrays the awareness of the world not as possibility but as constraint (imma-nence). Young writes that "feminine bodily existence is an inhibited intentionality, which simultaneously reaches toward a projected end with an 'I can' and withholds its full bodily commitment to that end in a self-imposed 'I cannot'" (146). In other words, even as she throws the ball, the little girl also holds back her throw. This needs a more precise analysis, which leads Young into the third modality of female embodiment.

3. The third modality, which Young calls the "discontinuous unity" of feminine bodily existence "with both itself and its surrounding" syn-thesises the first two. It is a rehearsal of the traditional idea of alien-ation. Just like in "ambiguous transcendence," the woman experiences her body as belonging not to her but to the external world (discontinu-ous unity "with itself"); in "inhibited intentionality," Young (1980) describes the world as a field of possibilities from which she is excluded (discontinuous unity from the world) (146).

This naturally leads Young into an analysis of the female experience no longer of her body but of space in general. As a reader of Merleau-Ponty,

Young regards the structures that organise spatial life as corresponding to those that organise embodiment. For being embodied is always minimally being spatial. However, distinguishing between the experience of embodiment and the experience of space has both pedagogical and practical uses: it allows us to understand more concretely why women move the way they do, among others, why they "throw like girls." Young suggests that the female embodied being experiences space as "double," as an enclosure as well as an open field. "In feminine existence there is a double spatiality as the space of the 'here' which is distinct from the space of the 'yonder'" (Young, 1980, 150). In other words, for the woman, the distant spatial areas are not experienced as accessible via the closer ones, but rather as lying disconnected from their realm of access. Not only does this suggest that the woman regards space as disconnected (from her) and discontinuous (from her surroundings), but it also shows how she regards the space she occupies as confined (Young, 1980, 149). This is a rather constant theme in the Western worldview, from Plato's prison analogy to the fantasies of high walls and enclosures conveyed by medieval poets and painters (with their obsession on virginity), through the confinement of the woman to the "home" as opposed to the "world" (Tagore, 1916/2005) all the way to the modern little girls observed by Erikson whom Young is citing here. It drives home Young's own critical point: experiencing the world as confronting is a culturally and historically determined way to be woman. If the world is confronting, it means that I can never ignore that the world is not just for me, I am also exposed to it. The world makes a claim on me. It puts me in my place, literally. And if that's the case, one can understand how gaining freedom will necessarily involve going through complex calculations about how to satisfy the demands of the world without allowing them to repress my freedom. In other words, the ideological system that controls access to gender membership presents the woman with the following *quid pro quo*: "I will give you agency if you internalise my demands." In other words, in order to achieve access to the world, the woman is meant to give up her freedom and play nice.

As a consequence, the woman experiences her body as positioned rather than positional: it exists according to coordinates of surrounding objects, and not the reverse. The woman's world is heterocentric, rather than egocentric as is the case in the genderless account of Merleau-Ponty for example. Merleau-Ponty argued that each body is naturally self-centered—that is, that it organises the space around itself and takes its own position as the fundamental coordinate. For Merleau-Ponty, the body is the original subject which constitutes space; and space is dependent on the embodied subject (102, 142). As the origin and subject of spatial relations, the body does not occupy a position coequal and interchangeable with the positions occupied by other things (143, 247–49). For the woman on the contrary, Young argues that the view of her spatial place is dependent on criteria which she values to the extent that they possess the authority of being "more" significant than herself; external criteria. Young adds: "the third modality of feminine spatiality is that feminine existence experiences itself as positioned in space." (147)

The Analytic Handicap

The discussion of the experience of embodied possibility and the experience of space remain unified within one single syndrome called "femininity in a patriarchal society." Let us make some effort towards finding out what remains the organising centre of this series of amputations that stake out the process of femininity-acquisition. Let us first note the constant recurrence of the theme of discontinuity cashed out as discontinuity of space, discontinuity between intention and gesture, discontinuity between possibility and interdiction, and discontinuity between subjectivity and objectivity. Let us also emphasise the constant competition between world and self, a sort of struggle that Sartre and Hegel would probably have dramatised as an existential struggle to the death. For the woman, all of this results in a distribution of the field of the virtual as either offering immediate possibility (the experience of sovereignty over a restricted inner space enjoyed by the little girl within her high walls) or a sense of mere impossibility (when it comes to events that take place in the distance). What is made inaccessible, however, is a sense of possibility proper, of possibility to be achieved by way of effort. More troubling yet, what has fallen by the wayside in the process of female subjectivation is any possible sense of *achievement*. Now, if we group the modalities of feminine comportment into the more fundamental elements that it organises, I think that we see that the separation of activity and passivity, in other words, the separation of the *I can* and the *I cannot*, is determinant for describing female embodied experience, at least according to Young. It brings with it the separation between the subjective side of me and the objective side of me, and further, the problem of objectification, and further still, the problem of guilt.

The woman's body is an object for another, but because it is *her* body it is an object that she must take responsibility for. This fallacious distribution of responsibility which characterises the experience of female embodiment carries with it a division between innocence and guilt too, which is toxic. If objectification is just seen as the recognition of a fact of the world, then the hurt it involves cannot be blamed on the objectifier who will always pretend that all they do is see things as they are; rather it is blamed on the objectified. We are familiar with the sexist defence of the type: "am I supposed not to see that so-and-so is attractive?" What that means is that when people objectify me, it's my responsibility! We are familiar with the victim-blaming that surrounds cases of sexual assault. This traps the subject of oppression into the obligation to take responsibility for those prejudices that oppress them.[1] In fact, the common practice of victim-blaming is really rooted in the ambiguity of the body. The body is ambiguous, it is both a subject and an object. Yet, our natural discomfort with such ambiguities means that we tend to register it as either object or subject. Because the woman's body is a subject, we use the fact that it's the subject of a person, as an excuse for blaming them for the objective side of their body, which is in fact objectified only by the other. Because it's an object, we regard objectification not as an offensive act but as a fact.

One might object to Young that much of what she attributes to the specifics of female embodiment are in fact central to Merleau-Ponty's own account of embodiment in general. Indeed, it is worth noting that Young's reading of Merleau-Ponty, for a series of contingent and historical reasons, goes through Beauvoir. As a result it remains a reading that regards ambiguity as an anomaly and in particular, her reading of Merleau-Ponty does not have a lot of room for Merleau-Ponty's idea that activity and passivity can exist at the same time at the same place as one thing. This is worth flagging as it may lead to confusion, for example, when she seems to consider "ambiguous transcendence," as a specificity of female embodiment, when a reading of Merleau-Ponty that takes seriously his difference from Beauvoir and Sartre would recognise that according to him, ambiguous transcendence is part of all embodiment.

All of this may be true, but it doesn't amount to reducing Young's analysis of female embodiment to the analysis of *all* embodiment, for even in Merleau-Ponty's account of embodiment—one that accommodates a wide array of combinations of activity and passivity reminiscent of the dualities that plague female embodiment—there remains a sense of normality according to which the woman as described by Young is abnormal, or as she says "handicapped." In the context of Merleau-Ponty, this is most visible in the case of Schneider, the World War I veteran, suffering from brain damage due to a shell injury. As we might remember, Schneider's condition was characterised by two prominent features: the first is his inability for abstraction, that is to say, his inability to respond physically to a mental stimulus. He will immediately salute if his commanding officer walks into the room, but is unable to give a salute when asked by his treating doctor. Second,

Schneider's gestures, Merleau-Ponty says, lack the "melodic" character that "normal" subjects exhibit. Instead of performing a gesture—a unified process made up of admittedly an infinity of micro-movements that are irrelevant to the performing subject—Schneider produces said gesture as a collection of these micro-gestures.

This should sound familiar: Merleau-Ponty describes Schneider the way Young describes the girl's embodiment. His way of reaching out to something, as you recall, was to mentally instruct his body to carry out all the right intermediary movements. Schneider relates to his body as if it was a robot. Or like one of those brilliant construction workers who manipulate mechanical arms. And Young is saying that it is also, tragically, the way that little girls think of their arms, when they are throwing a ball. They are doing all the right things, making all the right intermediary moves. But in the process, they lose what Merleau-Ponty calls the "melodic" dimension of the gesture and what Young calls its "harmonious" dimension, namely, the sense that this is *one* gesture. The resulting gesture is all broken down, but this breaking down is analytic, it results from the experience of movement as made of separable, discrete parts. This should also show us how seriously we must take Young's contention that the woman is "handicapped": it takes a shell shrapnel to do this to a man called Schneider, but it takes the patriarchy to do that to all girls and women.

This should allow us to synthesise a bit further Young's vision of the experience of female embodiment, as well as to understand better how the sense of ambiguity at work here cannot be recuperated entirely within the Merleau-Pontian framework. This is because the example of Schneider suggests that ambiguity has two senses. In the sense that Merleau-Ponty associates with the non-disabled body, ambiguity simply means the unity of notions that analytic thinking regards as incommensurable: body and mind, active and passive, subject and object. Call this "synthetic ambiguity" to account for the fact that thinking fails at understanding a synthetic fact which is nonetheless well established (e.g., the union of body and soul). In the crippling sense illustrated by Schneider and his female counterparts, ambiguity is existential, it is, in fact the tension between on the one hand the necessity to bring these opposites (e.g., thought and movement) together for the sake of a truly healthy life, and on the other hand the impossibility to do so. Call this "analytic ambiguity" to account for the fact that it results in "analytic movement," a self-conscious movement that doesn't reach the "melodic" stage in which parts are no longer analytically distinguishable. Analytic ambiguity, which coincides with disability, is the opposite of synthetic ambiguity, which corresponds to health.

Discourse

The reference to analysis could help us further, in order to address the next question which is a "how" question. It is one thing to note through phenomenological description that women's sense of embodiment and space is frustrated, but it is yet another thing to understand *how* this alienation occurred. The discussion of how the multifarious female syndrome is best reduced to analytic ambiguity suggests that this question must be rephrased: how can analyticity interfere with embodiment? Young's answer lies in her analysis of discourse. In order to work out how micro-power becomes a mediator in a woman's own relationship with herself, Young returns to the original sin of Western modernity: Cartesian dualism. When the world comes to speech, to speak like Merleau-Ponty, it becomes organised into subjects and objects. It becomes Cartesian. As you remember, Merleau-Ponty's critique of Descartes is that the world is not *given* along the Cartesian dualistic lines, but rather it *organises* itself along these lines. This organising process is called the "unmotivated springing forth of the world." In fact, Merleau-Ponty as well as the rest of the phenomenological tradition recognises that the Cartesian vision is the most appropriate analytically: Descartes's intellectualist presupposition, according to which the order or reasons (organised around clear and distinct ideas) corresponded to the order of causes (organised around fundamental objects, such as body and soul) is indeed satisfied by dualism. The objection lies in the belief that the analytical order has precedence over the existential order (which follows the regime of the union, not of the separation of body and soul). This precedence has a genealogy, but no justification. After Foucault and before Alcoff, Young regards discourse as the technology that enables ideologies to interfere with the harmonious arrangements of the self. Yet, discourses—through no fault of their own—are subjected to the formal requirements of analyticity and articulated on the basis of categories. In other words, thinking about embodied agency brings with it the bias for analyticity.

The insight from critical race theory and gender studies is to point out that this bias in favour of analysis is unfounded, and although it looks like an innocent enough piece of metaphysics, it is also politically and ethically oppressive. The organisation of the world into subject and object is the resource used by patriarchal structures to impose on women a certain view of themselves as an impossible combination of subjectivity and objectivity. It is the trick by which the patriarchy brands the female experience with the mark of impossibility. As women, the female subjects need to account for themselves in ways that neatly fit the Cartesian distinctions of subject and object and passive and active. A woman is, of course, neither a subject nor an object, neither passive nor active, or it is both. But this ambiguity will spontaneously tend to be erased at the level of discourse, for discourse doesn't accommodate ambiguity easily. The condition of female embodiment that we described so far, therefore, must be understood as the result of overthinking. It results from the fact that women need to analyse their conditions of existence in order to take action, in order to behave and move. In so doing, they subject their possible motions to the structures not of embodiment or of existence but to the structures of thought and language. As such, the basic mechanism that Young isolates as the mechanism by which women are made into women—or made into beings who strictly speaking *cannot live*—is discourse. The typical embodied style of the woman in the patriarchy is—like Schneider's—of an analytic sort: it is the kind of embodiment that is mediated by concepts (144).

Discourse and Internalisation
What Young shows, and that's typical of third-wave feminism (probably second wave too, depending on how you read Beauvoir), is that the oppression of women is not just an ethical or political problem. Rather, the political

> Feminists and philosophers seem to share a common view of the human subject as a being made up of two dichotomously opposed characteristics: mind and body, thought and extension, reason and passion, psychology and biology. This bifurcation of being is not simply a neutral division of an otherwise all encompassing descriptive field. Dichotomous thinking necessarily hierarchizes and ranks the two polarized terms so that one becomes the privileged term and the other its suppressed, subordinated, negative counterpart. . . . Most relevant here is the correlation and association of the mind/body opposition with the opposition between male and female, where man and mind, woman and body, become representationally aligned. Such a correlation is not contingent or accidental but is central to the ways in which philosophy has historically developed and still sees itself even today.— Elisabeth Grosz, *Refiguring Bodies*, pp. 3–4.

> Only when the relation between mind and body is adequately retheorized can we understand the contributions of the body to the production of knowledge systems, regimes of representation, cultural production, and socioeconomic exchange.—Elisabeth Grosz, *Volatile Bodies*, p. 19.

and ethical subjection of women is grounded in metaphysics, and therefore, it must be undone metaphysically. Young is not content with pointing out that little girls feel alienated, oppressed or devalued, her point goes further into the essence of subjectivity in general and how it is impaired in the case of girls and women. Little girls, she claims are taught to live an impossible life. For little girls it is impossible not to live, and it is impossible to live. It's impossible for little girls not to become gendered and turn into women (for they are exposed to discourses before they have any means to resist their influence), but being a woman is, rigorously, *unlivable*.

This is because the patriarchy demands of women to fulfil *the* impossible metaphysical task, the task of reconciling subject and object. In other words, women have been given the burden of modern philosophy, to resolve *in their own existence*. The girl's throw and the woman's motion is a metaphysical dance: it stages the tension between Cartesianism (on the side of analytic ambiguity) and existential phenomenology (on the side of synthetic ambiguity). The woman responds to her environment both with an "I can" and an "I cannot" both with the sense that she belongs in the world and with the sense that she is excluded from it (147–48). Worse: this predicament will remain unsurmountable as long as we remain within a regime of subjectivity and objectivity. "The modalities of feminine bodily comportment, motility and spatiality exhibit the same tension between transcendence and immanence, between subjectivity and being a mere subject" (141).

For Young, the experience of the woman confronted with impossibility takes place on two levels. The first level is concrete. "I need to hit that target with my ball, I need to throw the ball towards that target, but I can't do it." Young says that the girl in question objectively possesses the ability to do it. She has the strength to do it, she has the motor skills to do it, her body is energised enough to do it. But the objective body doesn't correspond to the body-schema: she experiences her body as unable to deliver the requisite throw. For Young the girl will typically respond to this sense of inadequacy by saying to herself: "I need to think carefully." "I need to think carefully about how to move my body in order to make this throw possible." By contrast, the boy's response, would predictably be of the kind: "Oh, I need to do this, let me try, let me give it a go." Unlike the boy's, the girl's response will not typically exude self-confidence. Rather it will exhibit *mistrust supplemented by intellectual work*. It is by appealing to this intellectual work that she opens Pandora's box: letting discourses rush in (142–43). This is how the relationship of the little girl with her bodily behaviour is mediated by discourse.

This allows Young to provide a very detailed account of the internalisation of gender through discourse. Crossing it with Merleau-Ponty allows us to understand that what Young is driving at is the fact that discourse mediates the relationship between the girl and her bodily behaviours. And that through this mediation, the whole weight of culture, history, and systems of values, rushes into the intimate realm and invades it. It steals the girl away from herself. This is a model, as has become increasingly visible, which also applies to many other kinds of identity-based subjections, based on sexuality, gender, race, age, ability or disability as well as those that take place at a more microlevel, and focus on different kinds of men, different kinds of girls, etc. What Young thus delivers is a generalisable model of normalisation.

Content and Structure of Discourse

Young brings out in precise ways the mechanisms through which discourse comes to interfere with the most intimate of experiences, the experience of embodied intentionality. But when we say that discourse "interferes," we might mean two things. Either we mean that the analytic understanding of the world which is reflected in Cartesianism forces us to live according to Cartesian dualism, or we mean that it is a certain content of discourse, namely, a discourse about woman or women, that is interfering with the girl's experience of embodiment. In the first case, it is discourse *as such* and regardless of its contents that disconnects the subject from their body. In this case, even emancipatory discourses such as feminism itself would fall foul of this critique. In the second case, it is a specific kind of discourse—that is, patriarchal discourse which is problematic. If Young meant "interference" according to the first case, her story would be incomplete, it would leave one question open: why is this kind of discursive interference more connected to the case of women and not men? Should we also seriously assume that discourse doesn't intervene in male embodiment? Young leaves this question open, but we can already see how answering it would need to appeal to another trope of critical philosophy (illustrated as we have seen in race and gender theory) namely that the dominant identity (white or male) generally doesn't racialise or gender itself. Rather, it regards itself as the standard according to which others are to be racialised or gendered. If this is true, we could complete Young's picture quite easily: In this sense, discourse doesn't interfere with male embodiment the way it interferes with female embodiment because there is no question to be had about the male subject's birthright to be in the world. The divide between male and female embodiment would therefore be cashed out in terms of self-conscious (female) and unself-conscious (male) embodiment. In fact, Young's emphasis on self-consciousness, shyness and fear seems to pull in this direction. This picture, however, leads into further trouble: it seems undecisive as to whether self-consciousness is the result or the cause of the damaged experience of female embodiment. In a sense, self-consciousness would have to come first insofar as it is only on the basis of such self-consciousness, such lack of confidence, that one can become susceptible to external discourses. If such is the case, self-consciousness seems to precede discourse and this would return us to dubious references to female nature, perhaps even some sort of "eternal feminine" (Beauvoir, 1961). On the other hand, if self-consciousness were to be construed as *the result* of discourses, it becomes hard to understand where this vulnerability to discourses could have come from.

In the second case, the difference between male and female embodiment is not to be cashed out in terms of their vulnerability to discourses, but in

How, then, is a different analysis of the body to proceed?

First, it must avoid the impasse posed by dichotomous accounts of the person which divide the subject into the mutually exclusive categories of mind and body.

Second, corporeality must no longer be associated with one sex (or race), which then takes on the burden of the other's corporeality for it. Women can no longer take on the function of being the body for men while men are left free to soar to the heights of theoretical reflection and cultural production. . . .

Third, it must refuse singular models, models which are based on one type of body as the norm by which all others are judged. A plural, multiple field of possible body "types," no one of which functions as the delegate or representative of the others, must be created.

Fourth, while dualism must be avoided, so too, where possible (though this is not always the case—one is always implicated in essentialism even as one flees it), must biologistic or essentialist accounts of the body. The body must be regarded as a site of social, political, cultural, and geographical inscriptions, production, or constitution. The body is not opposed to culture, a resistant throwback to a natural past; it is itself a cultural, *the* cultural, product. . . .

Fifth, whatever models are developed must demonstrate some sort of internal or constitutive articulation, or even disarticulation, between the biological and the psychological, between the inside and the outside of the body, while avoiding a reductionism of mind to brain. . . .

Sixth, instead of participating in—i.e., adhering to one side or the other of—a binary pair, these pairs can be more readily problematized by regarding the body as the threshold or borderline concept that hov-ers perilously and undecidably at the pivotal point of binary pairs. The body is neither—while also being both—the private or the public, self or other, natural or cultural, psychical or social, instinctive or learned, genetically or environmentally determined.— Elisabeth Grosz, *Volatile Bodies*, pp. 21–23.

terms of the contents of the dominant discourses about masculinity and femininity (i.e., female embodiment would thus be informed by a discourse of impossibility and male embodiment by a discourse of possibility). This solves the problems encountered previously by admitting that members of all genders are susceptible to the interference of discourse, although the result-ing alienation is of different valence. This option, however, seems to drift away from the contention that we find in Young and others that it is not the discourse about women, but the discourse about the body in general, which is responsible for the breaking up of the body-soul union and the resulting and crippling discontinued unity.

It seems either solution leaves us wanting. There is a third option how-ever. This requires that we return to an earlier point: gender-identity is constitutive: it happens to girls *as they learn to live in the world and in their bodies*, not afterwards. This means that by the time a child's ability or critical thinking has been achieved, gender is already there. This means also that we can find a middle way between option one, which involved that discourses as such interfere with embodiment, and option two, which blamed the in-terference on the content of these discourses. It can now be said that the female predicament results from a two-step process: the first step results from a specific discourse-content, namely the implicit order to be self-conscious given by the patriarchy to all girls. This doesn't have to raise the question mentioned earlier, about how discourses make their way into the girl's body-soul relationship, because this relationship is not yet established when this discourse intervenes. This first step, as has been illustrated by many historians of gender, has been articulated in naturalist terms: women must be self-conscious about their bodies because they may be assaulted, they risk becoming pregnant, their sexuality is socially threatening, etc. All of these in their own way are examples of the discourses that achieve the first step: to force women to engage with their bodies not spontaneously, but only via the mediation of discourses.

This, in turn achieves the second step: to make the female experience of life much more dependent on the structures of discourse (for more, see for example Butler, 2005). On the basis of this first step, the second step solidifies the girl's subsequent general vulnerability to *all kinds of discourses*. What all these discourses have in common, in spite of wildly varying contents, is that they all affirm the estrangement of body and soul. To be woman means to live according to the analytical separation of body and soul. This vulnerability to discourses reinforces, accompanies and informs the development of girls and women—their development, as Young would claim, into handicapped subjectivity. Henceforth, it will be part of female embodiment that it must justify, or engage in "female apologetics." This is an important point to bring out of the tradition that links Beauvoir, Sartre and Merleau-Ponty to Foucault and Young, because it provides insight into the importance of discourse analysis in subsequent studies about gender, especially in so-called third-wave feminism.

Third-wave of feminism is hard to define, but at the philosophical level, one of its chief features is the fact that it is organised by the view that, after a first wave focused on women's rights and a second wave focused on deconstructing the contents of patriarchal discourses about femininity, we must recognise that the patriarchal order is grounded not just in *certain* discourses, but in *all* discourses including those seemingly irrelevant to the condition of women. This allows third-wave feminism to interact fruitfully with other analyses of oppression, in particular homophobia and racism, and to accommodate intersectionality easily: the problem is not in contents (which target these group and not those) but in a universal structure. This is a tradition that combines the historicising pathos inherited from Foucault (and Marx) which exposes any claim to universality as false and ideologically motivated, with the emphasis on discourse inherited from second-wave feminism. The systematic combination of these two insights results in the argument that the patriarchy is not best understood as a set of prejudices about men and women, but as a set of wrong habits of thinking.

Elisabeth Grosz uses this approach to address the conundrum described previously. She denies the premise according to which Cartesianism is indeed a pure expression of analytic thinking in order to reject the distinction between the form of discourses and their content. She traces the ideological consequences of the Cartesian view and suggests that clear and distinct ideas do not neutrally reflect the structure of reason as a whole, but rather, that they construct a historical artefact called reason, one which has led to the inability to live a fulfilling life in the world of experience. For Grosz, it is the modern claim that rationality so described is universally representative (and the connected implicit claim that it is universally binding) and normatively neutral which is problematic. So we must think in new categories, and the old categories are (a) not necessary (not grounded in any universal sense of reason), and (b) essentially (and perhaps intentionally) sexist. Whether this third-wave approach appears as a sufficient conclusion, or whether one takes up the related worries about where this leaves the very ability for thinking and communicating, it is interesting to note how tightly this binds the debates around and within feminism with the question of Cartesian dualism, and therefore, with the question of the body: at stake is the way we conceptualise the relations of experience (which is unified) and thought (which abusively analyses this unified experience). The body is the site of both this unity and this separation. It unifies experience insofar as experience is always an experience of the physical world, to which our body gives us access, and yet it is always united with the experience of meaning. Similarly, it is our body that, as the "unmotivated springing forth of the world," generates and initiates the illusory categories of self and non-self, activity and passivity, and body and soul. The very categories that will come to fasten women and racial minorities to their chains.

Discourses normalise. In the case of gender oppression, the deeper point to stress is that once the first step is achieved, the normalisation doesn't even have to come from a discourse about women. Rather, it is discourse itself that reinforces the Cartesian tropes that make a fulfilling sense of embodiment impossible. This allows us to diagnose the deeper disease connected to gender oppression: the condition of women is a symptom of a Western illness, namely, the compulsion to live according to the structures of thought (clear and distinct ideas) and not of experience. As a result, the introduction of discourse as a mediator of our relationship with our own bodies is the basic form of alienation. The result, Young claims, is the girl's "mistrust" in her body (143). And so, the patriarchal prophecy that women's bodies are objects turns out to be self-fulfilling. The female internalisation of the patriarchal structures mandates that they adopt discourse as the middle-man in their relationship to their own body. The patriarchy's basic command to women is this: "don't be spontaneous." No wonder the little girl misses the target.

Further Readings
Judith Butler, *Giving an Account of Oneself.*
Iris Marion Young, *On Female Body Experience*, chapter 3: "Pregnant Embodiment: Subjectivity and Alienation" and chapter 6: "Menstrual Meditations."

Key Ideas

The patriarchy operates by disrupting the woman's spontaneous access to and use of her body.

This disruption is a two-step process: step one involves constituting the girl's subjectivity as susceptible to discourses, the second involves allowing the discursive structure in general to disable the body-soul union.

As a result, the woman's relationship to her body is characterised by mistrust and caution.

This is reflected in women's and girls' movements.

In the West, resolving the metaphysical split of body and soul is the condition for women and girls to live a fulfilled embodied life.

Note

1. This is a common trope in the analyses of exclusion. It animates Beauvoir's analysis of misogyny, Sartre's (1995) account of anti-Semitism, Fanon's (2008) account of racial violence in the colonial context, and Alcoff's (1999) account of racism.

~

Conclusion

The body changes everything. This mere fact, which the West has made every heroic effort at ignoring, dissolving, and avoiding by reducing it to the status of an epistemic disturbance, has now burst into metaphysics, into politics, into morals and into our everyday life in irreversible ways. This book has been tracing a history of thought eager to park the fact of embodiment in one of the nooks left unattended of their worldviews, while every effort has been made to sustain the fiction that the fact of our embodiment, a universal, constant, urgent condition of our life, was simply a quirk. What it found, however, is that this very same history has constantly been informed by the fact of embodiment, as a secret, a bad conscience, a demand, and finally an evidence. But our realisation that the system needed to be turned inside out to place the body as its centre has not completed the trajectory. It would be naïve to believe that the discomfort in which our embodiment throws us is simply the quirk or the sign of some ideological imitation of our canonical elders. This book also attempted to show that the story runs deeper: not just our own, contingent, Western worldview, but no possible worldview can lie comfortable with the fact of embodiment. For embodiment is irreducibly ambiguous, or to put it more simply: it doesn't obey the rules of thinking. The ambiguity of embodiment is not an accident to be corrected, it is a condition of our life.

The story we've been following is complex and rich, like the history which it informed and which informed it. One of the ways we can bring it to clarity is to recall that it is a story that obeys several logics. The first is the academic logic of professional philosophy. This is a logic motivated by a race to the best account. The second is the logic of history. This is a logic motivated by a constant process of reassignment of meanings and of emphases determined by contingent developments. The third is an existential logic. This is a logic in which the move from one conception of the body to another is mediated by existential discomfort and in which new ways to think of the body coincide with new ways to live in them, new discomforts. Plato was struck by how newborns were moving as if possessed, in compulsive spasms. Infants, he said, "would go forwards and backwards, then back and forth to the right and the left, and upwards and downwards, wandering every which way" (*Timaeus* 43b–c). The soul, Plato tells us, is too big for the small body in which it was born and it pushes and beats against the limits imposed by the body, trying to invest every part of it, irrigate it with life, and find some room to bloom. In terms of the existential logic, the history of the Western philosophical treatment of the body chronicles, on a civilisational scale, the spasms that endlessly seek for body and soul to make a home in and with each other. This is a history informed by the quest for a comfortable way to match the way we live in our body with the way we think about embodiment. The history of Western philosophy appears as a long and slow process of wriggling our body into place, one not unlike your instinctive movements when settling on your new sofa or in a new shirt.

In all three of these dynamics, some patterns emerge. In terms of the academic logic of philosophical debate, the chief pattern is an oscillation between intellectualism, which presupposes that mental structures are disclosive of the world, and experience, which violates these mental structures. This has a normative side, of course, for intellectualism also has an ethical dimension: it pre-establishes normative demands *a priori*. It has a political side too, for the notion of sovereignty is nothing but one such presupposition of perfection, the notion of a perfect power. Fundamentally, in both the metaphysical and the normative context, we see the temptation to posit a notion of perfection a priori as a standard for the world and for action. The fact of embodiment shatters this notion of perfection by demonstrating that in an embodied world, limitation disrupts any discourse of perfection, and renders the claims of the contingent insurmountable: norms now demand to be adjusted to experience, perfection needs to choose between being perfect but abstract or imperfect but concrete. What becomes out of the question, however, is the claim that a world without the imperfections brought about by the body is possible at all. With the body, notions of metaphysical perfection, moral purity and political sovereignty all come crashing down under the weight of their own contradictions. The philosophical movement, therefore, the constantly recurring debate around the body, is always this: an attempt to explain embodiment away on the basis of a transcendental factum fails. Rather, embodiment becomes the central factum on the basis of which the abstractions once presupposed are rejected. With these abstractions, an entire edifice collapses. Talk of essences, of purity, of ideals and of imperatives all become suspicious.

The historical pattern we observe corresponds to a constant struggle between the recognition of the fact of embodiment and the strategies deployed to neuter that fact, cover it up, or deny it. I hope to have begun to show that the results are dire. This ignorance of the fact of embodiment motivates untenable discourses of sovereignty, impossible and contradictory moral demands and most importantly, it constructs unliveable identities. For as we saw, it is the basic form of embodiment as a self-falsification, a unity that presents itself as a duality, or as Merleau-Ponty calls it, an "unmotivated springing forth of the world" that institutes the illusion of an in-itself-for-us and that thereby lends itself to all sorts of abuse. This is a view that recognises that our ownership of our own body is porous. Our body exposes us to alienation: in our childhood, it offers us to the other before we even take possession of it ourselves, it constantly reminds us that we own it, that we are it, and yet it constantly slips away by inducing the illusion that there are distinct subjects and objects, and that "we" belong to the former and they belong to the latter. Our bodies are "us" enough that we cannot bear to let them slip away from us; but they are independent of us enough that we regain them only via discourses. Discourses that we can only appeal to if we abide by them. As a result, the possibility for a life is dependent on the permission to live. We only acquire our body by accepting a fiction about ourselves and a fiction about it. The lot of the embodied subject is to live in this ambiguous relation with themselves: because we are embodied, we can never really hold ourselves in our grasp. This irreducible possibility to lose our own body is the space in which power rushes in to rule us.

Finally, this takes us to the third dynamic at play, the existential dynamic. It is this porosity of our body, this impossibility to take full ownership of ourselves, this daylight that always exists within ourselves that become the battlefield of history. It is through this non-coincidence that we are subjected to the winds of history. It is through them that history makes us members of our time, and this means, repressed, anxious and oppressed in our epoch's own special way. More urgently, it is through this daylight that the historical choices that determine who is racialised, who is gendered and how, and who shall be oppressed, make their way into our existence. This is not a desperate situation, but it is one that requires another form of ethics, one that wouldn't rely on the univocity of principles and moral standards. This is the question mark we now must deal with. I hope this book allowed us to think about the stakes of our relation to our body, perhaps to understand better the place and the weight of history in our embodied lives, and to begin to see where the intellectual battle lines and fault lines lie. If this is the case, we must congratulate ourselves by asking the next questions. The following few pages of apparatus are my invitation for you to take this next step.

~

Glossary

Affordance   In the context of the ecological approach to perception (chapter 8), an affordance is a set of possibilities that an object makes available to an organism. Gibson explains them in terms of "surfaces" insofar as these possibilities are made present to an organism that is external to it via its surface, "values" insofar as affordances are understood in terms of what they're usable or "good" for, and "meanings" insofar as objects only mean something to us if they afford anything to us and vice versa.

Alienation   The paradoxical experience of being estranged from what belongs to us or what we belong to. The theory of alienation begins with Marx (chapter 10), who points out that under capitalism, workers are estranged from themselves, from each other, from the objects they create and from nature. In the context of embodiment, alienation mostly emphasises that although we belong to our body and our body belongs to us, we also experience our body as an external object, one that we must compromise with. This enables the exercise of a host of powers that take advantage of this self-estrangement to intervene in a subject's relationship to themselves (see chapters 11 and 12).

Ambiguity   A phenomenon is ambiguous when it doesn't fit conceptual categories. The main way this occurs is when a phenomenon involves the unity of two objects that can only be conceived as distinct. In this sense, ambiguity in general has to do with the co-existence of identity and difference. In the case of embodiment, the mutual inherence of the body and the soul, which experience and perception testify to, but which

concepts regard as distinct, suggests that the resulting psycho-somatic being (i.e., ourselves) is ambiguous. The response of philosophy to ambiguity
is generally either to disqualify the ambiguous phenomenon or to revise
the conceptual categories that the phenomenon falsifies. In the case of
the body, we can recognise the first strategy in Cartesian dualism and the
subsequent reductionist strategies (reduction of the body to the soul in
idealism and of the soul to the body in materialism and physicalism); and
the second in later phenomenology, existentialism and embodied cognition (chapters 4, 5, 6, 7 and 8).

Bio-power In Foucault and his followers (including Agamben), bio-power
is defined as the power over life. It also characterises a certain era in the
exercise of power which coincides roughly with the modern era. It is
contrasted to the earlier era of the right of death. The difference between
right over death and bio-power is not merely in their objects. It is also a
different kind of power. The power over death is able to *bring about* (Foucault says "create") its object (death). The power over life cannot produce
its object (life), for life only occurs through natural means. Where power
over death creates, power over life *manages* life once it occurs. It does so
by organising the factors that favour or discourage fertility (the production
of life) and the biological lives of the subjects too. Bio-power is therefore
a less sovereign kind of power, but also one that requires a wider range of
procedures for its implementation. Eventually, the number and extent of
these procedures tends to coincide with the whole of the social norms and
structures in a society. It is therefore less absolute than the right of death,
but more total and all-encompassing (chapters 9, 10 and 11).

Body Politic The expression "body politic" is generally used in two senses
(chapter 9). In the first sense it refers to the whole of the society or polity
and it is meant to emphasis the solidarity between its members. It pro-
motes the idea that a society is an organic whole where everyone depends
on all. In the second, restricted sense, it refers to a mystical second body
possessed by individual kings, one that is withdrawn from the contingent
world. This mystical body doesn't die and is passed from one king to their
successor. This allows societies to achieve stability that exceeds the life
span of individual kings whose body natural, unlike their body politic, is
subject to illness and death.

Constitution In phenomenology, the constitution of an intentional object
is the process through which it becomes taken as an entity independent
from the subject (chapters 5 and 6). In the context of embodiment, constitution may result in the belief in the objective character of our body

(chapters 7 and 8), or in the attribution or self-attribution of a sexual, racial or gender identity (chapters 11 and 12).

Dualism   The metaphysical view that all existing objects are reducible to one of two basic substances, neither of which is further reducible. In the most famous, Cartesian version of dualism, the two substances are body ("res extensa") and mind ("res cogitans") (chapter 4). All dualistic metaphysics are exposed to questions concerning the possible interaction and commensurability between the two substances.

Eleatic Principle   Named after the Eleatic Stranger in Plato's *Sophist* (248c) (chapter 2), the Eleatic principle stipulates that things exist if they entertain causal relations with other existing things. In the context of embodiment, this suggests that any strict dualism will have to admit two ways for things to exist as long as the two basic substances must be said to both exist and be unable to entertain causal relations with each other. If we recognise that they act upon each other, this suggests that they share the same kind of existence, and this threatens to undermine dualism.

Enactivism   The view that "perception is something we do" (Noë, chapter 8). To perceive requires action and movement, and therefore a series of skills that can be learned. The basic skill in question is the skill of knowing how to live in one's body, or knowing how to use one's body for adequate perception. This opens up to an entire account of the world of experience defined as a context for action.

Existential   Relative to the qualitative experience of being a unity of body and soul.

Fall (of the soul)   Starting with Plato's *Phaedrus*, the theme of the Fall of the soul is an attempt at explaining the existence of the spatio-temporal world. Plato suggests that for each individual, their soul fell into their body. This suggests that the Fall is both the fall into one's body and the fall into the spatio-temporal world. The connotations related to the word "fall" naturally indicate that this is a regrettable event, which involves some sort of moral demotion for the fallen individual, and therefore some sort of imperfection. This leads Plato himself and his followers to debate whether the Fall into a body is the result of an imperfection of the soul, or whether it is the body itself which is responsible for imperfection in the world. In either case, this forces Plato to acknowledge that imperfection coincides with embodiment and that it is irreducible, thereby acknowledging that embodiment too is irreducible (chapters 2 and 3).

Flesh   Although this is a term with a long history, beginning in the Gospel and in Paul's commentaries, and pursued in Merleau-Ponty's later works, the notion of flesh indicates the body as involved in qualitative experiences. The flesh, unlike the body in the strict sense, can suffer, enjoy and desire. The notion of flesh in the literal sense suggests a certain thickness (as one might talk of flesh for meat, the flesh of a fish or of a plum). This thickness brings out that the flesh is two-sided: it enables qualitative experiences because in it both the owner of the flesh and the object touched by it are experienced at once.

Forms In Plato, the Forms, or ideas, are the universal models of spatio-temporal objects. As such, they are not spatio-temporal. They represent the perfection which the corresponding spatio-temporal objects fail to achieve. In the context of embodiment, Plato's theory of Forms is confronted with the necessity to take seriously that not all things that exist can have a perfect form: in particular, it looks like imperfection exists, suggesting that there are real things without a perfect form. Since the existence of imperfection is testified by the irreducibility of the body, Plato's theory of forms trips over the fact of embodiment (chapter 2).

Gestalt Literally, a form. *Gestalt theorie* is a psychological account of perception. It shows experimentally that perception is not the result of a process whereby sensations become ordered into graspable objects of perception, but rather, that the object appears to us immediately as a recognisable object. The form (or structure) of an object, which makes it understandable, graspable and recognisable, is not the result of any act of the mind. This suggests that there is no passive moment in perception, and that bodies directly interact with meanings and values (chapters 6, 7 and 8).

"In-itself-for-us" For Merleau-Ponty, who borrows the expression from Sartre, the problem of an in-itself-for-us is the problem of explaining why we take our perceptions to yield not percepts but objects taken to be independent from perception. For Merleau-Ponty, this doesn't prove that there are any such independent objects, but rather, it reveals a basic structure of our body: it is part of the body's essence to create the illusion of objectivity. We must therefore move from defining the body as a force of perception to defining it as a force of interpretation (chapter 7).

Intentionality In phenomenology, intentionality is the property that consciousness possesses of being "about" objects. Consciousness "intends" objects in the sense that it only exists (we are only "conscious") when we are conscious of something else. This means that self-consciousness takes the self to be other, and that any experience of being conscious presupposes a world (something that the consciousness is not). If the body is to be defined as intentional, then we must also define the body in reference to the world (chapters 5 and 6).

Irreducibility For the body to be irreducible means that it cannot be explained in terms of other entities (for example, in terms of the mind), and that it cannot be explained away (for example in terms of illusions). To say that the body is irreducible is the same as saying that it is positive.

Körper The body as an object, reducible to its objective features (temperature, measurements, etc). Although the expression *Körper* comes later, Cartesianism only admits bodies as *Körper*. Anything beyond this is part of the soul (chapters 5 and 6).

Leib The body as a subject and object of qualitative experience. As *Leib*, the body is indistinguishable from the subject. "Flesh" is sometimes used to translate *Leib* (chapters 5 and 6).

"Living according to Man" In Saint Augustine, living according to man is the definition of Evil. To live according to man means living as if the individual which we are is an end in itself. It involves the illusion that the individual is not part of god, and therefore "living according to man" is the opposite of "living according to god." Although the moral failing related to "living according to man" is spiritual—it involves *thinking* that our individuation is fundamental when in fact it is accidental—it is involved with embodiment because the body is nothing but this contingent spatio-temporal localisation called individuation.

Meaning Meaning is whatever understanding interacts with. To be understood or understandable is to have meaning. In the context of phenomenology and the ecological approach to perception, the body's nature is to interact with meanings: affordances, values (see above, Affordances) and objects-for-us interpreted as objects-in-themselves (see in-itself-for-us). This suggests that the body should be understood as a faculty of interpretation (chapter 7).

Mechanism The claim that bodies—living or dead—can be explained without any reference to qualitative experience, to life or to the soul. A mechanistic account contends that an account of the body is complete when all objective features in this body have been recorded. In mereological terms, mechanism regards bodies as nothing but the sum of their parts. Consequently, mechanism denies that *organisation* is relevant to the account of the body. As a result, a dead body is no different from a living body, and *Körper*, not *Leib*, is the proper definition of the body. As we saw in Descartes, mechanism encounters problems when it comes to explaining the inherence of the soul to the body mechanistically conceived (chapter 4).

Normalisation In Foucault, the processes by which individuals are made "normal"—that is, predictable and controllable. Normalisation is an instance of micro-power because it doesn't involve constraint and because it takes place during the personal development of each individual. It allows power to become internalised and to apply itself with the consent and active participation of the subject themselves. Normalisation, therefore, takes place during the process of identity and subjectivity-acquisition. It makes it all the more potent in maintaining people (including racialised minorities, sexual minorities and women) in a subjugated position (chapters 10–12).

Perception Sensation + meaning = perception. Unlike sensations, the objects of perceptions are recognisable entities (e.g., tables and chairs). In this sense, perception gives you access to an intelligible world of objects and possibilities. Whether perceptions result from a certain processing of sensations (as in transcendental idealism) or whether perception is immediate (as in later phenomenology and Gestalt theory) is an open debate, but it is worth noting that the first option tends to lead into the dualism of body and mind and the second tends to lean towards non-dualism (chapters 5–8).

Perfection The notion of perfection was made crucial by Platonism and then again by Christianity, which used it as a way of defining god. They define perfection as the unity of all attributes. This means that perfection unifies all that exists, and consequently, that there is no positivity to imperfection: ugliness is simply the absence of beauty, evil the absence of goodness, non-existence the failure of existence. In the context of embodiment, spatio-temporal localisation is seen as a mere imperfection (a limitation in time and space) and is thus reducible. The fact of embodiment conflicts with the metaphysics of perfection because it makes existence and perfection incompatible. One can maintain that the body doesn't exist and that the spatio-temporal is a mere illusion. If that is so, there is imperfection in the world, in the form of illusion. Or one may maintain that the body does exist but in a different mode than non-spatio-temporal entities (god or the forms). But one cannot hold both at a time. The irreducibility of the body therefore appears to the Platonist as an obstacle to the theory of forms and to the Christian as a limitation of god.

Phenomenology The philosophy that seeks to account for the world and the self as they are experienced. This does admit accounting for objects that are beyond perception but only insofar as our interaction with them is mediated by experience (e.g.: the experience of belief, or imagination). As a result, phenomenology tends to emphasise the fact that the world of experience is the world of the body, and therefore to regard the body as the true subject of experience.

Power (and micro-power)   Power is whatever generates obedience. As such it is distinct from constraint or force and it appeals to "freedom" (Foucault, chapter 10). It is not the kind of domination that denies or represses freedom, but the kind that collaborates with the free individual and coopts her freedom. It does so either by organising behaviors through incentives (think of the way the design of seats on a bus incentivise certain ways of sitting for example), or, most importantly, through influencing the formation of the subjects in ways that produce reliable and predictable subjects (see Normalisation). Since subjects use their freedom to act on their will and desires, power shapes these wills and desires by shaping who they think they are, by shaping their identity. This relies on a number of minimal acts of power that take place in the minute evolution of an individual into a subject, hence, Foucault and his tradition often refer to it as "micro-power." In the case of embodiment, the main way embodied subjectivities (like racialised or gendered ones) are created is through the intervention of micro-power in the relations between one's soul and their body (chapters 10–12).

Sensation   Perception – meaning = sensation. Sensations could be defined as the events that take place at the level of sensory organs. Whether sensations truly occur and provide the basic content further organised by the ego or the soul (as in transcendental idealism) or whether they are only retroactive illusions that we imagine when we analyse perceptions (as in *Gestalt theorie* and later phenomenology) is an open debate (see Perception) (chapters 5–7).

Union (of body and soul)   Descartes describes the human person as a union of body and soul. Yet, Cartesian dualism cannot provide an account of this union. In order to do so, it would have to establish some commensurability between the two substances. This commensurability presupposes at least one point of encounter between body and soul, and this point would have to belong to both—that is, it would have to be psycho-somatic. This is banned by dualism which establishes a principle of mutual exclusion between the physical and the spiritual. As a result, the human person as it experiences itself—that is, as a union—becomes an enigma. In fact, experience in general, which involves both the body (for sensing) and the mind (for understanding), becomes impossible to explain (chapter 4). Contemporary philosophy of mind refers to this problem as the problem of the "explanatory gap," or the "hard problem of consciousness."

"Unmotivated springing forth of the world"—Merleau-Ponty argues that the world's mode of being is self-presentation: in the case of the world, to be is to appear. This appearing means that the world springs forth for no external cause (for the world contains all causes). The way that this springing forth takes place is called the body. Since the world doesn't exist outside of this springing forth, Merleau-Ponty concludes that the body is the springing forth of the world. This makes the world and the body undistinguishable, and it leads Merleau-Ponty to think of the body as an act and not as an entity (chapter 7).

~

Bibliography

Readings (Recapitulative)

Agamben, Giorgio. (1998). *Homo Sacer, Sovereign Power and Bare Life*. (trans. Heller-Roazen). Stanford, CA: Stanford University Press.

Alcoff, Linda Martín. (1999). "Towards a Phenomenology of Racial Embodiment." *Radical Philosophy* 95: 15–26.

Augustine. (2001). *Genesis, against the Manichees*. (trans. Teske). Washington, DC: Catholic University of America Press.

Augustine. (2004). *The City of God*. (trans. Bettenson). London: Penguin.

Augustine. (2008). *Confessions*. (trans. Chadwick). Oxford: Oxford University Press.

Augustine. (1991–2019). Letter to Marcellinus, *The Works of Saint Augustine. A Translation for the 21st Century*. John E. Rotelle et al. (eds.). New York: New City Press.

Descartes, René. (2007). *Meditations on First Philosophy, With Selections from the Objections and Replies*. (trans.Cottingham). Cambridge: Cambridge University Press.

Descartes, René. (1640, 24 December). Letter to Mersenne, Bennett. (trans.) https://www.earlymoderntexts.com/assets/pdfs/descartes1619_1.pdf.

Descartes, René. (2000). *Treatise on the Passions*. In *Philosophical Essays and Correspondence*, Roger Ariew, ed. Indianapolis: Hackett.

Descartes, René. (2004). *The World and Other Writings*. (trans. Gaukroger). Cambridge: Cambridge University Press.

Descartes, René, and Elisabeth of Bohemia. (2007). *The Correspondence between Princess Elisabeth of Bohemia and René Descartes*. (ed. and trans. Shapiro). Chicago: University of Chicago Press.

Fanon, Frantz. (2008). *Black Skin, White Masks*. (trans. Philcox). New York: Grove Press.

Foucault, Michel. (1990). *The History of Sexuality, Volume I: An Introduction*. (trans. Hurley). New York: Vintage.

Freud, Sigmund. (2001). *Totem and Taboo*. (trans. Strachey). New York: Routledge.

Gibson, James. (1979/1986). *The Ecological Approach to Visual Perception*. Hillside, NJ: Erlbaum.

Grosz, Elisabeth. (1994). *Volatile Bodies: Towards a Corporeal Feminism*. Indianapolis: Indiana University Press.

Hurley, Susan. (2001). "Perception and Action: Alternative Views." *Synthese* 129: 3–40.

Husserl, Edmund. (1989). *Ideas Pertaining to a Pure Phenomenology and to a Phenomenological Philosophy: Second Book: Studies in the Phenomenology of Constitution*. (trans. Rojcewicz and Schuwer). Dordrecht: Springer, 1989.

Kantorowicz, Ernst. (1997). *The King's Two Bodies: A Study in Mediaeval Political Theology*. Princeton: Princeton University Press.

Marx, Karl. (2007). *The Economic and Philosophical Manuscripts of 1844*. (trans. Milligan). London: Dover Publications.

Merleau-Ponty, Maurice. (2012). *Phenomenology of Perception*. (trans. Landes). New York: Routledge.

Noë, Alva. (2004). *Action in Perception*. Cambridge: MIT Press.

Plato. (1997). *Cratylus*. 399a–400d (trans. Reeve), in Plato, *Complete Works*, John Cooper. (Ed.). Indianapolis: Hackett.

Plato. (1997). *Phaedo* (trans. Grube), in Plato, *Complete Works*, John Cooper. (Ed.). Indianapolis: Hackett 69e-72d and 95a-104c.

Plato. (1997). *Phaedrus* (trans. Woodruff and Nehamas), in Plato, *Complete Works*, John Cooper. (Ed.). Indianapolis: Hackett 246a-250d.

Rousseau, Jean-Jacques. (2018). *The Social Contract and Other Late Political Writings*. Cambridge: Cambridge University Press.

Young, Iris Marion. (1980). "Throwing Like a Girl: A Phenomenology of Feminine Body Comportment Motility and Spatiality." *Human Studies* 3: 137–56.

Additional Readings (Recapitulative)

Aristotle, *Physics*. (1984). (trans. Hardie and Gaye) in *The Complete Works of Aristotle*, Jonathan Barnes. (ed.). Princeton: Princeton University Press.

Aristotle, *On the Soul*. (1984). (trans. Ackrill), in *The Complete Works of Aristotle*, Jonathan Barnes. (ed.) Princeton: Princeton University Press.

Augustine. (1991–2019). *On Free Choice of the Will, On the Trinity, Letters*. In *The Works of Saint Augustine: A Translation for the 21st Century*, John E. Rotelle et al. (eds.). New York: New City Press.

Bermúdez, José Luis. (1995). "Ecological Perception and the Notion of a Nonconceptual Point of View." In *The Body and the Self*, Jose Luis Bermúdez, Anthony J. Marcel and Naomi M. Eilan (eds.), 153–73. Cambridge: MIT Press.

Bluck, R. S. (1958). "The *Phaedrus* and Reincarnation." *The American Journal of Philology* 79, no. 2: 156–64.

Butler, Judith. (1993). *Bodies That Matter: On the Discursive Limits of Sex*. New York: Routledge.

Butler, Judith. (2005). *Giving an Account of Oneself*. New York: Fordham University Press.

Descartes, René. (1998). *Discourse on Method*. (trans. Cress). Indianapolis: Hackett.

Descartes, René. (2001). *Dioptrics in Discourse on Method, Optics, Geometry, and Meteorology*. (trans. Olscamp). Indianapolis: Hackett.

Dodd, James. (1997). *Idealism and Corporeity: An Essay on the Problem of the Body in Husserl's Phenomenology*. Dordrecht: Kluwer Academic Publishers.

Dreyfus, Hubert. (2014). *Skillful Coping: Essays on the Phenomenology of Everyday Perception and Action*. Oxford: Oxford University Press.

Fortescue, John. (1997). "The Governance of England." In *On the Laws and Governance of England*, Shelly Lockwood (ed.). Cambridge: Cambridge University Press.

Genesis Ch. 2. In Prickett and Carroll. (trans.). *The Bible: Authorized King James Translation*, Oxford University Press, Oxford and New York, 2014.

Harding, Sandra. (1991). *Whose Science? Whose Knowledge?: Thinking from Women's Lives*. Ithaca, NY: Cornell University Press.

Hobbes, Thomas. (1839–1845). *De Corpore/On the Body*. In *The English Works of Thomas Hobbes*, Molesworth. (ed.). London: John Bohn.

Hunter, D.G. (2012). "Augustine on the Body." In *A Companion to Augustine*, M. Vessey (Ed.). London: Blackwell.

Husserl, Edmund. (1982). *Ideas Pertaining to a Pure Phenomenology and to a Phenomenological Philosophy*. Vol. 1. (trans. Kersten). Den Haag: Nijhoff/Springer.

James, William. (1983). *Principles of Psychology*. Cambridge, MA: Harvard University Press.

John of Salisbury. (1990). *Policraticus: Of the Frivolities of Courtiers and the Footprints of Philosophers*. Cambridge: Cambridge University Press.

Köhler, Wolfgang. (1969). *The Task of Gestalt Psychology*. Princeton, NJ: Princeton University Press.

Malebranche, Nicolas. (1997). *Dialogues on Metaphysics and on Religion*. (Jolley and Scott, trans.). Cambridge and New York: Cambridge University Press.

Mauss, Marcel. (1973). "Techniques of the Body." Economy and Society, 2:1, pp. 70-88.

McGibbon, D. D. (1964) "The Fall of the Soul in Plato's Phaedrus." *The Classical Quarterly*, vol. 14, no. 1, pp. 56–63.

Merleau-Ponty, Maurice. (1964). "The Philosopher and His Shadow." In *Signs*,. (trans. McCleary). Evanston IL: Northwestern University Press.

Merleau-Ponty, Maurice. (1968). *The Visible and the Invisible*. (trans. Lingis). Evanston, IL: Northwestern University Press.

Merleau-Ponty, Maurice. (2002). *The Incarnate Subject: Malebranche, Biran, and Bergson on the Union of Body and Soul*. (Milan, trans.). Amherst, NY: Humanity Books.

Mills, Charles. (2007). "White Ignorance." In Tuana and Sullivan. (Eds). *Race and Epistemologies of Ignorance*. Albany: SUNY Press, pp. 11–39.

Nightingale, Andrea. (2011). *Once Out of Nature: Augustine on Time and the Body*. Chicago: Chicago University Press.

O'Connell, R. (1963). "The Plotinian Fall of the Soul in St. Augustine." *Traditio*, 19, pp. 1–35.

Oksenberg Rorty, Amélie. (1992). "Descartes on Thinking with the Body." In J. Cottingham. (Ed.). *The Cambridge Companion to Descartes*, pp. 371-392. Cambridge: Cambridge University Press.

Plato. (1997). *Symposium* (Nehamas and Woodruff, trans.); *Gorgias* (Zeyl, trans.); *Republic* (Grube and Reeve, trans.); *Sophist* (trans. White) in Plato, *Complete Works*, John Cooper. (Ed.) Indianapolis: Hackett.

Plotinus. (2017). *Plotinus: The Enneads*. (trans. G. Boys-Stones, J. Dillon, R. King, A. Smith, & J. Wilberding) in L. Gerson. (Ed.). Cambridge: Cambridge University Press.

Sartre, Jean-Paul. (2012). *Saint Genet, Comedian and Martyr*. (trans. Frechtman). Minneapolis: University of Minnesota Press.

Shakespeare, William. (2008). *The Tragedy of Coriolanus*. Oxford: Oxford University Press.

Shapiro, Lisa. (1999). "Princess Elizabeth and Descartes: The Union of Mind and Body and the Practice of Philosophy." *British Journal for the History of Philosophy* 7(3): 503–20.

Varela, Francisco, Evan Thompson, and Eleanor Rosch. (1991). *The Embodied Mind: Cognitive Science and Human Experience*. Cambridge: MIT Press.

Zahavi, Dan. (1994). "Husserl's Phenomenology of the Body." *Études Phénoménologiques* no. 19: 63–84.

Zoller, Colleen P. (2019). Plato and the Body: Reconsidering Socratic Asceticism. Albany: SUNY Press.

Works Cited

Beauvoir, Simone de. (1961). *The Second Sex*. (trans. Borde and Malovany-Chevallier). New York: Grune and Stratton.

Bettini, Maurizio. (2014). *Elogio del politeismo. Quello che possiamo imparare dalle religioni antiche*. Bologna: Il Mulino.

Bodin, Jean. (1955). *Six Books on the Commonwealth*. (trans. Tooley). Oxford: Blackwell.

Chemero, Anthony, and Stephan Käufer. (2016). "Pragmatism, Phenomenology, and Extended Cognition." In *Pragmatism and Embodied Cognitive Science: From Bodily Interaction to Symbolic Articulation*, Madzia and M. Jung. (eds.). Berlin: De Gruyter.

Gallagher, Shaun. (2005). *How the Body Shapes the Mind*. Oxford: Oxford University Press.

Gallagher, Shaun. (2009). "Philosophical Antecedents of Situated Cognition." In P. Robbins and M. Aydede. (eds.), pp. 35–51. *The Cambridge Handbook of Situated Cognition.* Cambridge: Cambridge University Press.

Goldstein, Kurt. (1939). *The Organism: A Holistic Approach to Biology Derived from Pathological Data in Man.* New York: American Book Company.

Hobbes, Thomas. (1996). *Leviathan.* Cambridge: Cambridge University Press.

Kant, Immanuel. (1999). *Critique of Pure Reason.* (trans. Guyer and Wood). Cambridge: Cambridge University Press.

Lefort, Claude. (1986). *The Political Forms of Modern Society: Bureaucracy, Democracy, Totalitarianism.* (trans. Thompson). Cambridge: MIT Press.

Locke, John. (1999). *Two Treatises of Government.* Cambridge: Cambridge University Press.

Mace, W. M. (2015). Introduction in J.J. Gibson. (1979/2015). *The Ecological Approach to Visual Perception.* New York: Psychology Press.

Marenbon, John. (2015). *Pagans and Philosophers. The Problem of Paganism from Augustine to Leibniz.* Princeton, NJ: Princeton University Press.

Marx, Karl, and Engels, Friedrich (2002). *The Communist Manifesto,* (trans. Jones). London and New York: Penguin Classics.

Nietzsche, Friedrich. (1967). *The Will to Power,* (trans. Kauffmann). London, Vintage.

Noë, Alva. (2015). *Strange Tools, Art and Human Nature.* New York: Hill and Wang.

Plato. (1997) *Timaeus.* (trans. Zeyl). in Plato, *Complete Works,* John Cooper. (Ed.) Indianapolis and Cambridge: Hackett.

Rawls, John. (1971). *A Theory of Justice.* Cambridge: Harvard University Press.

St. Paul. (2014). *Letter to the Corinthians,* in Prickett and Carroll. (trans.). *The Bible: Authorized King James Translation.* Oxford: Oxford University Press, 2014.

Sartre, Jean-Paul. (1995). *Anti-Semite and Jew: An Exploration of the Etiology of Hate.* (trans. Becker). New York: Schocken.

Straus, Erwin. *The Upright Posture: Phenomenological Psychology.* New York: Basic Books, 1966.

Tagore, Rabindranath. (1916/2005). *The Home and the World.* (trans. Tagore). New York: Penguin.

Tambornino, John. (1999). "Locating the Body: Corporeality and Politics in Hannah Arendt." *Journal of Political Philosophy* 7: 172–90.

van Mazijk, Corijn. (2020). *Perception and Reality in Kant, Husserl and McDowell.* New York: Routledge.

Weber, Max. (2004). *The Vocation Lectures.* (Eds. Tracy Strong and David Owen, trans. Rodney Livingstone). Indianapolis: Hackett.

Wittgenstein, Ludwig. (1969). *On Certainty/Über Gewissheit.* (trans. Paul and Anscombe). London and Oxford: Blackwell.

Additional Sources

Other Classical Texts

Arendt, Hannah. (1958). *The Human Condition*. Chicago: Chicago University Press.

Bachelard, Gaston. (2014). *The Poetics of Space*. (trans. Jolas). New York: Penguin.

Bailey, Cyril. (1926). *Epicurus: The Extant Remains*. Oxford: Clarendon Press.

Bloch, Marc. (2015). *The Royal Touch, Sacred Monarchy and Scrofula in England and France*. (trans. Anderson). Abingdon: Routledge.

Butler, Judith. (1990). *Gender Trouble: Feminism and the Subversion of Identity*. New York: Routledge.

Butler, Judith. (2004). *Undoing Gender*. New York: Routledge.

Canguilhem, Georges. (2012). *On the Normal and the Pathological*. (trans. Fawcett). Dordrecht: Reidel.

Chalmers, David. (1996). *The Conscious Mind*. Oxford: Oxford University Press.

Clark, Andy. (1997). *Being There: Putting Brain, Body and World Together Again*. Cambridge: MIT Press.

Fanon, Frantz. (1963). *The Wretched of the Earth*. (trans. Farrington). New York: Grove Press.

Fichte, Johann Gottlieb. (1994). *Introductions to the Wissenschaftslehre and Other Writings*. (trans. Breazeale). Indianapolis: Hackett.

Foucault, Michel. (1995). *Discipline and Punish: The Birth of the Prison*. (trans. Sheridan). New York: Vintage.

Foucault, Michel. (2005). *Hermeneutics of the Subject: Lectures at the Collège de France, 1981–1982*. (trans. Burchell). New York: Picador.

Frazer, James George. (2009). *The Golden Bough, A Study in Magic and Religion*. Oxford and New York: Oxford University Press.

Gallagher, Shaun. (2005). *How the Body Shapes the Mind*. Oxford: Oxford University Press.

Gallagher, Shaun, and Zahavi, Dan. (2008). *The Phenomenological Mind: An Introduction to Philosophy of Mind and Cognitive Science*. New York: Routledge.

Heidegger, Martin. (2008). *Being and Time*. (trans. MacQuarrie and Robinson). New York: Harper and Row.

Kant, Immanuel. (1999). *Critique of Pure Reason*. (trans. Guyer and Wood). Cambridge: Cambridge University Press.

Levinas, Emmanuel. (1969). *Totality and Infinity*. (trans. Lingis). Pittsburgh: Duquesne University Press.

Machiavelli, Niccolò. (2019). *The Prince*. (trans. Price.). Cambridge: Cambridge University Press.

Maine de Biran, Pierre. (1929/1970). *The Influence of Habit on the Faculty of Thinking*. (trans. Donaldson Boehm). Philadelphia: Williams and Wilkins.

Merleau-Ponty, Maurice. (1983). *The Structure of Behavior*. (trans. Fisher). Pittsburgh: Duquesne University Press.

Merleau-Ponty, Maurice. (1993). *Eye and Mind.* (trans. Smith) in Johnson. (Ed.). *The Merleau-Ponty Aesthetics Reader.* Evanston, IL: Northwestern University Press.

Nietzsche, Friedrich. (2005). *Thus Spoke Zarathustra.* (trans. Parkes). Oxford: Oxford University Press.

Nietzsche, Friedrich. (2006). *On the Genealogy of Morality.* (trans. Diethe). Cambridge: Cambridge University Press.

Noë, Alva. (2012). *Varieties of Presence.* Cambridge, MA: Harvard University Press.

Origen. (1936, 1973). *First Principles.* (trans. Butterworth). Gloucester, MA: Peter Smith.

Ravaisson, Félix. (2008). *Of Habit.* (trans. Carlisle and Sinclair). London: Bloomsbury.

Sartre, Jean-Paul. (2018). *Being and Nothingness: An Essay on Phenomenological Ontology.* (trans. Richmond). Abingdon: Routledge.

Spinoza, Baruch. (2018). *Ethics.* (trans. Silverthorne). Cambridge: Cambridge University Press.

St. Paul. (2014). *Epistles to the Corinthians, Galatians, Romans,* in Prickett and Carroll. (trans.). *The Bible: Authorized King James Translation.* Oxford: University Press, 2014.

Stein, Edith. (1989). *On the Problem of Empathy.* (trans. Stein). Washington, DC: ICS Publications.

Thompson, Evan. (2007). *Mind in Life: Biology, Phenomenology, and the Sciences of Mind.* Cambridge, MA: Harvard University Press.

General Reference

Blackman, Lisa. (2008). *The Body: The Key Concepts.* New York: Berg.

Corbin, Alain, Jean-Jacques Courtine and Georges Vigarello. (eds.). (2005–2006). *Histoire du corps.* Paris: Seuil.

Grosz, Elisabeth. (1995). *Space, Time and Perversions: Essays on the Politics of Bodies.* New York: Routledge.

Lock, Margaret, and Judith Farquhar. (eds.). (2007). *Beyond the Body Proper.* Durham, NC: Duke University Press.

Ruberg, Willemijn. (2019). *History of the Body.* New York: Red Globe Press.

Smith, Justin. (ed.). (2017). *Embodiment: A History.* Oxford: Oxford University Press.

Weiss, Gail, and Honi Fern Haber. (eds.). (1999). *Perspectives on Embodiment: The Intersections of Nature and Culture.* New York: Routledge.

Welton, Donn. (1998). *Body and Flesh: A Philosophical Reader.* Oxford : Blackwell.

Aesthetics

Johnson, Mark. (2007). *The Meaning of the Body: Aesthetics of Human Understanding.* Chicago: University of Chicago Press.

Sobchack, Vivian. (2004). *Carnal Thoughts: Embodiment and Moving Image Culture*. Berkeley: University of California Press.

Dance

Foultier, Anna Petronella, and Cecilia Roos. (eds.). (2013). *Material of Movement and Thought: Reflections on the Dancer's Practice and Materiality*. Stockholm: Firework.

Fraleigh, Sondra Horton. (1996). *Dance and the Lived Body: A Descriptive Aesthetics*. Pittsburgh: University of Pittsburgh Press.

Fraleigh, Sondra Horton. (2015). *Moving Consciously: Somatic Transformations through Dance, Yoga, and Touch*. Champaign: University of Illinois Board of Trustees.

Fraleigh, Sondra Horton. (2018). *Back to the Dance Itself: Phenomenologies of the Body in Performance*. Champaign: University of Illinois Press.

Franko, Mark. (ed.). (2011). *Dance as Phenomenology: Critical Reappraisals*, Special issue, *Dance Research Journal* 43(2).

Katan, Einav. (2016). *Embodied Philosophy in Dance: Gaga and Ohad Naharin's Movement Research*. London: Palgrave Macmillan.

LaMothe, Kimerer. (2009). *What a Body Knows: Finding Wisdom in Desire*. Ropley: O Books.

LaMothe, Kimerer. (2015). *Why We Dance: A Philosophy of Bodily Becoming*. New York: Columbia University Press.

Osumare, Halifu. (2018). *Dancing in Blackness: A Memoir*. Gainesville: University Press of Florida.

Sheets-Johnstone, Maxine. (1966). *The Phenomenology of Dance*. Madison, WI: University of Wisconsin Press.

Shusterman, Richard. (2008). *Body Consciousness: A Philosophy of Mindfulness and Somaesthetics*. Cambridge: Cambridge University Press.

Shusterman, Richard. (2012). *Thinking through the Body: Essays in Somaesthetics*, Cambridge: Cambridge University Press.

Williamson, Amanda, et al. (2014). *Dance, Somatics and Spiritualities: Contemporary Sacred Narratives*: Bristol: Intellect.

Disability

Goodley Dan, et al. (eds.). (2012). *Disability and Social Theory: New Developments and Directions* London: Palgrave Macmillan.

Mintz, Susannah. (2007). *Unruly Bodies: Life Writing by Women with Disabilities*. Chapel Hill: University of North Carolina Press.

Tremain, Shelley. (ed.). (2005). *Foucault and the Government of Disability*. Ann Arbor: University of Michigan Press.

Tremain, Shelley. (2017). *Foucault and Feminist Philosophy of Disability*. Ann Arbor: University of Michigan Press

Wendell, Susan. (1996). *The Rejected Body: Feminist Philosophical Reflections on Disability*. London: Routledge.

Embodied Cognition

Cappuccio, Massimiliano. (2019). (ed.). *The MIT Handbook of Embodied Cognition and Sports Psychology*. Cambridge: MIT Press.

Durt, Christoph, Thomas Fuchs and Christian Tewes. (eds). (2017). *Embodiment, Enaction and Culture: Investigating the Constitution of the Shared World*. Cambridge: MIT Press.

Gibbs, Raymond. (2006). *Embodiment and Cognitive Science*. Cambridge: Cambridge University Press.

Lakoff, George and Mark Johnson. (1999). *Philosophy in the Flesh: The Embodied Mind and Its Challenge to Western Thought*. New York: Basic Books.

Nagel, Thomas. (2012). *Mind and Cosmos: Why the Materialist Neo-Darwinian Conception of Nature Is Almost Certainly False*. Oxford: Oxford University Press.

Noë, Alva. (2009). *Out of Our Heads, Why You Are Not Your Brain, and Other Lessons from the Biology of Consciousness*. New York: Hill and Wang.

Overton, Willis et al. (ed.). (2007). *Developmental Perspectives on Embodiment and Consciousness*. Hove: Psychology Press.

Zahavi, Dan, and Gallagher, Shaun. (eds.). (2007). *The Phenomenological Mind*. New York: Routledge.

Existential Readings

Bladow, Kyle, and Jennifer Ladino. (2018). *Affective Ecocriticism: Emotion, Embodiment, Environment*. Lincoln: University of Nebraska Press.

Busch, Thomas. (1999). *Circulating Being from Embodiment to Incorporation: Essays on Late Existentialism*. New York: Fordham University Press.

Ihde, Don. (2001). *Bodies in Technology*. Minneapolis: University of Minnesota Press.

Ihde, Don. (2010). *Embodied Technics*. Copenhagen: Automatic Press/VIP.

Kearney, Richard, and Brian Treanor. (eds.) (2015). *Carnal Hermeneutics*. New York: Fordham University Press.

Nettleton, Sarah, and Jonathan Watson. (1998). *The Body in Everyday Life*. London: Routledge.

Gender

Conboy, Katie et al. (eds.). (1997). *Writing on the Body: Female Embodiment and Feminist Theory*. New York: Columbia University Press.

Diprose, Rosalyn. (1994). *The Bodies of Women, Ethics, Embodiment, and Sexual Difference*. New York: Routledge.

Heinämaa, Sara, and Robin May Schott. (2010). *Birth, Death, and Femininity Philosophies of Embodiment*. Bloomington: Indiana University Press.
Hunt, Lynn. (1991). *Eroticism and the Body Politic*. Baltimore: Johns Hopkins University Press.
Tuana, Nancy, et al. (eds.). (2002). *Revealing Male Bodies*. Bloomington: Indiana University Press.

Health and Medicine

Aho, James and Kevin Aho. (2008). *Body Matters: A Phenomenology of Sickness, Disease, and Illness*. Lanham, MD: Lexington Books.
Aho, Kevin. (ed.). (2018). *Existential Medicine: Essays on Health and Illness*. Lanham, MD: Rowman and Littlefield International.
Benner, Patricia. (1994). *Interpretive Phenomenology: Embodiment, Caring and Ethics in Health and Illness*. London: Sage.
Carel, Havi. (2013). *Illness: The Cry of the Flesh*. Durham, UK: Acumen.
Carel, Havi. (2016). *Phenomenology of Illness*. Oxford: Oxford University Press.
Feldenkrais, Moshe. (2005). *Body and Mature Behaviour: A Study of Anxiety, Sex, Gravitation and Learning*. (trans. Ginsburg). Berkeley, CA: North Atlantic Books.
Kay Toombs, S. (ed.). *Handbook of Phenomenology and Medicine*. Dordrecht: Springer.
Slatman, Jenny. (2014). *Our Strange Body: Philosophical Reflections on Identity and Medical Intervention*. Amsterdam: Amsterdam University Press.

Non-Western Perspectives

Berger, Douglas. (2015). *Encounters of Mind: Luminosity and Personhood in Indian and Chinese Thought*. Albany: SUNY Press.
Csiszentmihalyi, Mark. (2005). *Material Virtue: Ethics and the Body in Early China*. Leiden: Brill.
Holm, Jean. (1994). *Picturing God*. London: Pinter.
Kit Wah Man, Eva. (2019). *Bodies in China: Philosophy, Aesthetics, Gender, and Politics*. Albany: SUNY Press.
Khuri, Fuad. (2001). *The Body in Islamic Culture*. London: Saqi Books.
Kugle, Scott. (2011). *Sufis and Saints' Bodies: Mysticism, Corporeality, and Sacred Power in Islam*. Chapel Hill: University of North Carolina Press.
Nagatomo, Shigenori. (1992). *Attunement through the Body*. Albany: SUNY Press.
Ram-Prasad, Chakravarthi. (2018). *Human Being, Bodily Being: Phenomenology from Classical India*. Oxford: Oxford University Press.

Race and Embodiment

Lee, Emily. (ed.). (2014). *Living Alterities: Phenomenology, Embodiment and Race*. Albany: SUNY Press.

Pinn, Anthony. (2010). *Embodiment and the New Shape of Black Theological Thought*. New York: NYU Press.

Pinn, Anthony. (2020). *Black Theology, Black Bodies, and Pedagogy*. Philadelphia: University of Pennsylvania Press.

Yancy, George. (2008). *Black Bodies, White Gazes: The Continuing Significance of Race in America*. Lanham, MD. Rowman and Littlefield.

Sexual Identity

Fuss, Diana (ed.). (1991). *Inside/Out: Lesbian Theories, Gay Theories*. New York: Routledge.

Kosofsky Sedgwick, Eve. (1990). *Epistemology of the Closet*. Berkeley: University of California Press.

Prosser, Jay. (1998). *Second Skins: The Body Narratives of Transsexuality*. New York: Columbia University Press.

Salamon, Gayle. (2010). *Assuming a Body: Transgender and Rhetorics of Materiality*. New York: Columbia University Press.

Violence, Trauma and Sexual Violence

Beauvoir, Simone de, and Gisèle Halimi. (1962). *Djamila Boupacha: The Story of the Torture of a Young Algerian Girl Which Shocked Liberal French Opinion*. (trans. Patrick Green). London: Weidenfeld and Nicolson.

Halwani, Raja. (ed.). (2007). *Sex and Ethics: Essays on Sexuality, Virtue, and the Good Life*. New York: Palgrave Macmillan.

Mann, Bonnie. (2013). *Sovereign Masculinities: Gender Lessons from the War on Terror*. Oxford: Oxford University Press.

Nussbaum, Martha. (1999). *Sex and Social Justice*. Oxford: Oxford University Press.

Sade, the Marquis de. (1965). *Three Complete Novels: Justine, Philosophy in the Bedroom, Eugénie de Franval and Other Writings*. (trans. Seaver and Wainhouse). New York: Grove Press.

du Toit, Louise. (2008). *A Philosophical Investigation of Rape: The Making and Unmaking of the Feminine Self*. Oxford: Routledge.

van der Kolk, Bessel. (2015). *The Body Keeps the Score*. New York: Penguin.

Index